ECHOES TO THE AMEN

Echoes to the Amen

ESSAYS AFTER R. S. THOMAS

Edited by

DAMIAN WALFORD DAVIES

UNIVERSITY OF WALES PRESS
CARDIFF
2003

© The contributors, 2003

British Library Cataloguing-in-Publication Data
A catalogue record for this book is available from the British Library.

ISBN 0–7083–1789–8

2481000

The rights of the Contributors to be identified as authors of their contributions have been asserted by them in accordance with sections 77 and 78 of the Copyright, Designs and Patents Act 1988.

Published with the financial support of the Welsh Books Council

Typeset by Bryan Turnbull
Printed in Great Britain by Dinefwr Press, Llandybïe

In Memory of R. S. Thomas
1913–2000

'In a green April'
2003

We stand looking at
Each other. I take the word 'prayer'
And present it to them. I wait idly,
Wondering what their lips will
Make of it. But they hand back
Such presents. I am left alone
With no echoes to the amen
I dreamed of.

('Service')

With the cathedrals thundering
at him, history proving
him the two-faced god, there were
the few who waited on him
in the small hours, undaunted
by the absence of an echo
to their Amens.

('Nuance')

The question
teases us like the undying
echo of an Amen . . .

('Fugue for Ann Griffiths')

There come times when it is necessary to evacuate the ear of the echoes of
cloying Amens.

(*The Echoes Return Slow*)

Contents

A Note on Texts

The publication in 1993 of R. S. Thomas's *Collected Poems, 1945–1990* was a landmark event in contemporary poetry which confirmed Thomas's status as one of the twentieth century's greatest poets in English. The *Collected Poems* is, however, far from complete. Ten years on, the need for a complete edition of the published and unpublished poetry is keenly felt by students of Thomas, if not, perhaps, by the general reader. In addition, two further volumes have appeared since 1993 – *No Truce with the Furies* in 1995 and the posthumous *Residues* in 2002. For these reasons, Thomas's poems are cited from their original volumes. Thomas's occasional prose is cited from *Selected Prose*, ed. Sandra Anstey (3rd edn; Bridgend: Seren, 1995) and his autobiographical writings from *Autobiographies*, ed. and trans. Jason Walford Davies (London: J. M. Dent, 1997).

Acknowledgements

Grateful acknowledgement for permission to quote from the work of R. S. Thomas is due to the following: Gwydion Thomas, Kunjana Thomas, and Rhodri Thomas; Marie de Lantsheere and J. M. Dent; Peg Osterman and Bloodaxe Books.

Material from *The Collected Poems of Wallace Stevens*, copyright 1954 by Wallace Stevens and renewed 1982 by Holly Stevens, is quoted by permission of Faber & Faber Ltd and Alfred A. Knopf, a division of Random House, Inc.

Sylvia Plath's poem, 'Mirror', is quoted by permission of Faber & Faber Ltd and HarperCollins Publishers Inc.

Research Centre Wales (University of Wales, Bangor) generously provided financial support in respect of copyright.

I would also like to thank Alice Goodman; Gwydion Thomas; M. Wynn Thomas (literary executor of the unpublished work of R. S. Thomas); and Jason Walford Davies for their assistance and advice.

My greatest debt, as ever, is to my wife, Francesca Rhydderch.

Damian Walford Davies

Notes on Contributors

JOHN BARNIE was born in Abergavenny, Monmouthshire. He taught in the English Department of Copenhagen University from 1969 to 1982, becoming assistant editor of the cultural magazine *Planet: The Welsh Internationalist* in 1985 and editor in 1990. A well-known commentator on political and environmental issues, he is the author of fourteen collections of poetry, fiction and essays, including *The King of Ashes* (Gomer, 1989), *The City* (Gomer, 1993), *No Hiding Place: Essays on the New Nature and Poetry* (University of Wales Press, 1996) and most recently *Ice* (Gomer, 2001), a novel in verse.

TONY BROWN is Reader in English at the University of Wales, Bangor, where he is also co-director of the R. S. Thomas Study Centre. His work on R. S. Thomas includes the co-editing with Bedwyr Lewis Jones of *Pe Medrwn yr Iaith ac Ysgrifau Eraill* (1988), several articles, and a forthcoming monograph in the Writers of Wales series. He has also written widely on other Welsh writers in English, most notably Glyn Jones, whose *Collected Stories* and seminal study, *The Dragon has Two Tongues*, he edited in 1999 and 2001 (both University of Wales Press). He is the editor of *Welsh Writing in English: A Yearbook of Critical Essays*.

PATRICK CROTTY is Professor of Irish and Scottish Literary History at the Academy for Irish Cultural Heritages at the University of Ulster's Magee campus. He has published many articles on Irish and Scottish poetry and on Welsh writing in English and is a regular reviewer for the *Times Literary Supplement*. His translations from seventeenth-, eighteenth- and twentieth-century Irish verse have appeared in many anthologies. He is editor of *Modern Irish Poetry: An Anthology* (Blackstaff Press, 1995) and recent publications include essays on the fiction of John McGahern and the songs of Bob Dylan. He is currently editing *The New Penguin Book of Irish Verse* and is co-editor with Alan Riach of the annotated three-volume *Complete Collected Poems of Hugh MacDiarmid* (Carcanet Press).

KATIE GRAMICH is a Literature Staff Tutor with the Open University. Born in Ceredigion, she received her education at the University of Wales, Aberystwyth, and at the universities of London and Alberta. She has published widely on Welsh writing in English and has a particular interest in women's literature. She has edited Allen Raine's *Queen of the Rushes* (Honno, 1998) and Amy Dillwyn's *The Rebecca Rioter* (Honno, 2001), and co-edited *Dangerous Diversity: The Changing Faces of Wales* (University of Wales Press, 1998) and *Welsh Women's Poetry, 1460–2001: An Anthology* (Honno, 2003).

GEOFFREY HILL, born in 1932 in Bromsgrove, Worcestershire, is University Professor, Professor of Literature and Religion, and co-director of the Editorial Institute at Boston University. He is a Fellow of the American Academy of Arts and Sciences and an Honorary Fellow of both Keble College, Oxford, and Emmanuel College, Cambridge. His scholarly and critical works include *The Lords of Limit: Essays on Literature and Ideas* (André Deutsch, 1984), *The Enemy's Country: Words, Contexture, and Other Circumstances of Language* (Stanford University Press, 1991) and *Style and Faith: Essays* (Counterpoint Press, 2003). Widely admired as one of the most distinguished English poets of the twentieth century, he is the author of *For the Unfallen* (1959), *King Log* (1968), *Mercian Hymns* (1971), *Tenebrae* (1978), *The Mystery of the Charity of Charles Péguy* (1983), *New and Collected Poems, 1952–1992* (1994), *Canaan* (1996), *The Triumph of Love* (1998), *Speech! Speech!* (2000) and *The Orchards of Syon* (2002), the last two published by Counterpoint Press.

JOHN PIKOULIS is Senior Lecturer in English Literature in Cardiff University's Centre for Lifelong Learning. He is the author of *The Art of William Faulkner* (Macmillan, 1982) and *Alun Lewis: A Life* (Seren, 1992), and editor of *Alun Lewis, A Miscellany of his Writings* (Poetry Wales Press, 1982). He has published numerous articles on aspects of English literature from Walter Scott to Louis MacNiece and, in the field of Welsh writing in English, on R. S. Thomas, Edward Thomas, Lynette Roberts, Lewis Jones and Glyn Jones. He is co-chair of Academi, the Welsh Literature promotion agency, and founder chair of the University of Wales Association for Welsh Writing in English, for whom he is series editor of a number of *Collected Works*.

M. WYNN THOMAS, literary executor of the unpublished work of R. S. Thomas, is Professor of English and Director of CREW (Centre for Research into the English Literature and Language of Wales) at the University of Wales, Swansea. He is the author or editor of twenty books (in both Welsh and English) on American literature (Walt Whitman in particular) and on the two literatures of modern Wales, including *The Page's Drift: R. S. Thomas at Eighty* (Seren, 1992), *Internal Difference: Twentieth-Century Writing in Wales* (University of Wales Press, 1992), *Corresponding Cultures: The Two Literatures of Wales* (University of Wales Press, 1999) and studies of Morgan Llwyd, John Ormond and James Kitchener Davies. He is a Fellow of the British Academy.

DAMIAN WALFORD DAVIES is Lecturer in the English Department at the University of Wales, Aberystwyth. He is the author of *Presences that Disturb: Models of Romantic Identity in the Literature and Culture of the 1790s* (University of Wales Press, 2002) and a number of articles on Romantic and Victorian literature and on the two literatures of Wales. He is the editor of *Waldo Williams: Rhyddiaith* (University of Wales Press, 2001; winner of the 2002/2003 Sir Ellis Griffith and L. W. Davies Prizes) and of *William Wordsworth: Selected Poems* (Dent, 1994), and co-editor of *The Monstrous Debt: Modalities of Romantic Influence in Twentieth-Century Literature* (Wayne State University Press, forthcoming). He is currently preparing the 'Penguin English Poets' edition of the poetry of Gerard Manley Hopkins.

ROWAN WILLIAMS is Archbishop of Canterbury. He was born in Swansea and studied theology at Cambridge. After research at Oxford in Russian religious thought, he worked as a priest and teacher of theology for seventeen years, becoming Lady Margaret Professor of Divinity at Oxford in 1986. From 1992 to 2002 he was Bishop of Monmouth, and from 1999 to 2002 Archbishop of Wales. A Fellow of the British Academy, he is the author of several books, including *The Wound of Knowledge* (1979; 2nd edn, 1990); *The Truce of God* (1983); *Arius: Heresy and Tradition* (1987; 2nd edn, 2001); *Teresa of Avila* (1991; 2nd edn, 2000); *Open to Judgement: Sermons and Addresses* (1994); *On Christian Theology* (1999); *Lost Icons: Reflections on Cultural Bereavement* (2000); *Christ on Trial* (2000); and *Writing in the Dust: Reflections on 11 September and its Aftermath* (2000). He has published a number of articles on R. S. Thomas, Vernon Watkins and other English-language Welsh writers, as well as three collections of poetry, the latest being *The Poems of Rowan Williams* (Perpetua Press, 2002).

Abbreviations

AL	*An Acre of Land* (Newtown: Montgomeryshire Printing Co., 1952)
Autobiographies	*R. S. Thomas: Autobiographies*, ed. and trans. Jason Walford Davies (London: J. M. Dent, 1997)
BHN	*Between Here and Now* (London: Macmillan, 1981)
BT	*The Bread of Truth* (London: Hart-Davis, 1963)
C	*Counterpoint* (Newcastle upon Tyne: Bloodaxe Books, 1990)
CP	*Collected Poems, 1945–1990* (London: J. M. Dent, 1993)
Critical Writings	*Critical Writings on R. S. Thomas*, ed. Sandra Anstey (Bridgend: Seren, 1992)
D	*Destinations* (Halford: Celandine Press, 1985)
EA	*Experimenting with an Amen* (London: Macmillan, 1986)
ERS	*The Echoes Return Slow* (London: Macmillan, 1988)
F	*Frequencies* (London: Macmillan, 1978)
Fr	*Frieze* (Schondorf am Ammersee: Babel, 1992)
H'm	*H'm* (London: Macmillan, 1972)
LP	*Later Poems, 1972–1982* (London: Macmillan, 1983)
LS	*Laboratories of the Spirit* (London: Macmillan, 1975)
M	*The Minister* (Newtown: Montgomeryshire Printing Co., 1953)
MHT	*Mass for Hard Times* (Newcastle upon Tyne: Bloodaxe Books, 1992)
Miraculous Simplicity	*Miraculous Simplicity: Essays on R. S. Thomas*, ed. William V. Davis (Fayetteville: University of Arkansas Press, 1993)
NBF	*Not That He Brought Flowers* (London: Hart-Davis, 1968)
NTF	*No Truce with the Furies* (Newcastle upon Tyne: Bloodaxe Books, 1995)
P	*Pietà* (London: Hart-Davis, 1966)
Page's Drift	*The Page's Drift: R. S. Thomas at Eighty*, ed. M. Wynn Thomas (Bridgend: Seren, 1993)
PS	*Poetry for Supper* (London: Hart-Davis, 1958)

R	*Residues* (Tarset: Bloodaxe Books, 2002)
Selected Prose	*R. S. Thomas: Selected Prose*, ed. Sandra Anstey (3rd edn; Bridgend: Seren, 1995)
SF	*The Stones of the Field* (Carmarthen: Druid Press, 1946)
SP	*Selected Poems, 1946–1968* (London: Hart-Davis, MacGibbon, 1973)
SYT	*Song at the Year's Turning* (London: Hart-Davis, 1955)
T	*Tares* (London: Hart-Davis, 1961)
WA	*Welsh Airs* (Bridgend: Poetry Wales Press, 1987)
WI	*The Way of It* (Sunderland: Coelfrith Press, 1977)
WW	*What is a Welshman?* (Llandybïe: Christopher Davies, 1974)
WWE	*Welsh Writing in English: A Yearbook of Critical Essays*, Vols 1– (1995–)
YO	*Young and Old* (London: Chatto & Windus, 1972)

Introduction

DAMIAN WALFORD DAVIES

Poet's Family Condemns Plan for Woodland Road
The family of R. S. Thomas, one of Britain's greatest 20th-century poets, has condemned plans for a road through the ancient wood that inspired some of his finest work. The proposal would split the ancient woodland of Coed y Rhiw and pass close to the Grade II listed home where one of the great voices of Welsh literature spent most of his latter days. The family of Thomas . . . said he would have been 'appalled' at the proposal that would see 38 trees uprooted to re-align a road made impassable because of a landslip.

Independent, 18 November 2002

More than all the elegies, obituaries and tributes that began to appear a few days after R. S. Thomas's death on 25 September 2000, it was perhaps this article in the *Independent* two years later that brought home the fact that Thomas was dead rather than merely *absconditus*, and that our way of citing him had to change tense. For the first time, he was being ventriloquized on an issue of public concern: 'he would have been "appalled" '. His intensely private – or, as urbanite commentators often had it, eremitic – existence notwithstanding, Thomas had always seemed a permanent feature of Wales's cultural landscape. He may have been chastened by the experience of measuring his transitory self against the ancient Precambrian rocks of Llŷn, as he records in *Neb*,[1] but many in Wales did not feel compelled to distinguish between those two entities. The third-person narration of his autobiography – 'R.S. realised that he was in contact with something that had been there for a thousand million years' – served to heighten this view of him as a natural phenomenon. The statement 'he would have been "appalled" ', then, had the force of a geological shift. Critical writing avoids such past subjunctives, speaking instead in an eternal present. *Echoes to the Amen: Essays After R. S. Thomas* is similarly inflected. But as the first collection of critical essays on Thomas's work to appear since his death, it is also conscious that its present tense must now invoke a 'presence in absence' (*NTF*, 33). Punning in the face of death, as Thomas often does in the poetry, the subtitle *After R. S. Thomas* registers that absence, while also expressing a continuing search for the poet and a sense of following a great original (as Thomas put it, discussing one of his 'translations' from the Welsh: 'the best we can do is to call one's effort "after the original" '[2]).

What Thomas said of himself in 1966 in 'A Welshman at St James' Park' became increasingly true during the course of a long life: he was not a member of the public, and had come a long way to realize it. From the late 1970s, he took on iconic status in Wales. Internalized as part of the Welsh literary, cultural and political psyche, he became, not 'plain and / out there, but dark rather and / inexplicable, as though he were in here' (*F*, 52) – something Tony Conran attributed to a 'prophetic stance' which is 'familiar to Welsh people as a subliminal part of their inheritance'.[3] Explicitly or implicitly, consciously or unconsciously, so many of the debates with ourselves about cultural identity and national allegiance became debates with Thomas. Freeing up imaginative space and forging a style as a poet inevitably involved writing oneself out from under his shadow. For many younger poets, however, Thomas seemed a distant, in a curious sense almost foreign, voice.

There were some who, as late as 1993, could even regard the poetry as being 'beside the point of / [its] sharpness' (*LP*, 178). Something of Thomas's status as cultural irritant can be gauged from Robert Minhinnick's comments in a tendentious essay published in a special 'R. S. Thomas at 80' issue of *Poetry Wales* in 1993. It was no conventional birthday greeting. 'For me', Minhinnick stated, 'Thomas as a poet is not important . . . R. S. Thomas the cultural icon has eclipsed R. S. Thomas the poet.' Minhinnick declared Thomas's poems 'a banquet of crumbs', his Wales 'unlocatable' and his strictures on Welsh identity wounding. Here was a baleful, intimidating presence whose pronouncements were capable of making the younger poet 'reel' out of lecture theatres feeling like 'a cancer in [his] own society'. A visit to Aberdaron, made oppressive by Thomas's presence in absence, caused Minhinnick to feel 'somehow diminished . . . almost unwell'. Such cultural valetudinarianism was obviously melodramatic. The essay, however, is an important one. For Minhinnick, the poet's legacy was likely to be his 'chilling', 'lacerating' and 'bitter' mapping of Wales's cultural and linguistic divisions – his 'breathtaking cartography of the difference between us' – rather than anything the poetry (or prose, which Minhinnick said he preferred) might have to offer. The essay was entitled 'Living with R. S. Thomas', and living without him is unlikely to have altered Minhinnick's assessment. However, opening as it does with the words 'Surprisingly, the church door was open', Minhinnick's piece is a version of Larkin's 'Church Going' (a parallel between Thomas and Larkin is at one point explicitly invoked). 'Living with R. S. Thomas' follows the trajectory of Larkin's poem, ultimately arriving with awkward reverence at an acknowledgement of the serious house that Thomas, as stern critic of the 'runaway marriage with the spirit of the age'[4] and the 'disinfected ersatz' (*R*, 46) of modern culture, undoubtedly represented:

> [I]t is not now for literary reasons that this man is important to Wales. Like it or not, the challenges laid down by R. S. Thomas are impossible to ignore. Ultimately concerned with language, they yet address the quality of the lives we seek to live. In a monoculture, he preaches diversity. In a consumer-state, he describes how we might practise the art of citizenship. In the empire of mammon, he evokes values.[5]

Minhinnick, however, remained hurt, sceptical of the value and achievement of the poetry.

Thomas could play that game himself, of course, offering typically ambiguous assessments of what the poetry was worth, now and in times to come. It is tempting to read the punning title of *Residues* (2002) – mere leftovers? or precious precipitate? – as Thomas's wry comment on becoming posthumo(ro)us. He had imagined being modified in the guts of the living more than once (indeed, all of Thomas's poetry is, on a certain view, epitaphic): 'Will they say on some future / occasion . . . / . . . This was Prytherch country? / Nothing to show for it now' (*F*, 34); 'keep these pieces / of me that in better / poets my pride may be mended' (*R*, 49); 'The poem in the rock and / The poem in the mind / Are not one. / It was in dying / I tried to make them so' (*PS*, 48 – in 1958, a very premature epitaph); 'now he dies / Intestate, having nothing to leave / But a few songs, cold as stones / In the thin hands that asked for bread' (*PS*, 31); and, mischievously, to one who asked him about literary life after death: ' "I don't mind at all . . . It's quite immaterial" '[6] (did the questioner get the pun?).

Once he had immaterialized, however, many rushed to place him above Dylan – a year younger than R.S., we were reminded (an uncanny thought, that). Most felt obliged to pronounce on precisely which 'pieces /

of [him]' represented the lasting legacy. In recent years, R. S. Thomas criticism has gained in conceptual stringency by enlisting the meta-perspectives of critical theory (deconstruction, feminist and post-colonial theory most especially) and by sharpening its engagement with the theological ground of the poetry. The resulting insights have made the received narrative of Thomas's career – the sour materiality of Prytherch displaced by a metaphysical quest – seem unconvincing. Indeed, the academic judgement arrived at a decade or so before Thomas's death was that the oeuvre was, in important respects, all of a piece.[7] Many of the writers in the present volume, now in a position to see Thomas's career whole, explore that fundamental unity from new angles.

In addition, growing international interest in Thomas's work has meant that the Wales–London axis along which discussion of Thomas was once conducted has developed during the past decade into a lively transatlantic forum in which one can speak of Thomas's 'Americanized . . . sense of form' and suggest that 'American readers and critics familiar with the poetics of William Carlos Williams's vein of Modernism may in fact be best equipped to appreciate the most innovative elements of Thomas's verse technique'.[8] Such affinities deserve further exploration. At the same time, we are also being equipped to appreciate the full extent of Thomas's formative debts to the Welsh-language literary tradition.[9] A regional or national Thomas is being replaced by a transnational Thomas whose 'local particularity' and 'parish placement' illuminate a representative, global predicament.[10] As Thomas reaches a wider audience through translation (into French, German, Italian, Swedish, Catalan and Japanese), critical discussion of the poetry is likely to be energized in the coming years by fresh cultural perspectives. A remarkable instance of Thomas's translatability and of the contexts in which he can now be invoked is the novel *Somersault* (English translation, 2003) by the Japanese Nobel laureate, Kenzaburo Oe. The book explores religious mania and the quest for the spiritual in the modern world, focusing on the fortunes of a religious cult. In a chapter entitled 'Reading R. S. Thomas', Kizu, an artist and academic dying of cancer, discusses various Thomas poems (along with passages of his prose and even samples of critical writing on Thomas) with one of the cult's leaders, Patron. This is international Thomas as therapy and enlightenment: his work provides both men with a purchase on their lives at a time of personal upheaval. Steven Poole's review in the *Guardian* (2 August 2003) bore a witty and insightful title: 'The Cult of R. S. Thomas'.

There is a recognizable Thomas and a Thomas who remains to be fully appreciated and understood. Critics are faced with the challenge of reading Thomas in more nuanced – in some cases, less adversarial – ways. Those who consider Thomas's work limited in its ploughing of narrow furrows would do well to reassess it as a great poetry of return, echo and repetition ('As has been said . . .' (*LS*, 46)) and, indeed, of the *fear* of repetition ('why / from verbal ranks // do I force the same adjectives / to volunteer?' (*R*, 26)). Despite his admission, late in life, that 'My failure, perhaps, / was to have had no sense of smell / for the holiness suspiring from forked humans' (*MHT*, 23), he deserves to be reconsidered as a great poet of fierce Christian love. And despite characterizing himself in 1990 as a 'diffident' love poet ('I shy at the word "darling" '[11]), he has emerged as a major poet of secular love. Commentators will be better able to assess the grounds of his ambiguous response to the female once they have come to terms with the highly sensual nature of his imagination (see, for example, the smouldering 'Guests'; *NTF*, 73), his aliveness to what he calls 'the / Conjunction the flesh needs' (*H'm*, 29). Love poems and elegies should be recognized as a distinct and distinguished category of the later work; indeed, it was interesting to note how in the final years of Thomas's life, 'A Marriage' from *Mass for Hard Times* – that most diaphanous of his elegies to his wife, Mildred E. Eldridge – seemed to have displaced 'A Peasant' as the poem chosen by the press to represent him whenever he became newsworthy. The nature of the creative symbiosis between Thomas and his artist wife ('My wife is a painter; I should have been a musician so that we could have designed a church and made music in it'[12]) is yet to be fully elucidated, as, indeed, are many other aspects of his life.[13]

Any consideration of Thomas within the frame of life writing is bound to acknowledge the startlingly innovative ways in which he articulated the self as an entity in and out of time. He is yet to receive the attention he deserves as a major poet of the postmodern who meditated eloquently on the 'failure of language' (*LS*, 43) and on the 'retreat of meaning' (*R*, 17). He was one of the boldest experimenters of the twentieth century not only with an amen but also with poetic form. Thomas may have begun a late poem with the lines 'Not to worry myself any more / if I am out of step, fallen behind (*MHT*, 23), and confessed himself a 'romantic' many times ('I have walked westward from Galway into the dark', he once mused to John Barnie[14]), but he was an anachronism in being ahead of the times, not behind them – troublingly *avant la lettre*. Recognizing the centrality of irony in the poetry should lead us to re-evaluate Thomas's humour and ludic verve. Many of these crucial aspects of Thomas's achievement are addressed in the present volume.

I suggest that what one might call 'second-generation' R. S. Thomas criticism should in the decade after the poet's death strive to see an iconic

Thomas anew and seek to *defamiliarize* its subject. This is why the most apt (and indeed, moving) tribute to appear on Thomas's death was in my view Peter Finch's droll elegy, cast in the form of a reference-work entry cum CD sleeve-notes. By enlisting and simultaneously transforming clichés, Finch asks us to see a familiar Thomas differently – as a late-twentieth-century Welsh gospel-singer and bluesman:

RNLD TOMOS (*vcl, hca, some prse*) aka Curtis Langdon. 1913–2000. Gospel. Austerity tradition. J[nd] Iago Prytherch Big Band (1959), gog, gap, bwlch, lleyn, tân, iaith, mynydd, mangle, adwy – mainly on Hart-Davis race label. Reissue Dent PoBkSoc Special Recommend. Concert at Sherman support Sorley Maclean (*gts, hrt clutching*) sold out. Fire Bomb tour Sain triple cd for D. Walford Davies (*vcl, crtcl harmonium*) new century highspot. A pioneer of dark wounds and internal tensions. In old age bird song and reliable grouch. Stood, was counted, still no change. To live in Wales is to become unassailable. 'An angel-fish' (Clarke). Expect retrospective, marvelling and statue. [15]

Here, a familiar Thomas salutarily shifts in and out of focus. It is a suggestive template for future ways of reading him.

'He is our capital of echoes', John Davies proclaims in a poem on Thomas.[16] Appropriately, the essays in *Echoes to the Amen* suggestively echo one another, setting up a dialogue and debate across the volume.

Emphasizing that Thomas's Iago Prytherch poems have not been 'systematically analysed', Patrick Crotty offers a reading of them as an 'interlinked series' of lyrics which 'echo and qualify' one another. Deprecating the 'extra-textual' pursuit of Prytherch, he sees Thomas's peasant-persona as 'a sort of bundle of associations, a poetic shorthand' whose resonance shifts throughout the sequence. This variation in the figure's 'secondary qualities', together with the use of 'personal pronouns with indeterminate or shifting referents', enable Thomas to explore 'quandaries' and 'dichotomies' relating not merely to the condition of a depopulated Wales (with Prytherch as a 'historicized' figure) but to a range of other concerns including war, the threat posed by technology and 'the nature of the poetic act'. Crotty's reading – which suggests illuminating parallels between Thomas and writers such as Caradoc Evans, Patrick Kavanagh, Wallace Stevens and Hugh MacDiarmid –

serves to foreground the 'continuity of [Thomas's] interests throughout his long career'. The Prytherch poems are found to be ironizing, self-reflexive texts which pose hermeneutic challenges and anticipate the strategies of the later poetry.

No contemporary poet was more highly regarded by Thomas than Geoffrey Hill, whose *Mercian Hymns* he acknowledged as an influence on the form of *The Echoes Return Slow*.[17] For Thomas, Hill's acute ethical consciousness, his exploration of the 'moral and immoral pressures'[18] of the world and of words – of history's, and the tongue's, atrocities – his demanding ironies and his subtle religious sensibility made him one of the most authoritative and *necessary* poets (and critics) of the twentieth century. 'Serious' is the word Thomas used of Hill[19] (who, like Thomas, has been seen as standing 'ec- / centric as a prophet', in the words of Hill's own 'De Jure Belli ac Pacis'[20]). Hill, for his part, holds Thomas's work in high esteem, and has spoken of a 'fan letter' sent to the Welsh poet, care of the Druid Press at Carmarthen, in the late 1950s – of which Thomas remained unaware until he initiated a correspondence with Hill many years later. A comparative study of the work of Hill and Thomas would reveal significant and surprising affinities. As Hill emphasizes, his essay in the present volume is 'uttered from a sense of common predicament' with Thomas, from 'a keen sense of fellow feeling'. It therefore represents an illuminating meditation on Hill's own poetry. At the same time, it offers a provocative and honest critique of Thomas's 'political– existential–pastoral modes'. As ever, Hill is alive to the ethical and aesthetic resonances of 'forms of speech', of 'the exact contour[s]' of poetic language, and he perceptively enlists James Hanley's *Grey Children: A Study in Humbug and Misery in South Wales* (1937) and John Cowper Powys's remarks on Huw Menai in order to get a purchase on Thomas and Alun Lewis as 'writers of conscience'. Suggestive comments are offered in this lapidary piece on Lewis's 'in-betweenness'; on his reinvention of 1930s political pastoral in his poems from India; on 'complete gratification of the self' – surprisingly, perhaps – as the 'clue to much of [Thomas's] best writing'; on the 'studied artlessness' and suspect 'spiritual aesthetics' of Thomas's 'writing about Wales' and about identity; and on how a Kierkegaardian Thomas runs poems down 'into a condition of inertia'.

In 'Was R. S. Thomas an Atheist Manqué?', John Barnie boldly approaches Thomas's work from the perspective of a scientific atheist. Barnie is interested in the ways in which Thomas's poems are troubled by the 'background radiation' of the neo-Darwinian synthesis of evolutionary theory, genetics and geological 'deep time'. He sees Thomas, whom he memorably describes as 'a lapwing feigning injury', evasively negotiating the problematic dualities of a pitiless natural order which exists 'outside the bounds of any possible set of moral categories'. Thomas can also be open-eyed about this pitiless existence, as in the mythopoeic poetry of *H'm*, in which he articulates the inescapability of humankind's 'subjugation to impersonal algorithmic processes'. Thomas's vision becomes 'a vortex funnelling down' to such harsh perceptions, but, for Barnie, the poet never arrived at a satisfactory or consoling resolution of the problem, and Christianity cannot ultimately square itself with nature. Barnie mounts a spirited defence of his own position against the 'liberal humanist' charge of being 'unimaginative' – 'the old objection of Keats to Newton'. The essay concludes that Thomas remained within 'a firmly Christian frame of reference' but that this was not 'an entirely frank position'; all too evident in the poetry is an 'unspoken position' which points in a very different direction. Nature, a vital component in Thomas's quest for God, was also, paradoxically, the source of his deepest religious doubts.

While Patrick Crotty's discussion draws attention to the significance of the stellar imagery invoked by Thomas as a 'cosmic frame' for Iago Prytherch, John Pikoulis's essay sees the stars as, *from the outset*, Thomas's 'primary theme' – his 'metasubject' and central topos – 'by force of utterance'. Thus, the essay dramatically and persuasively collapses the distinction between 'early' and 'late' Thomas. We are reminded that in Thomas's rural parishes, no light pollution obscured the stars, from whose distant fires the poet's astonishingly heterodox 'theo-sci' is seen to 'tak[e] its cue'. Pikoulis locates Prytherch, the stars and Thomas at the end of history; they all face 'a crisis of the grand narrative of Creation' and the stars become for Thomas *the* site of metaphysical anxiety. Offering valuable parallels with the work of Alun Lewis and some keen observations on Thomas's filial resentment and internal disturbances, the essay charts in detail how Thomas 'measure[d] the new cosmos' – a post-Darwinian universe 'queered' by science (thus activating a dialogue with John Barnie's essay). Pikoulis emphasizes the 'pseudo-irony' of these disturbing, stargazing poems: the space-navigating Thomas 'implies scepticism' about his subject but, held by a fascinated dread, can only lend 'credence to what [he] mocks'. By the later poetry, soul has become science – 'black holes, atomic weights and all'.

As already suggested, the 'American element' in Thomas's work has recently begun to attract serious critical attention. Tony Brown's essay seeks to initiate a discussion of Thomas's response to Wallace Stevens, who remained a significant and enabling figure for Thomas for over half a century. Brown's discussion of Thomas's early poem, 'Wallace Stevens' (*The Bread of Truth*, 1963), suggests that its 'partial' and 'inadequate' portrait of the American reveals more about the anguished Thomas of the Eglwys-fach period than about Wallace Stevens; this portrait was to be revised in the more 'assured' 'Homage to Wallace Stevens', published in *No Truce with the Furies* (1995). Brown considers the shared Romantic inheritance of Stevens and Thomas and the emphasis both poets placed on the centrality of the poetic imagination. But, as Brown stresses, Stevens's rage for order and his creation of imaginative 'fictions' were conducted under an 'empty heaven' in a universe very different from Thomas's. The essay moves on to examine Thomas's 'antiphonal' responses to Stevens (for Thomas, the 'high-priest' of the imagination), which include the strikingly uncharacteristic early poem, 'Mrs Li'.

Commentators have noted Thomas's obsession with images of mirrors, windows and pools. Katie Gramich's essay brings psycho-analytical and feminist theory to bear on this tortured poetry of reflections. Her discussion of Sylvia Plath's chilling poem 'Mirror' provides an intriguing comparison with Thomas's own mirror-games; significant gender-determined differences are revealed, and insightful incidental comments are offered on Thomas's 'tender regard for the signs of age' on the female face. Having considered Thomas's ambivalent response to the figure of Narcissus, Gramich enlists the psychoanalytical theories of Freud, Abraham, Lacan and Kristeva to posit the existence of 'a narcissistic wound' from which Thomas's tormented Narcissus poems emerge. Thomas's mirror images are now seen to interrogate not only 'personal identity' and the relationship with the *deus absconditus*, but also 'repressed familial tensions, particularly between mother and child'. This 'problematic bond' between a guilty and resentful Thomas and his mother provides a suggestive way of interpreting the mythological refer-ences of the late poetry. Gramich dramatically invokes an Orestes–Thomas, harried by the 'inescapable, terrible' image of the lost mother.

Doubleness, games and a measure of torment and fury are also at the heart of my own essay on Thomas's puns. I see Thomas's obsessive deployment of puns as constituting a 'double-entry poetics' which amounts to nothing less than 'a whole cognitive method'. Under the rubric of the 'cultural politics', 'ontology' and 'theology' of the pun, the first half of the essay forges a theory of the pun and seeks to establish why Thomas should have been so drawn to verbal equivocation. For Thomas, the quibble – an agent of his characteristic mode of irony and scepticism and part of his wider interest in echoes, reflections and narcissistic doubles – is an inscription of the 'dualities and tensions at the heart of his cultural, linguistic and religious experience'. The essay locates Thomas's poetry within the context of a post-structuralist concern to pluralize and destabilize meaning and the certainties of faith, and contends that the pun should also be viewed as a Kierkegaardian figure of 'double reflection'. The second half of the discussion shows Thomas's 'Janus-faced words' in savage, humorous, probing and neurotic action. I examine Thomas's punning response to Prytherch, Wales, applied technology, the juggling god and the female. The pun emerges as a vital aspect of Thomas's poetics – a subtle and exploratory cognitive tool and a fraught reflex response.

The final two essays in the volume discuss a Kierkegaardian Thomas. M. Wynn Thomas's ' "Time's Changeling": Autobiography in *The Echoes Return Slow*' can be considered a pendant to his seminal 1998 essay, 'Irony in the Soul: The Religious Poetry of R. S[ocrates] Thomas'. There, the author spoke of the 'double narrative' operations of *The Echoes Return Slow*, and his essay here develops this concern, showing how Thomas's innovative 'spiritual autobiography' in prose and verse is written against conventional modes of 'narrating the progress of the self'. *The Echoes Return Slow* is seen to enact a Kierkegaardian process of 'self-relating': for one conscious of the paradoxical – temporal and eternal – ground of existence, autobiography becomes 'authentic' only by means of a 'judge-ment of the self by the self' as one 'relate[s] objectively to one's own subjectivity'. This is achieved in *The Echoes Return Slow*, Wynn Thomas contends, through a complex discourse of radical 'doubleness' enacted by the interplay between prose and verse, 'the "interference" of present with past', puns and other equivocations of language, echoes, and 'repetition' in the transformative, redemptive Kierkegaardian sense. Wynn Thomas's analyses of these autobiographical strategies and categories highlight the fact that *The Echoes Return Slow* is a '*poet's* autobiography' – 'not merely incidentally or contingently' – which self-reflexively scrutinizes the process by which 'life' becomes 'art'.

Rowan Williams, too, is concerned with Thomas's 'questioning about subjectivity', and his essay offers further insights into the precise nature of Kierkegaard's centrality for Thomas. As in Gramich's essay, Thomas's 'metaphors of reflection and after-image' feature prominently; here, however, they are viewed in the context of Thomas's metaphysical quest, which Williams reads through the illuminating aperture offered by one of the most dramatic accounts of faith in modern theological writing – Kierkegaard's meditation in *Fear and Trembling* on the 'suspension of the ethical' involved in Abraham's 'abortive sacrifice of Isaac'. Williams shows how Thomas's poetry – especially that of the magisterial late volumes, *The Echoes Return Slow*, *Counterpoint* and *No Truce with the*

Furies – dramatizes tangled Kierkegaardian paradoxes and refigures 'quintessentially' Kierkegaardian metaphors of faith in its articulation of 'the becoming self . . . a self poised in tension'. Kierkegaard's distinction between the 'ethical' and the 'religious', Williams suggests, allows us to understand the motivations behind Thomas's deployment of 'post-ethical' language. 'Authentic' faith, for Kierkegaard's Abraham, exists in a realm beyond verbal and physical 'performance', in the absence of an 'audience'; one might suggest that this has teasing implications regarding Thomas's 'performance' of his religious quest in front of an 'audience' of readers. Williams concludes with a discussion of the Kierkegaardian underpinning of the very 'action of poetry', highlighting how poetry articulates 'a more deeply and resourcefully intelligible self' by pushing language towards 'new discoveries in form and metaphor'. For Williams, poetry seeks to present a world 'from something other than the simply human, readily available perspective . . . which is why good poetry is never *simply* autobiographical as one usually understands that word' – a comment that reflects back suggestively on M. Wynn Thomas's discussion of *The Echoes Return Slow*.

Similarly, *Echoes to the Amen* as a whole 'reflects back' on Thomas's career. It is also meant to echo forward, opening avenues of enquiry for future Thomas criticism. Janus-faced, this collection both celebrates a writing life that has come to an end and marks the beginning of a vital literary afterlife.

Aberystwyth, 2003

Notes

[1] See *Autobiographies*, 78.

[2] *Wales: A Problem of Translation* (The 1996 Adam Lecture; Adam Archive Publications/Centre for 20th-Century Cultural Studies, King's College, London, 1996), 12.

[3] 'The Death of R.S.T.', *The David Jones Journal* (R. S. Thomas Special Issue; Summer/Autumn, 2001), 121.

[4] *Miraculous Simplicity*, 38.

[5] See 'Living with R. S. Thomas', *Poetry Wales*, 29:1 (July 1993), 11–14.

[6] Quoted in Thomas's obituary in the *Daily Telegraph*, 27 September 2002.

[7] See, for example, *Page's Drift*, 19.

[8] See David Lloyd, 'Making It New: R. S. Thomas and William Carlos Williams', *WWE*, 8 (2003), 121–40.

[9] See Jason Walford Davies, *Gororau'r Iaith: R. S. Thomas a'r Traddodiad Llenyddol Cymraeg* (Cardiff: University of Wales Press, 2003).

[10] See Dennis Brown, *The Poetry of Postmodernity: Anglo/American Encodings* (London: Macmillan, 1994), 125 and 130.

[11] See *Miraculous Simplicity*, 44–5.

[12] 'Probings: An Interview with R. S. Thomas', originally published in *Planet*, 80 (April/May 1990); *Miraculous Simplicity*, 25.

[13] For comments on the Thomas–Eldridge creative relationship, see Peter Lord, 'Parallel Lives?', *Planet*, 128 (June/July 1998), 17–26.

[14] *Miraculous Simplicity*, 35.

[15] *New Welsh Review*, 51 (Winter 2000–1), 11. The first version of this piece, published in Finch's collection *Useful* (Bridgend: Seren, 1997), 45, ended with 'Still recording'.

[16] John Davies, *North by South: New and Selected Poems* (Bridgend: Seren, 2002), 117.

[17] *Miraculous Simplicity*, 44.

[18] Hill's words in *Viewpoints: Poets in Conversation with John Haffenden* (London: Faber & Faber, 1981), 87.

[19] See, for example, *Miraculous Simplicity*, 41.

[20] *Canaan* (London: Penguin, 1996), 33.

1

Extraordinary Man of the Bald Welsh Hills: The Iago Prytherch Poems

PATRICK CROTTY

R. S. Thomas's so-called Iago Prytherch poems have occasioned a good deal of comment, though they have not, so far as I know, been systematically analysed.[1] The appropriateness of treating them as a discrete area of the oeuvre is perhaps open to question, given that the poet never saw fit to bring them together as a sequence. Rather, he interspersed most of them throughout his early volumes, and apparently thought so little of them as to represent them extremely sparely in his *Selected Poems, 1946–1968* (1973). *Collected Poems, 1945–1990* (1993), however, reprints all but two of the Prytherch lyrics, including one, 'Iago Prytherch', which disappeared from the canon when most of the contents of *The Stones of the Field* (1946) and *An Acre of Land* (1952) were subsumed into *Song at the Year's Turning* in 1955.[2] As employed in this essay, the term 'Iago Prytherch poems' refers to the eighteen texts by Thomas published from 1946 to 1969 which cite the Prytherch character by name, in addition to a belated nineteenth, 'Gone?' (from *Frequencies*, 1978), which meditates on the transformation of the Welsh hill-country in a mechanized future and questions whether posterity will show any interest in Prytherch and in the poems that generated him. The list below indicates the first inclusion of each poem in an individual volume (or periodical in the case of the eighteenth, uncollected item) along with subsequent appearances in *Song at the Year's Turning*, *Selected Poems, 1946–1968* and *Collected Poems, 1945–1990*:

'A Peasant' (*SF*; *SYT*; *SP*; *CP*)
'Iago Prytherch' (*SF*; *CP*)
'The Gap in the Hedge' (*AL*; *SYT*; *CP*)
'Memories' (*AL*; *SYT*)

'Lament for Prytherch' (*SYT*; *CP*)
'Invasion on the Farm' (*SYT*; *SP*; *CP*)
'Temptation of a Poet' (*PS*; *CP*)
'Green Categories' (*PS*; *CP*)
'Iago Prytherch' (*PS*; *CP*)
'Absolution' (*PS*; *CP*)
'The Dark Well' (*T*; *CP*)
'Too Late' (*T*; *CP*)
'Portrait' (*T*; *CP*)
'Which?' (*T*; *CP*)
'Servant' (*BT*; *CP*)
'For the Record' (*P*; *CP*)
'Aside' (*P*; *SP*; *CP*)
'The Grave' (*Anglo-Welsh Review*, 18:41 (Summer 1969))
'Gone?' (*F*; *CP*)

While these are the Prytherch poems proper, it would be foolish to consider them in isolation from other early pieces by Thomas with manifestly related concerns. Particularly relevant are the lyrics, roughly equal in number, focusing on unnamed farmers and farm workers who may legitimately be identified with (and sometimes as) Prytherch: 'A Labourer', 'Affinity', 'Peasant Greeting' (all *SF*; *SYT*; *CP*), 'The Hill Farmer Speaks' (*AL*; *SYT*; *CP*), 'Soil' (*AL*; *SYT*), 'Enigma' (*AL*; *SYT*), 'The Labourer' (*AL*; *SYT*; *CP*), 'The Slave' (*SYT*), 'Autumn on the Land' (*SYT*), 'The Last of the Peasantry' (*SYT*; *CP*), 'The Muck Farmer' (*PS*), 'Power' (*PS*; *CP*), 'The Cry' (*PS*; *SP*), 'To the Farmer' (*T*; *CP*), 'The Parish' (*T*; *CP*), 'The Face' (*T*; *SP*), 'Truth' (*BT*; *CP*) and 'The Face' (*P*; *SP*; *CP*). Some of the pieces on this 'B-list' develop images and motifs introduced in the poems on the main list, while one of them, the second bearing the title 'The Face', can be read as a gloss on the contents of both lists and as an admission by the poet of the obsessional nature of his concern with Prytherch. It is of course the case that any 'B-list' of Prytherch poems must be provisional, and would probably be constituted differently by different critics. The list above is a conservative one: the grounds of detail (in relation to physical appearance and domestic or economic circumstance) upon which I have omitted 'Man and Tree' (*SF*; *CP*), 'Valediction' (*AL*; *SYT*; *CP*), 'Age' (*PS*; *CP*) and 'Hireling' (*T*; *SP*; *CP*) – to cite examples only of poems with strong claims for inclusion – might appear overscrupulous to another commentator, particularly in the light of the considerable inconsistencies of detail between the poems on the main list. Then there are poems featuring characters who are clearly not Prytherch, having different names or circumstances, but who share his rudimentary living conditions and virtual aphasia, and who, like him, are employed by the poet to dramatize questions about the relationship between articulacy, consciousness and definitions of the human. Tomos in 'The Airy Tomb' (*SF*; *SYT*; *CP*), the Evans who survives almost as long as Prytherch from the early work into the middle decades of Thomas's production,[3] and the grotesque dramatis personae of 'Meet the Family' (*PS*; *SP*; *CP*) and 'On the Farm' (*BT*; *SP*; *CP*) are among the most prominent of such figures. A very substantial portion of Thomas's early poetry, then, portrays or evokes radically inarticulate, uneducated rural labourers and small farmers whose lives are marked by toil and unreflecting suffering. The poetry offers us portraits of more morally repugnant characters also, victimizers rather than victims. Job Davies, the boorish deacon of the long poem *The Minister* (broadcast on the BBC's Welsh Home Service on 18 September 1952; published in 1953 and reprinted in *SYT*, *SP* and *CP*) is the most notable of these: he reappears in the lyrics 'Chapel Deacon' (*PS*; *CP*) and 'Lore' (*T*; *SP*; *CP*). He is not to be confused with the Davies – or Davieses – of 'Death of a Peasant' (*AL*; *SYT*; *CP*), 'Priest and Peasant' (*SYT*; *CP*) and 'Dialectic' (*T*), despite the latter poem's reference to Job. The eponymous speaker of 'Walter Llywarch' (*T*; *SP*; *CP*), as churlish as Job Davies, should presumably be considered as a separate character from the sparely etched but apparently docile farmer of the same surname in *The Minister*.

All of these poems, along with many others in the early volumes, can be said to have grown out of the struggle of the poet to come to terms with the unprepossessing actualities of his ministry in a rural parish. After curacies in Chirk and Hanmer, the twenty-nine-year-old Thomas became rector of Manafon, Montgomeryshire, in 1942. From the perspective of four decades later, *Neb*, the most extended of his autobiographical writings, offers a laconic portrait of the artist as a bookish and slightly priggish pastor who 'had to learn' in Manafon 'the craft of being a young rector amongst rough and hardened farmers who expected more from him than he could give; while they in turn failed to meet his own ideals' (*Autobiographies*, 51). The Rhiw valley and surrounding uplands provided much of the local colour not only of the poems written during Thomas's twelve-year stay in Manafon, but of a good number of those composed in the following dozen or so years as well. It was in those uplands that he saw the man who became his model for Iago Prytherch.[4] His account of the sighting in *Neb* suggests that he considered the Prytherch figure to be representative of the hardness and intractability of his parishioners generally:

Manafon scarcely existed. There was no village there, only a church, a school, a public house and a shop. The farms were scattered along the slopes, smallholdings on the whole, with the occasional more substantial farm. The people were English–Welsh, with Welsh names and a Shropshire accent. They became the subject of his poetry. For him, the countryside and its surroundings were beautiful. He wanted to continue to sing poems of praise to them. But how to reconcile with this the life and attitude of the farmers themselves? On a dark, cold day in November, on his way to visit a family in a farm over a thousand feet above sea-level, he saw the farmer's brother out in a field, docking mangels. The thing made a profound impression on him, and when he returned to the house after the visit he set about writing 'A Peasant', the first poem to attempt to face the reality of the scenes around him.

(*Autobiographies*, 52)

This essay focuses on 'A Peasant' and the eighteen other poems which name Prytherch; the material on the 'B-list' is referred to when it provides clarification or amplification of matters arising in the Prytherch poems proper. While the poems of the 'A-list' should not be thought of as a sequence, they *do* constitute an interlinked series. The manner in which they echo and qualify one another makes treatment in chronological order of their appearance seem apposite. For example, the closing sentence of the fourth lyric, 'Memories', includes the phrase 'When I was a child', and the next piece, 'Lament for Prytherch', responds by opening: 'When I was young, when I was young!'. Indeed, 'Lament for Prytherch' might be said to sustain the argument with its predecessor through to the closing lines. In the seventh poem, 'Temptation of a Poet', the 'green' of 'nature's / Lore' on Prytherch's tongue, and the 'flaw' attributed to what Thomas calls the 'first premise' of his argument, set the terms for the nature versus philosophy antithesis proposed in the eighth, 'Green Categories'. As is to be expected, the poems comment on each other across the range of the series also. 'For the Record', the sixteenth lyric, reaches back to the beginning to reactivate the martial metaphor of lines 17–21 of the first piece, 'A Peasant'. Similarly, the 'planets' which 'have seen more ills than yours' in 'Aside' (the seventeenth) recall and perhaps ironize the 'curious stars' of that opening poem's concluding line. A number of other seams of imagery run through the series, while variations are played throughout on a kind of four-way relationship between Prytherch, other denizens of Prytherch's world (varying in status from neighbours to tourists), the poet/speaker and the reader.

In the course of a lecture in 1968, Thomas observed: 'One of my objections to the so-called critics . . . is that they do not show . . . that they know much about poetry, mainly because they nearly always go over what the poems are about.'[5] Commentary on the Prytherch series has perhaps been particularly guilty of concern with subject matter at the expense of technique. That subject matter has in my view been mis-construed, however, or at least defined too narrowly in terms of the stringencies of rural life in Wales in the middle of the twentieth century. The poems are not in any exclusive sense 'about' the hard lives and restricted horizons of the 'peasants' to whom Thomas ministered. Rather, they take those lives and horizons as the starting point for their exploration of a wide range of concerns, some of which are identified by the poet in *Neb*, where he speaks of their attempt 'to understand the countryman in Manafon as a man, and mak[e] him a symbol of the relationship that existed between man and the earth in the contemporary world of the machine' (*Autobiographies*, 55). Too much critical and exegetical energy has been expended on explaining and even explaining away what the Prytherch series tells us about Thomas's attitude to his flock. This is particularly true of early responses to the poems. No less a commentator than Pennar Davies suggested, in the face of what one might consider overwhelming textual evidence, that Prytherch is 'a representative of the Welsh *gwladwr*, the ideal peasant'.[6] (One would not wish to deny, however, that Thomas measures his peasant, with varying degrees of irony, against that ideal.) Raymond Garlick developed this sentimental strain in 1952 in a review of *An Acre of Land* in *Dock Leaves*, where he restated the *gwladwr* identification and described Prytherch as '[w]ise with the wisdom of the earth, and kind with its charity'.[7] It is difficult not to read 'Autumn on the Land', a 'B-list' poem from *Song at the Year's Turning*, as a rebuke to that comment:

> You must revise
> Your bland philosophy of nature, earth
> Has of itself no power to make men wise.
> (*SYT*, 106)

Hailing *Song at the Year's Turning* in 1955 in a landmark *Dock Leaves* editorial, Garlick helpfully drew attention to Thomas's essay 'The Depopulation of the Welsh Hill Country'[8] but perhaps less helpfully asserted that it provides 'the context into which the characters of the poems are to be fitted'.[9] Certainly, the essay displays a deeply informed and humane concern for the welfare of the hill folk and of the country they inhabited, and conveys, as Garlick says, the poet's 'passionate par-tisanship' and his 'identification' with the 'life' of the country people.

Whether it – or indeed any other evidence relating to Thomas's day-to-day attitudes to his neighbours and parishioners – has more than incidental bearing on the meaning of the poems must remain open to question, however.

The extra-textual pursuit of the poems' themes was taken up by other critics, who joined debate on such topics as whether or not Iago Prytherch spoke Welsh. H. J. Savill, in the first full-length treatment of the poems, declared that Prytherch must be thought of as 'a monoglot English-speaking man', as he lacks 'the cultural background of a Welsh-speaking countryman who has a literary and poetic tradition stretching far back into time and giving him roots which nourish his daily life'.[10] (Where genuinely ignorant peasanthood is concerned, it would seem, no Welsh-speaker need apply.) A quarter of a century later, in his useful, if journalistic, *Furious Interiors: Wales, R. S. Thomas and God*, Justin Wintle seemed just as convinced that Prytherch is a creature of flesh and blood who somehow has an existence outside the texts.[11] Even today, students can speak of Prytherch as a person rather than as a persona or cypher, though none perhaps so touchingly as Raymond Garlick, who in the *Anglo-Welsh Review* in 1959 supplied an up-to-the minute report on how the Reverend Thomas and Mr Prytherch were getting along: 'In later poems the poet bridges [the] chasm patiently and painfully, warms with fellow-feeling for Prytherch, ranges himself beside him . . .'.[12] They were getting along just fine, that is to say, thanks to the efforts of the saintly rector.

I do not intend to suggest that the problems posed by the poems did not arise from first-hand experience, or that the Iago Prytherch figure whom Thomas invented to facilitate an imaginative probing of those problems was not in important respects 'drawn from life'. Prytherch is a literary creation rather than a person, however, and the question as to which of the languages of Wales he employed is, strictly speaking, a meaningless one, or at least one to which contradictory answers can be given. While he is implicitly presented as a monoglot English-speaker in the majority of the lyrics, he would appear to be a Welsh speaker in 'Too Late'. Similarly, there is no way of reconciling the vacant mind of the protagonist of 'A Peasant' with the full heart of the addressee of 'The Dark Well', or the hard blue eyes of 'Portrait' with either the blurring moist eye of 'Which?' or the colourless eyes of the haunting visage of the second 'The Face' (one which it seems unreasonable to believe belongs to anyone but Prytherch). Many of the issues that exercised commentators on the early volumes vanish if we approach Prytherch according to the one-poem-at-a-time regimen of the recovering naive realist. He then emerges as a character who displays traits in some lyrics he lacks in others. If he is consistently ragged, unsophisticated and less than fragrant, he is inconsistently Welsh – a deracinated brute, ignorant of his country's past, in some embodiments and a last representative of the old Wales in others. In order to highlight Prytherch's primary quality of immunity to high cultural and consumerist values alike, Thomas varies his secondary qualities as the occasion requires. After his introduction in 'A Peasant' – a work to which all the subsequent poems implicitly refer – Prytherch functions as a sort of bundle of associations, a poetic shorthand enabling the poet to get on with what he does best throughout his career: exploring quandaries, projecting dichotomies.

Certainly, some of those quandaries and dichotomies relate to the condition of Wales, and to the hard lives of the uneducated hill-farmers of the border country. Iago Prytherch is, to a degree at least, a 'historicized' figure painted against the background of the depressed, depopulated rural Wales of the 1940s. He is, however, much else besides, and the 'content' of the Prytherch poems encompasses not only rural hardship but also youth and age, the limits of 'culture', the devastation of war, the menace of technology, the extent to which depth of awareness confers value on life, and such staple concerns of modernist verse as the relationship between consciousness and the non-conscious domain, and the nature of the poetic act. These are topics Thomas's later poetry would approach with a bleak minimalist directness, and their presence in the Prytherch series highlights the continuity of his interests throughout his long career. (The disjunction between his poetry up to the 1960s and his subsequent work can be exaggerated.) Even in the 1950s, Thomas had as much in common with Wallace Stevens as with Patrick Kavanagh, and my comments below will indicate some of the many points of contact between the Prytherch poems and the work of a range of twentieth-century practitioners.

'A Peasant' can be thought of as Thomas's 'breakthrough' poem, the first to sound his characteristic tonalities (which may account for the fact that he chose it to open *Selected Poems*). The concern with fallen humanity, the tempering of sympathy with an austere and even embittered distaste, the insistence that the apparently unfallen of the world are in as abject a state as the obviously wretched, the conflation of ecological and religious categories: perspectives and attitudes that would be recurring and near staple features of Thomas's verse over the next fifty years are here brought into rich confluence. On the one hand, the title exhibits a peremptory matter-of-factness we recognise as typical; on the other, it draws frisson from the problematic status of a word already laden with dangerous overtones long before the phrase 'political correctness' entered the language. 'Peasant' had become an insulting term in industrial Britain by 1946; in the Celtic countries of the archipelago it was doubly problematic, being tied up positively with notions of national purity and negatively with stereotypes of the slow-wittedness and backwardness of the Irish and Welsh. In the English-language literatures of those countries, representations of 'peasant' life had been at the centre of high-profile literary controversies. The dispute surrounding the production of John Millington Synge's *The Playboy of the Western World* at the Abbey Theatre in Dublin in 1907 is the best-known of these internationally – a dispute ultimately to be understood less in terms of philistines ganging up on aesthetes than in the light of the emerging Catholic middle classes' touchiness in the face of what they saw as an Anglophile Protestant's misrepresentation of the mores of their immediate forebears. Longer-lasting and arguably more bitter was the trouble successfully courted (if that is a fair way of putting it) by Caradoc Evans when he developed an Anglo-Welsh version of Synge-speak, as cacophonous and reductive as its prototype was lyrical and extravagant, to pillory west Walian rural society in the stories of *My People* (1915) and later books. The sensibilities of a new middle class anxious for respectability were, in this case too, central to the quarrel, and resentments deriving from the historical disadvantages suffered by Roman Catholicism and Noncon-formity played their respective and parallel roles in the Irish and Welsh controversies. As recently as 1942, Patrick Kavanagh's long poem *The Great Hunger* had challenged the (quite distinct) idealizations of Irish country life in the works of Synge, Yeats and other writers of the Literary Revival on the one hand, and of nationalist rhetoricians like Eamon de Valera on the other, offering in their place a roughly naturalistic portrayal of a sexually and emotionally starved small farming community. (Thomas certainly knew Kavanagh's poem, which to some degree he used as a template for *The Minister*,[13] though whether he had read it by 1946 is unclear.) Evans and Kavanagh each in his own way offered an anti-pastoral vision of the countryside where their nations' qualities were conventionally thought to be found at their purest, and each in doing so drew on the experience of growing up disadvantaged in the national heartland. The idealizing distortions of Celticism and literary national-ism were among the particular targets of both writers.

Thomas is as anti-idyllic as either, but he is an outsider to the community he describes – if his parade of solitaries can be called a com-munity – and his assault on prettification in 'A Peasant' and elsewhere serves a deep-seated and (many would argue) backward-looking nationalism. The concern with Wales is intimated by the phrase 'though, be it allowed', a syntactic formulation which posits a contrast between the exotic possibilities of the peasant's name and the bareness of his reality. (A similar contrast is stated, more explicitly and thus less powerfully, at the opening of 'Rhodri': 'Rhodri Theophilus Owen, / Nothing Welsh but the name' (*P*, 7)). The first four words of 'A Peasant', that is to say, constitute a romantic flourish glumly qualified in everything that follows. (The name Iago Prytherch is neither as symbolically resonant as Justin Wintle argues nor as immaterial as Anne Stevenson suggests.[14] 'Cynddylan on a Tractor' provides a rare instance of an early Thomas lyric that exploits the specific legendary associations of a Welsh name, as it traces the declension from the tragic grandeur of the hero of the early medieval *englynion* cycle *Canu Heledd* to the boisterous materialism of the contemporary farmer who bears his name.) The details of Prytherch's work and appearance mark the degradation of an ideal of Welshness, and the fact that such repulsive and even grotesque qualities belong to someone who is 'just an ordinary man of the bald Welsh hills' – rather than to someone whose primitive condition is exceptional – underscores the slumped state of national life. Those details reverberate through many poems on the 'B-list'. Prytherch's mangel-docking and his 'half-witted grin / of satisfaction' link him to the swede-pulling, inscrutable protagonist of 'A Labourer', and to the mangold- and swede-docking toiler of 'Soil'. His sour clothes and 'half-witted' expression are paralleled in the 'stinking garments' and 'aimless grin' of the 'man in the field beneath' in 'Affinity'. The reference to Prytherch's 'spittled mirth', described as 'Rarer than the sun that cracks the cheeks / Of the gaunt sky perhaps once in a week', is recalled in 'The Muck Farmer':

> His rare smile,
> Cracked as the windows of his stone house
> Sagging under its weight of moss . . .
> (*PS*, 23)

The focus on physiognomy in 'A Peasant' and these related pieces will be sufficient to convince most readers that Prytherch is the subject of the two poems called 'The Face'.

In later presentations, Thomas's man of the hills will be reticent, but in 'A Peasant' he simply has nothing to say. The day's toil over, he sits 'fixed in his chair / Motionless, except when he leans to gob in the fire'. This cheerless description leads to the crucial reversal at the end of the poem:

There is something frightening in the vacancy of his mind.
His clothes, sour with years of sweat
And animal contact, shock the refined,
But affected, sense with their stark naturalness.
Yet this is your prototype, who, season by season
Against siege of rain and the wind's attrition,
Preserves his stock, an impregnable fortress
Not to be stormed even in death's confusion.
Remember him, then, for he, too, is a winner of wars,
Enduring like a tree under the curious stars.

The reader has up to this point accepted the neutral authority of the poem's narrative voice. That voice now turns on him/her, as the adjective 'affected' lodges an accusation of complacency and self-regard against the response Thomas's description of Prytherch has been evoking – the only response, be it said, it could reasonably be expected to evoke. The assault is driven home and personalised by the sudden lunge into the second person, '*your* prototype'. Thomas is sometimes said to be a Wordsworthian poet, the epithet conveying little beyond a recognition of his tendency to mention – as he does in this poem – sheep and clouds. The rhetorical strategies of 'A Peasant', though, recall in detail the procedures of some of the most revolutionary poems in *Lyrical Ballads*, texts in which Wordsworth unmasks the prejudices of his readers by cunningly playing Augustan notions of sensibility off against his own radically democratic attitude. Particularly relevant in this context is the ballad 'Simon Lee, the Old Huntsman', which apostrophizes its 'gentle reader' while expertly toying with the conventions of author–audience relationship to highlight the inadequacy of received responses to 'low' subject matter. If Thomas's lyric 'reads the reader' somewhat less subtly, it does so scarcely less powerfully.

The addressee whose prototype is identified in Thomas's peasant is, arguably at least, open to a number of identifications. (The Prytherch poems, as we shall see, characteristically employ personal pronouns with indeterminate or shifting referents.) 'Your' could conceivably be taken as a rebuke to the speaker himself, and certainly the dialectic developed throughout the series is ultimately to be understood in terms of the argument with the self out of which, as Yeats famously claimed, poetry grows. If we assume that the pronoun refers to the reader, however, it may be said to direct its accusation not just against the reader in general in his/her capacity as a representative of sophisticated humanity, but against the British reader in particular. The limitation is effected by the historic-ally specific nature of the extended martial metaphor upon which the poem ends. 'A Peasant' was composed in 1946, shortly after the end of the Second World War, and the public rhetoric of victory is borrowed by Thomas for his depiction of Prytherch as a hero of endurance: 'Remember him', he writes, rather than 'Think of him', extending the idiom of the cult of Remembrance the United Kingdom employs officially to honour her veterans and war dead. 'Siege', 'attrition', 'fortress', 'stormed', 'winner of wars' – the sheer profligacy of the martial terminology applied to the poem's ill-favoured protagonist ironizes the language of the state and registers a protest (of a kind which would become much more forthright as Thomas's work developed) against war, a protest linked to the rage against mercantilism, mechanization and mass culture sustained throughout the poet's career.

There are a number of key ambiguities in the poem's closing movement. Does the word 'stock' denote Prytherch's sheep – that is, his livestock – or the core of his person, however 'vacant' we might consider that to be? One of the passage's grimmer ironies, of course, is that it is by virtue of its blankness that Prytherch's personality is unassailable 'even in death's confusion'. And what of the word 'curious', the subject some years ago of a spirited debate in *The New Welsh Review* between Walford Davies and D. Z. Phillips?[15] There must be a sense in which the stars are *in*curious about Prytherch's fate, pursuing their courses without care for the welfare of an obscure peasant on a hillside in one of the smaller countries of a small planet millions of light-years below them. They are no doubt curious – mysterious, inducing to wonder – from the standpoint of the speaker, and their citation at this point not only provides a cosmic frame for the portrait of Prytherch but also expands from the social to the (concretely as well as abstractly) universal the grounds of the poem's concern with estrangement. (It is tempting to relate the role of stars here and elsewhere in the series to Hugh MacDiarmid's cultivation of interstellar perspectives as a measure of the depth and insignificance of human emotion in his Scots lyrics of the 1920s, lyrics Thomas appears to have admired.[16]) Davies and Phillips are no doubt right to draw attention to the older meanings of 'curious' as both 'made with care or art', 'patterned' (Davies) and 'exquisite' (Phillips), as instanced in Andrew Marvell's line in 'The Garden' about 'the nectarine and curious peach',[17] though to take any of these meanings as primary in Thomas's usage is to imbue the rhetoric of the poem with a gentility it otherwise seems at pains to eschew. The word order in the last line opens another interpretative crux. Are the stars part of the simile or do they share the same grammatical status, and consequently inhabit the same reality, as Prytherch? Does the peasant, in other words, simply endure – like a tree under the stars? Or endure under the stars like a tree? The lack of punctuation in the line vindicates both interpretations, though of course the second is as rich in implication as the first is poor, and most of the resonance of the image is lost if the stars are considered merely as a decorative addition to the tree simile. In my comments I have 'run with' the more promising reading that allows the rough countryman's life to be viewed *sub specie aeternitatis*, though in having recourse to that phrase I do not mean to imply that Thomas invokes his Christian faith at the end of the poem to resolve the enigma of Prytherch.[18]

If Thomas's peasant is the prototype of the winners of wars and of those who honoured them in Britain in the late 1940s, he is also, in terms of the wider application of 'your', the prototype of us all. Prytherch is terrible in Thomas's eyes not because he is sub-human but because he is human. The shock of 'A Peasant' is less a matter of the refined sensibility's encounter with the uncouth, unwashed and unlettered Prytherch than of the consequent realization that everything that divides the speaker from the half-witted labourer is contingent and inessential. The point is driven home in the poems of the 'B-list'. 'Listen, listen, I am a man like you', insists the protagonist of 'The Hill Farmer Speaks'. 'Affinity', significantly, uses a star image to restate the case:

> Don't be taken in
> By stinking garments or an aimless grin;
> He also is human, and the same small star,
> That lights you homeward, has inflamed his mind
> With the old hunger, born of his kind.
>
> (*SF*, 20)

There is a star in 'The Labourer' also, and if in this instance it is invisible to the countryman, the argument underlying the shifting imagery remains the same:

> What do you see? Notice the twitching hands,
> Veined like a leaf, and tough bark of the limbs,
> Wrinkled and gnarled, and tell me what you think.
> A wild tree still, whose seasons are not yours,
> The slow heart beating to the hidden pulse
> Of the strong sap, the feet firm in the soil?
> No, no, a man like you, but blind with tears
> Of sweat to the bright star that draws you on.
>
> (*AL*, 32)

These lines develop the tree simile of the end of 'A Peasant' with an almost programmatic single-mindedness, only to disavow it immediately in the assertion of the subject's human rather than botanical reality. (It is not the first ingenious figure of speech in twentieth-century verse to be dismissed by its creator with a brusque 'No, no' at the very moment of articulation, as if to suggest that figuration involves obfuscation, while nothing can be allowed to get in the way of poetry's commitment to reality – think of Yeats's 'No, no, not night but death' in 'Easter 1916'.)

The first poem's unsentimental and discomfiting recognition of the shared humanity of the speaker and Prytherch facilitates the hailing of the latter as 'friend' in 'Iago Prytherch', the second lyric of the series:

> Ah, Iago, my friend, whom the ignorant people thought
> The last of your kind, since all the wealth you brought
> From the age of gold was the yellow dust on your shoes,
> Spilled by the meadow flowers, if you should choose
> To wrest your barns from the wind and the weather's claws,
> And break the hold of the moss on roof and gable;
> If you can till your fields and stand to see
> The world go by, a foolish tapestry
> Scrawled by the times, and lead your mares to stable,
> And dream your dream, and after the earth's laws
> Order your life and faith, then you shall be
> The first man of the new community.
>   (SF, 38)

This is a strange text which, though difficult to interpret, hardly supports H. J. Savill's description of it as 'a beautiful Romantic poem with a strain of lyricism, almost of euphoria . . . a young man's poem'.[19] It is lyrical, certainly, but the conditional clauses ('if you should choose', 'If you can till your fields and stand to see . . .') control its long unspooling sentence and keep the proceedings from straying too far from Thomas's characteristic ironic mode. The first thing we notice is that the ignorance imputed to Prytherch in the first poem now afflicts others, those 'people' who had considered him the last of his 'kind'. Commentary has perhaps paid insufficient attention to the ludic dimension of Thomas's art, a dimension which must be invoked if we are to account for his lifelong practice of varying perspective in relation to given situations, deploying familiar tropes in subtly unfamiliar contexts, and otherwise well nigh systematically working his materials to their furthest potential by trying out their elements in new permutations and combinations. Thus this poem takes the three elements, Prytherch, ignorance and people, and proceeds to arrange them differently from the text in which they had been introduced. But who, precisely, are 'the ignorant people'? The third-person equivalents of the second-person readers of 'A Peasant', perhaps? Have Thomas's readers, that is to ask, already stepped into his fictive world, as they will certainly do in some of the later pieces in the series? (Thomas's early poetry is considerably more sly in its self-awareness, more self-reflexive and modern – or proto-postmodern – than accounts of its conventionality of technique would have us believe.) If so, they have received an accusation of ignorance for their pains – few poets have ever done less than Thomas to flatter their audience. The 'people' of the first line may alternatively be identified with the bourgeois dwellers 'in houses on the main road'[20] in 'The Parish', who comprehend nothing of the 'old violence' of nature their farmer neighbour (arguably Prytherch) understands so well. Not only is Prytherch now a 'friend' of the speaker, he is also someone who can share with him a sense of the futility of the contemporary world, that 'foolish tapestry / Scrawled by the times'. With his barns and mares and stable, the addressee of this poem seems more prosperous than the toiler of 'A Peasant'. He is also, possibly, more imaginative. The vacant-minded creature of the earlier lyric scarcely had a dream to dream, though it is not clear that even in this second manifestation Prytherch is capable of much in the way of aspiration (those are two very big *ifs* in the conditional clauses, after all[21]). The closing lines are particularly puzzling. Surely Prytherch – indicatively rather than conditionally, so to speak – already orders his life according to 'the earth's laws'? And it is difficult to appreciate the text's distinction between the 'life' and the 'faith' of someone who leads so rudimentary an existence. The climactic phrase about Prytherch's potential as the 'first man of the new community' presents a more substantial hermeneutical problem. How sardonic is Thomas being here? Any answer must be contingent on the definition of 'new community'. Prytherch is a solitary, who is only in the very loosest sense a member of the community constituted by his fellow parishioners. The community that could have such a person as its 'first man' would have to be radically different from the one on the edge of which he pursues his lonely and anti-social existence. And how 'first'? In time? In importance? The ending of the poem is perhaps best understood in relation to the war theme of some of the others in the series and on the 'B-list'. Though generalized fear of nuclear holocaust is a feature of the Cold War era rather than of the 1940s, the bombing of Hiroshima and Nagasaki had taken place a year before 'Iago Prytherch' was published, and Thomas's poetry was alert to the ecological threat posed by mechanization at least as early as 1952, when *An Acre of Land* appeared. 'To the Farmer', admittedly a much later poem on the 'B-list', disrupts its own optimism to warn that while one major war has been withstood by a worker of the earth, the next one will not be. Edwin Muir's famous poem on the aftermath of nuclear war, 'The Horses', was first published in 1955.[22] It is at least conceivable that Thomas anticipated Muir's healing vision of a post-apocalyptic return to 'primitive' farming nine years earlier. In such a world-building project, Prytherch's skills would be infinitely more valuable than those of his genteel neighbours on the main road, and the 'last of his kind' would have become 'the first man of the new community'.

The third poem, 'The Gap in the Hedge', is one of the best known and most anthologized of the group. While it presents no major challenge to interpretation, it playfully problematizes Prytherch's ontological status. 'I saw him often', declares the poet at the beginning, only to concede a few lines later that he may have seen no more than

> a likeness that the twigs drew
> With bold pencilling upon that bare
> Piece of the sky . . .
>
> (*AL*, 15)

The twigs' bold pencilling parallels the poet's bold penning. On one level, this poem belongs to the Romantic tradition, conjuring a personage by enumerating the natural phenomena into which he has become dispersed; Arnold's pursuit of the phantasm of the Scholar Gypsy in the poem of that name and Keats's glimpses of the personified season 'amidst [her] store' in the ode 'To Autumn' lie somewhere in its textual hinterland. On another level, it is a characteristically modern poem that draws attention to the imagined condition of its proposed reality – a poem about the beguiling procedures of poetry itself. It implies, if it does not state, that the flesh and blood protagonist of the first poem is no more and no less boldly penned than the vanishing, insubstantial 'man . . . with the torn cap' of this one.

The 'mild weather' of 'Memories', the fourth poem, is startlingly un-characteristic, at odds with those 'harsher conditions' Thomas has else-where suggested are proper to poetry ('Reservoirs'; *NBF*, 26). Prytherch, once again addressed as 'my friend', is enlisted to help the poet sing 'the land's praises'. This undue fulsomeness on his creator's part is explained in terms of the attempt to give voice to the peasant's 'strong feelings'. Agricultural plenitude is evoked by a series of images endowing plant life with an animal busy-ness – wheat gathers in 'shoals', there is a 'hissing swarm' of 'winged' oats, and so on. By the time we reach the reference to 'green and gold' patches in the snow we could be forgiven for thinking we have been transposed to the more opulent world of that other, slightly younger Thomas who famously celebrates those colours as badges of youth in 'Fern Hill'. (One is tempted to see this as a conscious echo.) Although Prytherch fails to express his joy amid all this evidence of 'the heart's rich harvest', his silence is neither puzzling nor disturbing in this instance, being a matter merely of his 'natural' and therefore entirely commendable reticence. 'When I was a child I thought as a child', said St Paul, and the sentimentality of 'Memories' may perhaps be explained in terms of the infantile stage of the speaker's development adverted to in the closing lines about the owl and the badger answering his young cry. Such indulgence, however, proved too much for the older man who wrote the subsequent lyrics and assembled *Selected Poems, 1946–1968*, and this commentator, at least, would not wish to argue with the omission of the lyric from *Collected Poems*.

Thomas may have been young once, but it is difficult to imagine that Prytherch ever was. 'Lament for Prytherch' employs a simple but extremely effective comparison of youth to wealth, eloquently dissuading us from imagining that Prytherch could once have been a rich and complacent young farmer as it sets the context for a striking description of his ruined face:

> You are old now; time's geometry
> Upon your face by which we tell
> Your sum of years has with sharp care
> Conspired and crossed your brow with grief.
> Your heart that is dry as a dead leaf
> Undone by frost's cruel chemistry
> Clings in vain to the bare bough
> Where once in April a bird sang.
> (*SYT*, 99)

The echo of Shakespeare's seventy-third sonnet is brilliantly exploited not so much to enrich as to thin out the texture of the verse.

'Invasion on the Farm', one of Thomas's most frequently anthologized pieces, like the previous four poems takes the form of an address in the second person, though the speaker this time is Prytherch himself. To whom is he talking? The obvious answer is the poet, whose swift thoughts and 'sharp eyes' leave the countryman no peace or hiding place. (The fact that in 'The Gap in the Hedge' it was Prytherch who had the 'sharp eyes' highlights the extent to which the relationship between poet and peasant is one of mutual torment.) The poet is now cast as an agent rather than a critic of the modern world, however – one of the careless tourists who leave gates open without thought for the consequences for those who have to make their living from the land. 'Invasion on the Farm' is another poem about poetry, this time about the politics of representation. To write about a social reality is to 'let the world in' on that reality, with the possibility of thereby changing it for the worse. This is a particular danger where literature about remote regions is concerned. Such writing constitutes a sort of virtual tourism which can, if it gains a readership of any size, lead to actual tourism: a poetry such as Thomas's can consequently become implicated in the commodification and consumerism it sets out to deplore. Thomas has often been accused of self-contradiction in his political pronouncements, but in his poetry at least he displays the most sophisticated awareness of the ironies involved in writerly intervention in the public sphere. One of the particular ironies of 'Invasion on the Farm' is that though it is the poet who has transgressed, it is Prytherch who asks for forgiveness.

Only the first six of the Prytherch poems were written during Thomas's rectorship at Manafon. He moved in 1954 to become vicar of Eglwys-fach in Cardiganshire, where he remained for a year longer than he had in Manafon. There is a retrospective quality about many of the poems in the last two-thirds of the series, as if to acknowledge that the encounter with Prytherch already belongs to the past and that even to ponder its significance is to surrender to nostalgia. Thus the first post-Manafon piece to feature Prytherch, 'Temptation of a Poet', struggles against the impulse to 'renew / The lost poetry of our talk'. We might object that while poetry may have flowed from the encounter staged in the earlier poems, there was very little in the way of 'talk' in evidence there, unless we construe the word in terms of the dialectic sparked in the poet's mind by the spectacle of the mute peasant. By the end of the poem, at any rate, the speaker can no longer resist the call of the past, with its 'cool smell / Of autumn leaves'. 'I am undone', he concedes, and so the 'talk' is resumed with renewed vigour in 'Green Categories', the next piece, which roughly challenges the countryman with an impossibly arch question:

> You never heard of Kant, did you, Prytherch?
> A strange man! What would he have said
> Of your life here, free from the remote
> War of antinomies; free also

From the mind's uncertainty faced with a world
Of its own making?
                    Here all is sure;
Things exist rooted in the flesh,
Stone, tree and flower. Even while you sleep
In your low room, the dark moor exerts
Its pressure on the timbers. Space and time
Are not the mathematics that your will
Imposes, but a green calendar
Your heart observes; how else could you
Find your way home or know when to die
With the slow patience of the men who raised
This landmark in the moor's deep tides?

His logic would have failed; your mind, too,
Exposed suddenly to the cold wind
Of genius, faltered. Yet at night together
In your small garden, fenced from the wild moor's
Constant aggression, you could have been at one,
Sharing your faith over a star's blue fire.
                                        (*PS*, 19)

The mind's solitary helplessness before a material reality it can never truly know but has an ineradicable need to render meaningful is the subject of some of the most resourceful and ambitious modernist poems, such as Wallace Stevens's 'The Idea of Order at Key West' and Hugh MacDiarmid's 'On a Raised Beach'. Both of those works implicitly draw on the Kantian distinction between *phenomenon* – a thing as it appears to us – and *noumenon* – a thing as it is in itself. Thomas makes more explicit and at the same time more reckless use of Kant's epistemology, significantly distorting it to highlight the stubborn, unreachable integrity of Prytherch's view of the world. Kant's 'Copernican revolution' in cognitive theory centred on the key insight that the mind does not, as earlier philosophers had assumed, conform to the world, but that the world conforms to the mind. We can perceive *phenomena* but we cannot know *noumena*. Things have to be located in the *a priori* particulars of space and time for us to experience them, and we can experience them only by imposing upon them four mental 'categories', namely Quantity (Unity, Plurality, Totality), Quality (Reality, Negation, Limitation), Relation (Substance, Causality, Interaction) and Modality (Possibility, Existence, Necessity). This imposition is effected by what Kant calls the pure self, and is necessarily anterior to the emergence of what he terms the empirical self, that seat of conscious experience and so-called 'self-awareness'. Kant's 'critical philosophy' attempts to describe the way perception works, and assumes that it works the same way for everybody. Thus while a twentieth-century Welsh sheep-farmer's empirical self may be very different from that of an eighteenth-century German philosopher, the pure selves of both men may be taken to operate in the same way to bring their distinctive empirical selves into being. That is why it is nonsense for Thomas to write of perception in terms of what the 'will / Imposes'. We perceive things the way we perceive them, and the will is a function of the empirical self, which has no control over cognitive processes. Stone, tree and flower are phenomenal emanations of the noumenal world whether Prytherch knows them to be so or not, and the pressure exerted by the dark moor on Iago's house offers no more convincing a refutation of Kant's epistemology than Dr Johnson's famous kicking of a stone did of George Berkeley's. (It might also be observed that 'antinomies' in Kantian logic are apparent rather than substantive contradictions, and that Thomas's application of the epithet 'warring' to them is therefore misleading.) 'Green Categories', then, is bad philosophy, but philosophical continence is hardly the point of the poem. Kant is recruited by the poet as the most sophisticated, least 'affected' representative imaginable of what 'A Peasant' had called 'the refined . . . sense', in order to facilitate the poem's genuinely warring antinomy between intellect on the one hand and Prytherch's particular form of mindlessness on the other. The Kantian term 'category' is adapted and adorned with the epithet 'green' to help Thomas body forth Prytherch's unshakeable country sense of things and ultimately to salute the dignity of his deeply ingrained, unexamined and yet in its way authoritative manner of looking at the world. The fact that both philosopher and countryman are locked into their disparate solipsistic visions provides the paradoxical ground for our imagining them sitting happily together at day's end. The closing lines, as has been pointed out by earlier commentators, allude to the concluding sentence of Kant's *Critique of Practical Reason*: 'der bestirnte Himmel über mir, und das moralische Gesetz in mir' – 'the starry heaven above me, and the moral law within me'.[23] The ending of the poem may not be entirely successful, however. How can Kant and Prytherch be said to share a 'faith' (singular)? While the recurrence of the star image is pleasing in terms both of the figurative coherence of the series as a whole, and of the particularity of its reference to Kant's writing in the context of this particular poem, the preposition that accompanies it is problematic. We can visualize the unlikely companions sitting 'over' a fire, but 'fire' here

exists on the secondary, metaphorical level of the text. How they could
contrive to sit 'over' a star is a question that seems to the present reader in
need of resolution as he struggles to make the poem conform to his
mind's perhaps too puritanical categories.

The ninth poem – the second with the title 'Iago Prytherch' – also
features a slight grammatical crux:

> no one will tell you
> How I made fun of you, or pitied either
> Your long soliloquies, crouched at your slow
> And patient surgery under the faint
> November rays of the sun's lamp.
>
> (*PS*, 36)

Syntactically, if not metrically, 'either' belongs after 'you', a full line
above where Thomas places it. The poem is nevertheless among the
strongest in the series, one that returns to the politics of representation
theme of 'Invasion on the Farm' in the light of criticism from an
unidentified source ('them') that Thomas's work exploits the plight of
the hill farmers. (It repeats and reverses that earlier poem's 'Forgive me',
now addressed from poet to peasant.) Thomas's defence against the
charge takes the form of the poetry's fullest description of Prytherch
since 'A Peasant', a description suffused with a sort of sacramental
tenderness entirely absent from that first poem. As 'patient surgery' of
the earth, Iago's work now has a holistic, vocational aspect difficult to
reconcile with the 'half-witted grin / Of satisfaction' of our initial
encounter with him. (Those 'long soliloquies' are news, too, though they
may of course consist of grunts and mutterings rather than Shakespear-
ian self-communings: Thomas can be thin-lipped and sardonic even in
the presence of the sacramental.) The lyric to some degree anticipates the
testimony of the second 'The Face' to the urgent, obsessive character of
the poetry's involvement with Prytherch – it is yet another Prytherch
poem 'about' the Prytherch poems. The sense that Iago has a 'real', extra-
textual existence is as strong here as it has been weak in some of the
intervening pieces, though it is to be noted that even in locating him once
again firmly in the empirical world, Thomas textualizes Prytherch's being
by making him look like a question mark:

> I passed and saw you
> Labouring there, your dark figure
> Marring the simple geometry

Of the square fields with its gaunt question.
My poems were made in its long shadow
Falling coldly across the page.

(*PS*, 36)

'Absolution' is very much a companion piece to the ninth poem, taking up the forgiveness trope and deepening and making more explicit its sacramental aspect. It is the peasant who is priestly now, at his 'stone altar on which the light's / Bread is broken', and the priest who is peasant-like in the 'thin' quality of his scorn. The redisposition of what I have earlier referred to as the 'elements' of the series reaches an extreme in this poem, in which the mind of the poet, rather than that of the representatives of mass culture, is described as a 'cheap gallery'. The abjection of the poet-speaker before the depth and dignity of Prytherch's suffering continues in 'The Dark Well', yet another lyric on the relationship between the poetry and its audience. 'I have . . . chosen', writes Thomas,

> for an indulgent world's
> Ear the story of one whose hands
> Have bruised themselves on the locked doors
> Of life; whose heart, fuller than mine
> Of gulped tears, is the dark well
> From which to draw, drop after drop,
> The terrible poetry of his kind.

(*T*, 9)

The 'terrible poetry of his kind', of course, is less the text the peasant figure elicits from Thomas than the text he represents in himself. Continuous with the earlier projection of him as a question mark, these lines elaborate a distinction between the poetry Prytherch features in and the poetry he *is*. They retrospectively license a reading of the 'long soliloquies' of the second 'Iago Prytherch' in terms of a contrast between the eloquence of Prytherch's actions – his 'patient surgery' of the soil – and the inarticulacy of his speech.

In 'Too Late', the twelfth lyric, everything is reversed again and Prytherch is rebuked for his shallow materialism. For the first time since 'A Peasant', his Welshness is highlighted – a Welshness he is accused of betraying by giving up his poverty-stricken life as a smallholder for more remunerative employment as a farm labourer:

The rain and the wind are hard masters;
I have known you wince under their lash.
But there was comfort for you at the day's end
Dreaming over the warm ash

Of a turf fire on a hill farm.
Contented with your accustomed ration
Of bread and bacon, and drawing your strength
From membership of an old nation

Not given to beg. But look at yourself
Now, a servant hired to flog
The life out of the slow soil,
Or come obediently as a dog

To the pound's whistle.
                    (*T*, 25)

This is not without its absurdity. Was Prytherch not also following the pound's whistle – in the more obvious sense of that pleasing pun – when in the old days he strove to make a living out of his smallholding? The real point of the poem emerges in the last two lines about 'the cold brain of the machine' that will destroy 'you and your race' (the last two words deftly partner 'his kind', the previous lyric's closing phrase). Wishing to write a poem on the cultural price to be paid for the mechanization of farming, Thomas reaches for the figure of Prytherch as a convenient peg upon which to hang his protest. In the process, Prytherch at last becomes the (albeit degenerate) 'representative of the Welsh *gwladwr*' Pennar Davies had seen in him in 1946. It is not the series' finest moment.

Neither, perhaps, is 'Portrait', though it memorably develops the stellar imagery of the group in its description of Prytherch as 'a man for whom / The stars' bridle was hung too high'. The first stanza poses a question, to which the second replies. The unsatisfactory aspect of the poem is the indeterminate identity of the 'You' addressed throughout, or rather the difficulty the reader experiences in positing *any* conceivable identity for the addressee. The poem nonetheless ends strongly with a contrast between the clarity of Prytherch's 'hard blue eyes' and the incoherence of his 'lips' slobber'. 'Which?', the fourteenth piece, once again raises questions about the peasant's status as anything other than a literary creation, and otherwise recapitulates the themes of the preceding poems without significantly deepening or extending them.

A sense that the series was running out of steam probably underlies the summarizing retrospection of the opening line of 'Servant' – 'You served me well, Prytherch' – a poem which then proceeds to revivify the entire enterprise magnificently, fully articulating the land-as-book figure adumbrated in some of the earlier pieces and seeking to balance their contradictory witness to the textuality and non-textuality of their central figure, and to the fullness and emptiness of his heart:

> Not that you gave
> The whole answer. Is truth so bare,
> So dark, so dumb, as on your hearth
> And in your company I found it?
> Is not the evolving print of the sky
> To be read, too; the mineral
> Of the mind worked? Is not truth choice,
> With a clear eye and a free hand,
> From life's bounty?
> Not choice for you,
> But seed sown upon the thin
> Soil of a heart, not rich, nor fertile,
> Yet capable of the one crop,
> Which is the bread of truth that I break.
>
> (*BT*, 41)

The climactic closing line here gave the volume in which the poem appeared its sacramental title. A case could perhaps be made for 'Servant' as the greatest of the Prytherch poems, so effective is its combination of rich figuration with plainness of address, and so successful its gathering of most – if not quite all – of the concerns of the series into a unitary, expertly modulated utterance.

The war theme, which does not feature in 'Servant', is taken up in 'For the Record', another piece that might merit inclusion even in a small selection of Thomas's verse. 'This will go onward the same / Though Dynasties pass' wrote Thomas Hardy in 1915 of a man following a plough-horse ('In Time of "The Breaking of Nations"'). 'How wrong can a writer be?' we might ask in relation to the English poet's observation, given that farming in Britain would be mechanized within a few years of his lyric's appearance. In time of the breaking of nations, however, fuel becomes scarce and mechanization has to be laid aside in favour of older, less ecologically expensive methods of tilling the land. Thomas appears to take a grim satisfaction in wartime exigencies in his depiction of Prytherch in 'For the Record', a lyric which, though published in 1966, reminds us that the Welsh poet's peasant exists in a sort of eternal mid-1940s, the period when his shadow first fell across his page:

> What was your war record, Prytherch?
> I know: up and down the same field,
> Following a horse; no oil for tractors;
> Sniped at by rain, but never starving.
> Did you listen to the reports
> Of how heroes are fashioned and how killed?
> Did you wait up late for the news?

We can assume that the answer to both those questions is in the negative. (Thomas elsewhere gives us to understand that farmers in his early parishes were in fact sharply aware of the war, sharing in the widespread fear of a German invasion and alert to the proximity of Luftwaffe aircraft on their way to bomb Merseyside.[24]) Yet the vacancy of Prytherch's mind, in this context at least, is a matter for congratulation, duly rendered in terms of the tillage-as-surgery conceit introduced in the ninth poem. The poor farmer now becomes a healer of the time's ills and an obstetrician to the future:

> Yet in your acres,
> With no medals to be won,
> You were on the old side of life,
> Helping it in through the dark door
> Of earth and beast, quietly repairing
> The rents of history with your hands.
> (*P*, 22)

'Aside', the seventeenth poem, plays a minor variation on the war theme, and recalls the heavenly bodies as witnesses to the timeless validity of Prytherch's solitary and uncomplaining working of the land:

> There is no forward and no back
> In the fields, only the year's two
> Solstices, and patience between.
> (*P*, 29)

If Prytherch was dying as a spur to Thomas's creativity by the mid-1960s, 'The Grave', published in the last year of that decade, and hitherto uncollected, buried him:

I pass your grave
Daily; walk up and down
On it. I know that under
The bright grass there is nothing
But your dry bones. Prytherch,
They won't believe that this
Is the truth. Rumours start
Like hill fires; empty minds
Blow on them. Someone has seen
You at a meeting; somewhere
A bomb grumbles. Echoes
Reverberate in the heart's
Hollows. Durable
As a tree in history's
Landscape, you are renewed
By wishes, by foliage
Of young hopes . . .
                                    It is the old
Failing, a skirmish seen
As a battle, a victory turned
To a legend before it is won.[25]

The 'Elvis is alive' scenario developed here makes sense in relation to the demands of Thomas's readers for more of the same rather than in terms of the logic of the fictive world once (and forever) inhabited by Prytherch. In that world, after all, the peasant was unremarkable and unknown even to his neighbours. The poet's readers were implicitly criticised in the first poem of the series and now, in a text probably intended as the last devoted (albeit off-handedly) to Prytherch, they are scarcely more favoured. The tree image comes full circle, and the very endurance of the tree, once a focus for admiration, becomes a matter of annoyance. (The extent to which the tree, here and elsewhere in the series, relates to the magic trees of Welsh mythology is a subject that deserves further discussion.) The rebuke in the closing lines is perhaps aimed at Thomas's admiring critics and in particular at their tendency to treat the Prytherch series as more significant and coherent than its creator believes it to be. Certainly, if the texts that bring Hugh MacDiarmid's Drunk Man and John Berryman's Henry to being are to be seen as battles, the Prytherch poems can hardly be said to constitute more than a skirmish. Some skirmishes are decisive, however, and Thomas's dismissive attitude towards his own creation is perhaps to be understood less as a guide to our estimation of the series than as an indication of his interest in moving on to another kind of poetry, an atonal art deliberately opposed to the seductions of lyricism and the constructions of fiction – an art of which 'The Grave', with its loose structure and brusque, rather underworked enjambments, provides a not particularly promising (and thus deceptive) foretaste. The 'meeting' and 'bomb' details probably involve a mordant comment on the protests and subversive activities surrounding the Investiture of the Prince of Wales in Caernarfon Castle in the summer of 1969. In the most famous incident, two members of Mudiad Amddiffyn Cymru, subsequently known as the Abergele Martyrs, lost their lives when the bomb they were carrying exploded prematurely in Denbighshire. The poem seems to imply that the nationalist excitements of the day were misguided, if only by virtue of their insufficiency of scale and achievement, and that the contribution of the Prytherch poems to the salvation of Wales has been no less exaggerated. (If the idea of Prytherch's attendance at a political meeting seems preposterous, that surely is Thomas's way of repudiating optimistic nationalist readings of his character's significance.)

The full significance of the Prytherch figure cannot be assessed without reference to some of the poems on the 'B-list' yet to be discussed. The early 'Enigma' explores the meaning of the peasant's silence, of his blindness, deafness and dumbness before the beauty and diversity of nature, rather as the later poetry probes the meaning of the silence of God. 'The Slave' takes up the same theme in terms which suggest that Thomas's interest in peasant inarticulacy involves a sort of displaced concern with the value of his own commitment to poetic articulation. 'The Last of the Peasantry' focuses on the peasant's visage, as do, obviously, the two pieces called 'The Face'. The first of these can be read as one of a number of attempted valedictions to Prytherch, and perhaps even as the first poem to mark his death. The second, a work of considerable power, recounts the haunting of the speaker's mind by the 'never absent' face of a ploughman (as Thomas's countryman is in this manifestation). It is perhaps significant that the locality in which the subject lives is evoked in terms remarkably consistent with the prose description of Manafon quoted earlier in this essay. There is a very faint suggestion of a peasant–Christ identification in this poem's realization of the tree image:

> I can see his eye
> That expects nothing, that has the rain's
> Colourlessness. His hands are broken
> But not his spirit. He is like bark
> Weathering on the tree of his kind.

The identification is repeated, at once strengthened and disallowed, in the final verse paragraph:

> He will go on; that much is certain.
> Beneath him tenancies of the fields
> Will change; machinery turn
> All to noise. But on the walls
> Of the mind's gallery that face
> With the hills framing it will hang
> Unglorified, but stern like the soil.
>
> (*P*, 41)

(The 'hills framing' the unglorified visage here recall the 'same hills' that 'crowd the horizon' round the Crucifixion scene in 'Pietà', the title poem of the volume in which 'The Face' was collected.)

Prytherch did indeed 'go on'. The poet may have 'buried' him in the lyric – or anti-lyric – appropriately called 'The Grave', but the peasant's face returned to haunt him in the late, last addition to the series in 1978. By the time he wrote 'Gone?', the nineteenth of the 'A-list' Prytherch poems, Thomas had assumed full mastery of the austere style towards which he had been groping in the penultimate piece:

> Will they say on some future
> occasion, looking over the flogged acres
> of ploughland: This was Prytherch country?
> Nothing to show for it now: hedges
> uprooted, walls gone, a mobile people
> hurrying to and fro on their fast
> tractors; a forest of aerials
> as though an invading fleet invisibly
> had come to anchor among these
> financed hills. They copy the image
> of themselves projected on their smooth
> screens to the accompaniment of inane
> music. They give grins and smiles
> back in return for the money that is
> spent on them. But where is the face
> with the crazed eyes that through the unseen
> drizzle of its tears looked out
> on this land and found no beauty
> in it, but accepted it, as a man

> will who has needs in him that only
> bare ground, black thorns and the sky's
>   emptiness can fulfil?
>
>   (*F*, 34)

Insofar as the question posed by the title relates to Prytherch, it elicits three possible answers, two positive, one ambiguous. Has Prytherch *gone?* He and his ilk have indeed – necessarily – departed from the machine-dominated, consumerist, hedgeless and soil-exhausted rural Welsh dystopia conjured here. By 1978 he had gone also, as we are now in a position to say, from Thomas's poetry, or at least from that portion of it placed in the public domain: the nine collections published between *Frequencies* and the posthumous *Residues* make no mention of him.[26] (That the old, numinous Wales has gone with him is suggested by the bathetic echo,[27] in the figure likening television aerials to the masts of an invading fleet, of the description of the hostile Welsh ships approaching Ireland in Branwen's tale in the *Mabinogi*.[28]) But, facilitating the third answer, there is a sense in which Prytherch will never be gone as long as there are readers to read the poems in which his being inheres. 'So long as men can breathe or eyes can see', wrote Shakespeare in his eighteenth sonnet, 'So long lives this, and this gives life to thee'. Thomas may never have been tempted to compare Prytherch to a summer's day, and the desolate time-scapes of his later poetry make a mockery of the Renaissance sonneteers' vaunting confidence in the perdurability of art. He was nonetheless interested in the matter of posterity, as poets perhaps inevitably are, and it can hardly come as a surprise that he communicated his interest in an oblique and sardonic manner. The 'Residues' label he attached to the sheaf of texts which was to form the basis of his posthumous collection suggests, on the one hand, that poems are mere scraps, leavings.[29] Yet, on the other, it registers a low-key but stubborn claim for the durability of language and art: words, for all their tricksiness and undependability, have more reality than we have, and our skilful arrangements of them outlast us. If the positive aspect of his choice of the term amounts to less than a Horatian boast of building a monument more lasting than bronze, it does at least acknowledge that verbal artefacts can have a measure of permanence. 'Gone?', published almost a quarter of a century before Thomas's death, and many years before he assembled the contents of *Residues*, opens with a conjecture about his poetic afterlife and about the fate of Prytherch, who might in this context be described as the best-known of his residues. Only those familiar with Thomas's poems, after all, will think of observing that the 'flogged acres' were once 'Prytherch country'. The 'they' of the opening line, however, cannot be identified as the poet's readers unless they make such an observation, and their making of it is rendered subject to the question mark at the end of the third line. The answer to that question is in turn bound up with the answer to the further question on which, nineteen lines later, the poem concludes. And in response to that final question we can say only that the face with the crazed eyes exists (and will exist in the future) not in the Welsh countryside where it was first seen or imagined but in the minds of the poems' readers. Thomas's vision of the permanence of his art is thus less a matter of haughty authorial claim than of tortuous speculation by way of a composite question, yet that question encompasses somewhere in its folds a sly confidence in at least the possibility of a continuing viability for his poems after his death, a confidence vindicated – *inter alia* – by the existence of the present volume of essays. If the ecological horrors adumbrated in the later poetry do not engulf humanity in the short to middle term (not·the first big *if* of this essay), it seems probable that that man Prytherch, with the torn cap, will still be there in the gap in the hedge for a very considerable number of mornings to come.

Notes

[1] There have been two dedicated essays on the Prytherch poems: H. J. Savill, 'The Iago Prytherch Poems of R. S. Thomas', originally published in the *Anglo-Welsh Review*, 20:45 (Autumn 1971) and reprinted in *Critical Writings*, 30–45; and Anne Stevenson, 'The Uses of Prytherch', in *Page's Drift*, 36–56. Stevenson uses the term 'Prytherch poems' to refer to Thomas's early work in general. See also M. Wynn Thomas, 'R. S. Thomas: The Poetry of the Sixties', *Internal Difference: Twentieth-Century Writing in Wales* (Cardiff: University of Wales Press, 1992), 111–20; and John Powell Ward, *The Poetry of R. S. Thomas* (2nd edn; Bridgend: Seren, 2001), 17–20, 23–34, 71–3, 75–6.

[2] Of the 18 poems from *SF* dropped from *SYT*, 6 are restored in *CP*, which excludes 20 poems from *SF* in all. Of the 6 pieces from *AL* excluded from the 1955 volume, 4 are re-admitted to the canon in *CP*, which excludes 12 poems from *AL* in total. The canonicity of *CP* is problematic, as the volume was compiled by the poet's son, Gwydion Thomas, rather than by R. S. Thomas himself.

[3] Evans is introduced in 'Evans' (*PS*, 15). Though he appears to be near death in that poem, he is a figure of brute health in the much later 'The Country' (*YO*, 25), where he strongly resembles Prytherch.

[4] Elsewhere, Thomas suggests that Prytherch was an 'amalgam' of a number of his parishioners. *Abercuawg*, his 1976 address at the National Eisteddfod, includes the following key passage: 'When I began writing I devised a character called Iago Prytherch – an amalgam of some farmers I used to see at work on the Montgomeryshire hillsides. In the opinion of some, he developed into a symbol of something greater. And yet I had to ask myself whether he was real at all. And there

was something else that would worry me as I saw him sweating or shivering hour after hour in the fields: "What is he thinking about? What's going on inside his skull?" And of course there was always the awful possibility that the answer was – "Nothing" ' (*Selected Prose*, 126).

[5] 'The Making of a Poem', a lecture delivered at the conference of Library Authorities in Wales and Monmouthshire, Barry, 1968; *Selected Prose*, 84. Thomas goes on to suggest that he is in no position to raise such an objection given that so much of his own poetry is theme-driven.

[6] Pennar Davies, *Our Modern Poets*, broadcast on the BBC Welsh Home Service, 21 November 1946.

[7] *Dock Leaves*, 3:7 (Spring 1952), 48.

[8] First published in *Wales*, 5:7 (1945) and reprinted in *Selected Prose*, 17–23.

[9] *Dock Leaves*, 6:18 (Winter 1955), 5.

[10] *Critical Writings on R. S. Thomas*, 33. Savill is responding to Pennar Davies's assumption that Prytherch is a Welsh speaker.

[11] See Justin Wintle, *Furious Interiors: Wales, R. S. Thomas and God* (London: HarperCollins, 1996), 184–94, 239–41 and 294–8.

[12] Editorial, *Anglo-Welsh Review*, 9:24 (1959), 6.

[13] For an account of the structural parallels and aesthetic and cultural divergences between Kavavagh's and Thomas's long poems, see the present writer's 'Lean Parishes: Patrick Kavanagh's *The Great Hunger* and R. S. Thomas's *The Minister*', in *Dangerous Diversity: The Changing Faces of Wales*, ed. Katie Gramich and Andrew Hiscock (Cardiff: University of Wales Press, 1998), 131–49.

[14] See Wintle, *Furious Interiors*, 189–92, and *Page's Drift*, 39–40.

[15] Walford Davies, 'R. S. Thomas: The Poem's Harsher Conditions', *New Welsh Review*, 11 (Winter 1990–1), 15–26; D. Z. Phillips, 'Poetry and Philosophy: A Reply', *New Welsh Review*, 12 (Spring 1991), 64–8; Walford Davies, 'Poetry and Philosophy: a Rejoinder', *New Welsh Review*, 12 (Spring 1991), 68–71.

[16] Thomas professed an admiration for MacDiarmid's Scots poetry. 'The English is, as it were, the water in the whisky, and I prefer my MacDiarmid neat', he observed in his little-known Preface to the catalogue of the exhibition held by the National Library of Scotland on the occasion of MacDiarmid's seventy-fifth birthday. See *Hugh MacDiarmid*, Catalogue No. 7 (Edinburgh: National Library of Scotland, 1967), 3. See also 'Some Contemporary Scottish Writing' (*Selected Prose*, 24–35), which first appeared in *Wales*, 6:3, in 1946, the year 'A Peasant' was composed.

[17] See *New Welsh Review*, 11 (Winter 1990–1), 21, and *New Welsh Review*, 12 (Spring 1991), 65 and 70.

[18] I should like to express my gratitude to Harri Pritchard Jones for a cheerful and stimulating exchange on the significance of Thomas's 'curious stars' image.

[19] *Critical Writings*, 38.

[20] It is perhaps worth bearing in mind that the gate of Manafon Rectory opens onto the main road.

[21] I am grateful to M. Wynn Thomas for the ingenious suggestion – independently corroborated by Damian Walford Davies (see p. 158 above) – that 'Iago Prytherch' (*SF*) offers a variation on the syntax of Kipling's 'If—'. Thomas's lyric gains in eirenic force when read against the imperial machismo of Kipling's too-well-known poem.

[22] *The Listener*, 80 (10 March 1955), 429. See *The Complete Poems of Edwin Muir: An Annotated Edition*, ed. Peter Butter (Aberdeen: The Association for Scottish Literary Studies, 1991), 226 and 353.

[23] See Raymond Garlick's editorial, *Anglo-Welsh Review*, 9:24 (1959), 6, and H. J. Savill, *Critical Writings*, 35.

[24] *Selected Prose*, 21, 45. For an illuminating discussion of the wartime context of the Prytherch poems, see M. Wynn Thomas, 'R. S. Thomas: War Poet', *WWE*, 2 (1996), 83–7.

[25] *Anglo-Welsh Review*, 18:41 (Summer 1969), 16.

[26] It would be interesting to learn whether there are any references to Prytherch among the 'not inconsiderable number of poems' in the keeping of M. Wynn Thomas, the literary executor of the poet's unpublished work. See 'Editor's Note', *R*, 9.

[27] The allusion to the *Mabinogi* was noted by Jason Walford Davies in ' "Thick Ambush of Shadows": Allusions to Welsh Literature in the Work of R. S. Thomas', *WWE*, 1 (1995), 103. See also the same author's discussion in *Gororau'r Iaith: R. S. Thomas a'r Traddodiad Llenyddol Cymraeg* (Cardiff: University of Wales Press, 2003), 272–4.

[28] On the subject of echoes: there is a striking, if questionably significant, chime between the closing lines of this poem and those of 'The Way of It', the title piece of Thomas's previous collection. That lyric – its rhetoric precludes our calling it a love poem – brings its qualified celebration of the relationship between the poet and his wife to rest with an account of their courtship (the italics are mine):

> I saw her,
> when young, and spread the panoply
> of my feathers instinctively
> to engage her. She was not deceived,
> *but accepted me as a girl*
> *will* under a thin moon
> in love's absence as someone
> she could build a home with
> for her imagined child.
> (*WI*, 30)

[29] See 'Editor's Note', *R*, 9.

2

R. S. Thomas's Welsh Pastoral

GEOFFREY HILL

For twenty-six years – from 1940 until he took early retirement in the mid-1960s – Rush Rhees, the philosopher most inward with Wittgenstein's thinking, lived in Swansea and taught there at the University of Wales. He was deeply drawn to Wittgenstein's theories of language, both in assent and dissent, and because he lectured at a Welsh university college, he used the context and situation of the Welsh language for purposes of illustration. He did not discuss any feature that makes Welsh Welsh, and if he had been lecturing in Germany, German would have served his purpose equally well. It is the weight of circumstance that brings me to begin my essay in this way; there are undoubtedly better ways, but a start has to be made. Rush Rhees could not read or speak Welsh, though he made attempts to learn; nor can I read or speak the language, except for a few of the most basic phrases. R. S. Thomas wrote autobiographical and polemical prose in Welsh and composed poetry in English, much of it on Welsh themes. Clearly, the complex issue of belonging and not belonging possessed Thomas's mind, politically in the Welsh prose as in the English lyrics, though the lyrics most often present themselves as pastoral or existential cogitations. The sense or perception that unites his poetry and prose is that of *hiraeth*. It is not inevitable that *hiraeth* will draw you into contemplation and expression of political vision, but it is not unlikely that it will.

Rush Rhees returns often to the theme of language and belonging. It is not so much that one learns, say, Welsh directly at one's mother's knee as that in the slow on-going of life one is gradually gathered up by it and into it: 'Language goes with a way of living'; 'If someone learns to speak, he does not just learn to make sentences and utter them'; 'Wittgenstein used to say that to imagine a language is to imagine a form of life.'[1] Rhees thinks that some of Wittgenstein's ideas about language remained unthought-through; but taking these phrases as they stand, I incline to the view that they go some way towards the illumination of R. S. Thomas's political–existential–pastoral modes. One of the chief functions of the poet is to imagine and project a form of life, whether of bird, beast and flower or of the righteous commonweal or kingdom; and one is entitled to require of poets that their language shall itself be a dimension of that imagining, not an uninflected, unreflective medium through which, in a neutral way, thought and feeling flow. The poet has to imagine the making of his own language in the immediate process of making it.[2]

Seen from a different angle, the poet's language is as much as he can make – and make of it – in the given circumstances, the unfinished and approximate as much in evidence as the perfected. This is a question with which Alun Lewis was much exercised, in his letters and in some of the poems. It is the kind of issue which writers of conscience can be expected to debate with themselves and with others, particularly if extreme circumstances have arisen which bring a search for meaning into a terrain of meaninglessness. R. S. Thomas is always in this sense a writer of conscience. In the polemical Welsh prose he is inclined to see himself as a keeper of consciences; he then becomes disdainful and hectoring.[3]

Rush Rhees contends, in much of his thinking about Wittgenstein, that 'language makes sense if living makes sense';[4] but if living ceases to make sense, does language decline with it in a symmetrical curve? Obviously not, because 'cease to make sense' is itself a figure of speech. I would ask the reader to bear this oxymoron in mind while I present the salient features (as they appear to me) of James Hanley's *Grey Children: A Study in Humbug and Misery in South Wales* (1937). This book is an account of a brief visit to a colliery village in south Wales during the worst of the Depression and of mass unemployment in the mining communities. *Grey Children* provides an essential means of understanding not only such poets as Huw Menai and Idris Davies but also writers of conscience born into more comfortable circumstances: I have in mind especially Alun Lewis and R. S. Thomas.

Among the tasks which Hanley sets himself is that of recording the forms of speech with which the destitute miners and their families try to register for themselves, and make cogent for the stranger, the abnormality of once normal lives (though many would say that mining was never normal in the accepted sense) and the abnormality of what now passes as 'normal' in the mining villages. The word 'farce', for example, becomes a term of oratory: 'We *don't* like it, it's a farce' (of the Social Centre);

'sometimes I just don't care, getting sick of the farce of the whole damned thing'. Hanley takes up the word – from them and on their behalf: 'going through the same old farce all over again'; 'The above case, quite a simple one, showing meanness and farce in the same breath, is the kind of thing that goes on day after day amongst the workless'.[5] In terms of grammar, farce can be represented by tautology and oxymoron: 'men and lads talking together, all the same things over and over again'; 'The worst of it is you wake up to the same old thing every morning of your life . . . Many men lie in bed . . . Many of them do nothing but walk, walk, walk'; 'The reader may notice here a tendency to the word terrible, and I add that it is just meant that way. For the thing *is* terrible, and the best way of forcing it home on people is to keep on saying so' (*Grey Children*, 27, 60, 77).

Hanley's prose is here self-abnegating: anyone who supposes that plodding repetitiousness is natural to this writer has not read his novel *The Welsh Sonata* (1954). Two terms applicable to the narrative form of *Grey Children*, which alternates between agitated and inert, are 'inure' and 'acclimatize'. I apply them because they are words that Hanley uses to describe men and women sinking into the conditions of their lives: 'True, there are some old people who are so used to this sort of thing that they have become quite inured to it'; 'He had completely forgotten the pits, what they looked and smelt like. He had become acclimatized to a new kind of life' (*Grey Children*, 151, 206). A further reason is that the two terms suggest equally well what happens to words, and what words make happen, when they are placed in service to a given narrative. There is a deep ambivalence caught up in our sense of inurement – almost too deep for articulation. To be inured is to endure by taking the obstructive-ness of things into one's essential being without in any way being diminished thereby. It is also to become impoverished, depleted, by the habitual bearing of that to which one has become acclimatized. This bi-fold strain is of greatest significance when it affects men and women; but it is not without significance when it affects the language that people use.

Alun Lewis and early R. S. Thomas are strikingly similar – and, to an extent, reminiscent of Hanley – in their depiction of inurement and acclimatization. Hanley and Thomas were friends;[6] Hanley wrote a letter of encouragement to Lewis after reading one of his short stories;[7] but the kind of resonances we catch here could have occurred without the slightest degree of personal acquaintance. Lewis, 'On Embarkation':

> And farther on the mortgaged crumbling farm
> Where Shonni Rhys, that rough backsliding man

> Has found the sheep again within the corn
> And fills the evening with his sour oaths . . .[8]

R. S. Thomas, 'A Peasant':

> Iago Prytherch his name . . .
> . . .
> His clothes, sour with years of sweat
> And animal contact . . .
>   (*SF*, 14)

I have observed that, in *Grey Children*, repetitiousness to the point of monotony, even tautology, is Hanley's way of presenting inurement and drab acclimatization with the greatest possible truthfulness of observation. I come to a less certain conclusion about the similarities between Lewis's lines and those by Thomas: 'his sour oaths', 'sour with years of sweat'. One is looking at a type of poetic diction here. 'Sour' usefully compounds the physical with the psychological and is a shorthand sign standing for a landscape at once real and symbolic, physical and mental – a variant of the early poems of Auden: 'the shut gates of works', 'silted harbours', 'strangled orchards', 'the children / At play on the fuming alkali-tip', 'the distortions of ingrown virginity'.[9]

Objection is sometimes made to the lordly insouciance with which the young Auden casts his vivid runes of injustice and suffering. As others before me have observed, there is something arbitrary, conscienceless, in the power of poetry to move us; one can sense that both Lewis and Thomas are somewhat uneasy with this aspect of their art, though Thomas less so than Lewis. The exact contour of the speech each is looking for lies somewhere between the lines marked out by Auden's *Poems* of 1930 and James Hanley's *Grey Children* of 1937. Hanley states:

> To study the psychology of the little thing is to get to the very roots of working-class mentality, to sound feelings, to understand them. The problem of the lost markets for coal is a big problem, but not as big as Mrs Johns' problem of not having sixpence to give her son to go to the pictures.
> (*Grey Children*, 70)

That is to say, Mrs Johns may be naive but the human rightness of her naive priorities is unarguable. I originally wrote 'unassailable', thinking to stress the ethical side of things, but found the irony intolerable. Mrs Johns is assailed from all sides.

The difficulty for any writer attempting to take the measure of the 'psychology of the little thing' is that the phrase is open to more than one interpretation. It shades into the Flaubert–Pound insistence that 'Good writing . . . uses the smallest possible number of words',[10] even though the philosophy behind the one statement may be radically at odds with the philosophy of the other. I believe that in the work of both Lewis and Thomas there is some attempt to view the two emphases as compatible. The attempt is more immediately evident in Lewis's writing: 'no expression of human life is powerless',[11] where 'expression of . . . life' is to be inclusive of people such as Hanley's Mrs Johns, keeping house against grim odds, and also of Lewis's own writing, such as his newly completed 'Post-Script: for Gweno':

> If I should go away,
> Beloved, do not say
> 'He has forgotten me'.
> For you abide,
> A singing rib within my dreaming side . . .
>
> (*Collected Poems*, 54)

Lewis's literary socialism, as expressed in his letters to Brenda Chamberlain and John Petts, understood the immediately personal as being also extensively representative; ideally and practically, poems need to be printed as broadsheets which 'should look forward all the time, beyond individual love and or failure or defeat, and should speak for a whole nation, all humanity in their small way.' 'This project [the *Caseg Broadsheets*] is to reach *the people* – with beauty, and love. Sell them at 1d or 2d each'.[12]

It is not difficult to see how Lewis's social idealism differs from Thomas's sacramental nihilism, though it is far from easy to exhibit the minute particulars of the distinction. In other ways, they resemble each other. Lewis's 'Post-Script: for Gweno' and Thomas's 'The Unborn Daughter' read like the two parts of an existential diptych:

> On her unborn in the vast circle
> Concentric with our finite lives;
> On her unborn, her name uncurling
> Like a young fern within the mind;
> On her unclothed with flesh or beauty
> In the womb's darkness, I bestow
> The formal influence of the will,
> The wayward influence of the heart,

> Weaving upon her fluid bones
> The subtle fabric of her being,
> Hair, hands and eyes, the body's texture,
> Shot with the glory of the soul.
>
> (*AL*, 21)

This is, however, a much lonelier poem, lonely in its own perfected being, than are Lewis's poems of parting addressed to his wife. It is an intense poem of the imagination: the imagination subsumes the reality of the newly-conceived child while it (seemingly) works to proclaim that the child is real even if never to be realised except by the imagination. The 'fluid' bones partake at once of the nature of the biological, the embryonic, and of that which is inchoate, awaiting the shaping spirit of imagination. Of the *incantatory* imagination, moreover. Lewis, in 'Post-Script: for Gweno' uses syntax, rhythm and variable line-length to lay bare affirmation against the odds; Thomas uses rhythm and syntax to protect the imagination's sequence as much as to assert it. Thomas's poem is at once tender and authoritarian – 'The formal influence of the will, / The wayward influence of the heart' – as is Yeats, a clear influence on Thomas's early writing. Lewis speaks of himself much more as a poet of in-betweenness, at its most negative in 'the moody half-tones of thought and longing and impatience', at its most self-consciously positive in turns of phrase like 'Acceptance seems so spiritless, protest so vain. In between the two I live', a phrase which nonetheless builds into a sentence ending 'the certainty that we have exalted ourselves into an indestructible love'.[13] Lewis writes well of in-betweenness; at times he fails to see, or chooses not to accept, the peril inherent in such verbs as 'exalted'. By contrast, Thomas's prose in *A Year in Llŷn*[14] has absolute confidence in its exaltations, not always justifiably. This is a way of saying that, dissimilar as they finally are as writers, in matters of rhetorical detail they have weaknesses as well as strengths in common. Reviewing *Ha! Ha! Among the Trumpets*, Lewis's second collection of poems, in December 1945, W. D. Thomas made two observations of particular acuteness. In Lewis's short stories, he suggests, 'the ideal in human personality becomes one with instinctive need. In one and the same action there is both complete gratification of the self, and complete unselfishness or selflessness.' He adds that Lewis 'created character and situation imaginatively in which unity of personality is achieved or destroyed. It seems to have been his personal problem.'[15]

These words put cogently some of my own half-formed thoughts in response, not to Lewis, but to the poetry and prose of R. S. Thomas.

Complete gratification of the self is, I think, the clue to much of his best writing. It is the gratification of the self's image of its own irreducible integrity and an act of witness to self-determined unity of personality. In the poems this fuses so completely with the gratification of technical problems overcome that the resulting work is in a restricted but true sense 'selfless', as, by analogy, in Welsh, 'someone' may be 'no one' and 'no one' 'someone'.[16] But this kind of selflessness is far from being synonymous with unselfishness. And what I earlier called Thomas's sense of belonging and not belonging affects him in ways that do not finally resemble Lewis's recurrent ambivalence, his hovering between a sense of domestic self-alienation and the objective alien nature of India and its peoples. In the finest of Lewis's poems from India, the existential does not appear to be a category distinct from the political; that is to say, Lewis reinvents 1930s political pastoral in such poems as 'The Mahratta Ghats', 'The Journey', 'The Jungle', and in the short story 'The Orange Grove'. It is as though he has discovered an extension, or rather a twinning, of Eliot's objective correlative. A private malaise of spirit and the public malaise of late imperialism reinforce each other in the achieved textures of the poems and of 'The Orange Grove'. The political vision of late Lewis makes his 'Caseg' socialism appear callow.

A knowledge of his late work also affects our – or, I had better say, my – reading of Thomas's political pastoral. I return to the matter of 'sour' and 'sourness', of the significance of 'bleak' and 'gaunt' in his oeuvre. To recall Keats's definition of negative capability: I do have the impression, in reading Thomas, of an 'irritable reaching after fact and reason';[17] in reading Lewis I do not. But, is my saying this an attempted value-judgement or is it a description of two kinds of rhetoric, each effective in its way? If one were to conclude that the emphasis on 'sour', 'bleak', 'gaunt', 'cold', and so on, declines into a mannerism then one would have to accept that a judgement is implied – that is, a soured vision or a bleak projection is a poorer thing than is the Keatsian exercise of negative capability upon the world's recognized harshness. Thomas's *Collected Poems, 1945–1990* is a book of over 500 pages and no two or two hundred people are going to agree as to what constitutes an acceptable, or an unacceptable, proportion of reiterated mood words. I constantly propose to myself that the intrinsic value of a poem is securely demonstrable; in my experience, however, the clinching demonstration is one of the most difficult achievements in the field of poetics.

'To imagine a language is to imagine a form of life', said Wittgenstein. Before he knew Welsh, Thomas imagined a form of life – Welsh landscape and culture – and through the slow process of learning the language was brought to a self-realization within a realized sense of nationhood that, shocks notwithstanding, was still recognizable as the imagination's truth. In a piece published in *The Listener* in 1974, he remarked that 'if a national identity were sufficiently valuable, it would be completely fulfilling to live to serve it, and to die knowing that it would survive one.'[18] Posing as a diffident *Sais*, I put 'remarked' rather than 'affirmed' only because of the prefatory 'if' and the conditional 'were', but it is an affirmation nonetheless and of a piece with the studied artlessness of all Thomas's writing about Wales and about the isolated and interlocking natures of identity.

Thomas seeks the true identity of Wales as Cobbett sought the true identity of England. We hear of 'the old heart of Wales', 'hardy and extremely individual people . . . who are attuned to the old, traditional life of the earth'; the trouble with 'the majority of the English-language Welsh' is that 'too many of them come from the industrial areas'. For Thomas, 'the true Wales is still to be found in the country'.[19] English incomers are to Thomas what rich landowning Jews are to Cobbett.[20] The true Wales is Welsh speaking, and Welsh speakers are country folk.

Yet, when Hanley was in the South Wales Coalfield in 1937, his guide, an out-of-work miner who had given no indication that he spoke anything other than English, on entering a mate's house 'made some remark in Welsh which was quite beyond me'. Hanley subsequently discovered that his companion was 'interested in the various Welsh societies that inculcate a love for the ancient culture and learning of his country . . . Penury does not in any way [affect] his devotion to these things' (*Grey Children*, 58, 144). When Alun Lewis was born, in 1915, in the Glamorgan mining village of Cwmaman, most of the inhabitants, including his own father, a schoolteacher, were bilingual. I find it hard to accept that Hanley's guide or Lewis's father is less truly Welsh than Thomas's idealized country-dweller. I find it hard to accept that a statement such as Thomas's 'it was the small, plain, unassuming things that appealed to him [R.S.T.]' (*Autobiographies*, 72) carries the same weight as Hanley's 'psychology of the little thing'; the first is spiritual aesthetics, the second a recording of existence barely at subsistence-level.

There is appropriate irony in the fact that Thomas came to understand himself as in some major sense Kierkegaardian. Kierkegaard pondered aesthetics but understood God to be 'so infinitely exalted that the only thing he looks upon is ethics'.[21] In the course of writing this essay I have come to think that whereas Thomas saw himself as an existential nationalist he was in fact closer to being a politicized aesthete, as were

Yeats, Eliot and Pound. And as was Rupert Brooke, it needs to be said. The distinguishing factor here is not to be sought in varying degrees of political attachment or detachment but in the degrees of achieved self-realization within the dimension of language. Self-realization is an ambiguous term and is placed here precisely because it is so.

To indicate the range of distinctions I am endeavouring to make requires the introduction of a few sentences from John Cowper Powys's *Obstinate Cymric* – from a chapter, 'The Simple Vision', which was originally the preface to a collection with that title by Huw Menai (1946):

> Between the 'coal face' and his home, or between the factory and his bus, varied by years of twilight-monotony in a 'depressed area', the genius of a poet gets into the habit of what might be called 'taking the Muse as she comes'; and to any patient student of the deeper psychological levels of poetic inspiration few things are more interesting than to note all that is implied in the differences between a writer like Wordsworth whose whole life was one long leisure of waiting for 'emotion remembered in tranquillity'; and a writer like Huw Menai.[22]

At this point, let me attempt to take stock of what I appear to be saying. Kingsley Amis remarked that Thomas's example 'reduces most modern verse to footling whimsy'[23] – a just assessment. He is a poet of the essentials and an essential poet. Re-reading him, I am amazed by the splendour of his economy. But like the rest of us, he is a flawed human being. Insofar as the human flaws enter into the textures of his work, they are relevant matter in any discussion of his achievement. Referring now to Powys's remarks on genius and habit, I am not suggesting that Thomas enjoyed a life of Wordsworthian 'long leisure', though he managed his circumstances adroitly enough: 'throughout his career R. S. chose the care of small parishes, thereby securing the conditions that are essential to a poet, namely time and peace' (*Autobiographies*, 80–1). Time and peace are not 'essential to a poet'; they are essential merely to persons of a particular cast of mind. That the gifts of a poet so circumstanced as was Huw Menai (working in a Royal Ordnance Factory – probably the same one referred to in *Grey Children*[24] as having been recently opened) should be held so unremittingly at bay, his phrases 'written in pencil between factory or pit's head and the train or bus or when its poet is "laid-off" ', is as effective a representation of the 'true' Wales as are Thomas's representations of the Manafon 'smallholder in his fields' (*Autobiographies*, 59) or the *haecceitas* of the Llŷn peninsula – 'a branch of rock suspended between the sea and the heavens' (*Autobiographies*,

133). If one is determined to invest one's art in elemental things, both language and contingency must be understood to be as elemental as one's favourite rock and unharmonious (unlike the Llŷn seasons), perpetually out of kilter with our potentialities and desires. Powys observes that Huw Menai's poetry 'contains both the tragic thoughts of the Rhondda at work and the still more tragic thought of the Rhondda out of work' (*Obstinate Cymric*, 120).

Powys also observes – and it is possible that he is here indebted to a major strand in the texture of *Grey Children* – that 'the sensation of walking for the sake of . . . pleasure' is to be distinguished from 'noting the impressions left upon us by what we catch sight of on our way to work'. Powys associates walking for the sake of pleasure with 'the experiences of many of our English poets' (*Obstinate Cymric*, 126). Had he been aware, in 1947, of Alun Lewis's Caseg letters he could have inserted 'and Anglo-Welsh': 'Oh, for the mountains and the vigour of walking where there is resistance of rock and elation of grass.'[25] By contrast, the sensation of walking to which Hanley persistently reverts in *Grey Children* is virtually synonymous with a sensation of imprisonment: 'Miners are great walkers, but then, look at the state of things. That's all some of the poor b——s *can* do'; or, 'Many men . . . do nothing but walk, walk, walk. It's rotten, really'; or ' "I was in gaol once", remarked Jones, "and when I see these chaps walking round in their large circles it reminds me of a big prison yard where you exercise. Some of those chaps are up here as early as six in the morning, walking, walking" ' (*Grey Children*, 21, 60, 144).

To leave the debate in the form of an unresolved antithesis between James Hanley and Alun Lewis, and to overlook certain key sentences in Thomas's *Autobiographies*, would be to deal out injustice all round. In the prose account of his time as rector of Manafon, Thomas is scrupulously open about the fact that his experiences of freedom on the hill slopes run athwart – at best parallel to – his parishioners' experiences of servitude amid the unremitting cycles of crop and season; that 'The horizons of some of them lay no further than the far side of the slope of the valley where they lived. But the rector would sometimes climb to the hilltops, and from one of their peaks a completely different world would open out in front of him' (*Autobiographies*, 52–3). His poem 'Relay' – though not among his most striking – is an effective paradigm of all this, where 'lack of the oxygen / of the spirit' somehow equates with 'the complacencies of being / half-way up', where one man's toil 'to release / his potential' from the 'stench' of 'the valley' is in some way diminished by the 'bright flags' that 'other / climbers of other mountains / have planted' (*LS*, 9). And all this understood as a metaphor of the evolution of the varieties of human speech, and the evolution of the varieties of human speech understood as a metaphor for the coexistence of extinction and survival, of perpetual entrapment and an enduring kind of Bergsonian élan.

I know that, in his minor as well as in his major statements, Thomas remains aware of the simultaneity in human terms of bafflement and creative coinherence. I happen to think also that frequently he confuses creative coherence with 'the normal amenities of the life of the middle classes' (*Autobiographies*, 52), and that this tendency is at its most etiolated and repetitious in *A Year in Llŷn*.

Every good poem – my earlier caveat notwithstanding – is in its own way a statement of value. Such statements may get confused or overlaid with a concern for values – 'the condition of man', 'to secure an answer, through poetry, to some of the great questions of life' (*Autobiographies*, 148, 150). If, in deference to Thomas's vocation, we say that the great questions of life are Christian questions, then we must add that there is no answer to these that can be truthfully secured through poetry. The fantasy to which Thomas here lends his eloquent support is one of the peripheral amenities of the life of the middle classes. The stature of his best poetry is secured by the fact that it is not dependent on the mannered ruralities of the prose.

Thomas says that 'A Peasant' is his 'first poem to attempt to face the reality of the scenes around him' when he was rector of Manafon: 'He asked himself about the condition and function of the smallholder in his fields. What was he thinking about, if about anything? Was he of equal value to the important learned people of the world? What was nature to him?' (*Autobiographies*, 59). The concluding questions here are little better than postures, affectations; the *faux-naif* tone of 'the important, learned people of the world' is wretched. Such prose affects rawness but is in fact urbane, in the sense that Horace or Machiavelli are urbane when writing about their rural estates, or that Yeats is when describing the eccentric characters of Sligo and Gort. Such writing stresses 'condition' because this is at once atmospheric and ethical; condition is of significance if you are 'attempt[ing] to face . . . reality'; at the same time facing reality may easily translate into such phrases as 'searching for a symbol of mankind' (*Autobiographies*, 76). 'Function' is something other than 'condition'; and it may be a mistake to try to equate – even self-critically – the way a man or woman works when docking mangels and the way a mind works itself around and into the making of a poem. The attempt is suggestive of values rather than of value. The power that is evident – spasmodically but also cumulatively – in the early poem 'The Airy Tomb' stems from the fact that here value exists in terms of function; by which I mean, principally, Thomas's sure control of narrative pacing. I also mean by the term 'value' the articulacy of the concluding lines, where the rhyme and the rhythm of syntax are no longer mere ancillaries of the fable but assume a kind of arbitrary eloquence that can take on anything we or the 'odd tale' itself may hurl at it – or Thomas's needless, derivative intrusion of middle-class anxieties ('And you, hypocrite reader, at ease in your chair . . .'; 'No, no, you must face the fact . . .'). The one fact properly in the poem is the extraordinary structural finality that is emotionally or philosophically right only because it is absolutely right in itself; in its building up and dissolution of a life that in terms of narrative itself is a lucid resolution:

> where youth and age
> Met in the circle of a buzzard's flight
> Round the blue axle of heaven; and a fortnight gone
> Was the shy soul from the festering flesh and bone
> When they found him there, entombed in the lucid weather.
>
> (SF, 46)

To return one more time to the Kierkegaardian element in Thomas's work – and I do so in the belief that it is a genuine characteristic, not a middle-class amenity – requires, appropriately enough, a leap of context. The leap is away from thought and into structure, which is technique weighing and moving imagination's density – the poet's equivalent of the Archimedean point. This equivalent in Thomas is more truly Kierke-gaardian than are his several poems directly addressed to, or with allusions to, the Danish theologian. Kierkegaard's journal entry number 1338, in Dru's translation, begins: '*The imagination* is what providence uses in order to get men into reality, into existence, to get them far enough out, or in, or down in existence. And when imagination has helped them as far out as they are meant to go – that is where reality, properly speaking, begins.'[26] Applied to poetry and poetics, the second sentence can be understood only in relation to the very greatest writers – Homer, Dante, Shakespeare. However, the first sentence implies gifts of perception and self-perception that are far from negligible. Thomas's 'A Country' from *Experimenting with an Amen* (1986) reads like a sketch-plan of the process, as do a significant number of Thomas's early and late poems.

I think here particularly of the way in which he can appear, through management of metre combined with syntax and phrase-rhythm, to run a poem down into a condition of inertia – an effect, however, that does not diminish the final impression of something essential being positively *struck*. In its fine balance between exhaustion and resolution it is a significant technical discovery and an appropriate example of Thomas's mastery of the medium.[27] The 'Archimedean point' to which Kierkegaard alludes in the *Journals*[28] is the hypothetical station from which it would be possible to move the earth. For the poet, the Archimedean point has to be not imaginary or hypothetical but actual, perhaps some arbitrariness of rhythm or syntax – more even than of image – which establishes beyond question the alienness of the poetic statement, its refusal of, even its obliviousness to, such matters as finding answers to 'the great questions of life'. A further entry from Kierkegaard's *Journals* – number 351 – reads as follows: 'Next after stripping myself naked, possessing nothing, not the smallest thing in the world, and then leaping into the water, I like most of all to speak a foreign language, preferably a living one, so as to become quite foreign to myself.'[29] On occasions throughout his work, Thomas, like other good poets, discovers that to write a poem is to write a living foreign language, and that in the writing one becomes quite foreign to oneself. The inevitable conclusion is that Thomas found salvation as a poet by moving in a direction diametrically opposite to the course that he had (not without political sentimentality) set himself to follow: that is, self-identification with a nation, a history and a people.[30]

Among the sixteen thousand manuscript pages left by Rush Rhees at his death, his executors found a number of commentaries on Wittgenstein's thinking about religion. From those papers, I take the following two statements: Wittgenstein's 'The common behaviour of mankind is the system of reference by which we interpret an unknown language'; and Rhees's 'Most ritual acts and utterances corrupt or contaminate what they present'.[31] Speaking as a politicized aesthete, I suggest that what we are pleased to call the truth of poetry is in fact an approximation, shifting in sense between the emphases of those two sentences. Or, to try again, the truth of poetry resides in forms of coinherence that are drawn from, and relapse into, incoherence.

Where this view may differ from Eliot's is in its conceiving the incoherence not as debility and bathos but as essential to the tripartite nature of creativity. The truth of poetry is in part corruption and contamination, in part a field of reference by which to interpret an unknown language, in part the unknown language itself. Poetry as utterance – both genuine and fraudulent – is part of 'the common behaviour of mankind', even though people are commonly oblivious to its peculiar attractions and demands.

Archimedean points, in a context of poetry and poetics, are points of intersection and of purchase at which potentiality, whether inchoate or incoherent, is taken hold of by a particular series of acts of will. Such formal acts, activity moved by intuition, may, if successful, be seen in retrospect as having formed the necessary Archimedean points of focus and distribution by which the economy of the poem is established. Coherence and incoherence, taken together, are not as evenly matched as Mill's 'mutually checking powers',[32] however. They more resemble the activities of Achebe's intransigent *chi*.[33]

Poetic diction is an attempt to regulate incoherence by way of short-cuts or a kind of prepared tape-loop. Among modern instances I note 'bone' and 'blood' in the poetry of Yeats, Eliot, and of those strongly influenced by them. Edith Sitwell is a case in point. R. S. Thomas, a much finer poet, is another.[34] The real austerities of R. S. Thomas's craft are at times corrupted and contaminated by a desire to demonstrate the austere or by a desire to grasp austerity as a principle by which to conduct oneself as priest and poet.

If my remarks are to be read as a radical criticism of elements deeply embedded in Thomas's understanding of poetry's capacity and calling, they are, even so, uttered from a sense of common predicament, with a keen sense of fellow feeling, and from a shared belief in the reality of original sin.

Notes

[1] Rush Rhees, *Discussions of Wittgenstein* (London: Routledge & Kegan Paul, 1970), 64, 79, 83.

[2] The theme, essentially, of Wallace Stevens's 'The Idea of Order at Key West'. Thomas's poem 'Wallace Stevens' (*BT*, 25–6) regards Stevens only in the aspect of thought or opinion; and therefore cannot move beyond the impression of 'cold' ascribed to a despairing hedonist. One could as well call Thomas a despairing hedonist.

[3] In criticizing Thomas's Welsh writings I am of course speaking of them as they appear in English translation. What, if any, details of tone – preservation or loss of association and nuance – are the result of the translation process I am unable to judge.

[4] Rush Rhees, *Wittgenstein and the Possibility of Discourse* (Cambridge: Cambridge University Press, 1998), 6: D. Z. Phillips's introductory summary and appraisal.

[5] James Hanley, *Grey Children: A Study in Humbug and Misery in South Wales* (London: Dent, 1937), 84, 190, 209, 46.

[6] See *Autobiographies*, 65 and 184, and John Fordham, *James Hanley: Modernism and the Working Class* (Cardiff: University of Wales Press, 2002), 208. Fordham's book was brought to my attention when my essay was at proof stage. The given page reference was added by the editor.

7 Alun Lewis, *Letters to My Wife*, ed. Gweno Lewis (Bridgend: Seren, 1989), 184.

8 Alun Lewis, *Collected Poems*, ed. Cary Archard (Bridgend: Seren, 1994), 116.

9 W. H. Auden, *Poems* (1930) (2nd edn; London: Faber, 1933), 71, 87, 65, 89.

10 Ezra Pound, *Literary Essays* (London: Faber, 1954), 50.

11 Lewis, *Letters to My Wife*, 44.

12 Brenda Chamberlain, *Alun Lewis and the Making of the Caseg Broadsheets* (London: Enitharmon Press, 1970), 31, 7.

13 Lewis, *Letters to My Wife*, 359, 327.

14 *Autobiographies*, 113–74.

15 *The Welsh Review*, 4:4 (December 1945), 293.

16 See *Autobiographies*, x–xi.

17 Letter of December 1817; see *The Letters of John Keats, 1814–1821*, ed. Hyder E. Rollins (2 vols; Cambridge: Cambridge University Press), I, 193.

18 *Selected Prose*, 118.

19 *Selected Prose*, 21, 22, 43.

20 See William Cobbett, *Rural Rides* (2 vols; London: Dent, 1968), I, 8, 95, 97, 160, 173; II, 130.

21 *The Journals of Søren Kierkegaard*, ed. and trans. Alexander Dru (London: Oxford University Press, 1938), 346, entry 997.

22 John Cowper Powys, *Obstinate Cymric: Essays, 1935–47* (1947; new edition, London: Village Press, 1973), 125.

23 Quoted in publisher's advertisement for *Selected Poems, 1946–1968*.

24 Powys, *Obstinate Cymric*, 124; Hanley, *Grey Children*, 75.

25 Chamberlain, *Caseg Broadsheets*, 17.

26 Kierkegaard, *Journals*, 519.

27 See such poems across the oeuvre as 'Iago Prytherch' (*PS*), 'Expatriates', 'Anniversary', 'Ninetieth Birthday', 'A Welsh Testament', 'Sailor's Hospital', 'That', 'Pavane', 'Revision', 'Geriatric', 'Lunar', 'The Lost', 'Symbols' and 'Homage to Wallace Stevens'.

28 Kierkegaard, *Journals*, 1, 2, 13, 61, 86, 249.

29 Kierkegaard, *Journals*, 89.

30 I should guess that an article by Keidrych Rhys first published in *Wales* and reprinted in *Little Reviews Anthology, 1945* (London: Eyre and Spottiswoode, 1945), 126–9, was an early influence on Thomas's nationalist-literary thinking. Rhys makes several basic points that are subsequently picked up and developed by Thomas: 1) the role played by the traditional 'Poet's Corner' of the typical Welsh newspaper and by the ministers of religion and village poets who keep the tradition going for good and ill; 2) the significance of Saunders Lewis and Gwenallt Jones in contrast to the 'academic poets' writing in Welsh; 3) the importance of Welsh-language publications such as *Y Faner*; 4) the question – the problem – of Anglo-Welsh writers and writing; 5) 'For Wales the permanent medium of literature should always be Welsh.'

31 *Rush Rhees on Religion and Philosophy*, ed. D. Z. Phillips (Cambridge: Cambridge University Press, 1997), 66, 84.

32 In the essay on Coleridge; see *Mill on Bentham and Coleridge*, ed. F. R. Leavis (Cambridge and New York: Cambridge University Press, 1980), 104.

33 Chinua Achebe, *Morning Yet on Creation Day* (London: Heinemann, 1977), 97; *chi* is 'personal spirit' or 'spirit double' (see 93).

34 *Literature on Line* records 'blood' 83 times in Yeats's poems; entries for 'bone' occur 33 times. There are 20 occurrences of 'bone(s)' in Eliot's poems. I have noted 70 uses of the word in Thomas's *Collected Poems, 1945–1990*. Typical uses include 'Men of bone' (13), 'our small bones' (36), 'a bone whitening' (44), 'the bone beneath the

skin' (72), 'the bone's wharf' (142), 'bone belfry' (168), 'unmanageable bone / Of language' (192), 'bone tent' (476), 'bone thrones' (479), 'bone / ladder' (482), 'all bones and in rags' (489), 'the bone the island / is made of' (499). At a rough count there are 66 occurrences of the word 'blood' in the *Collected Poems*. In the case of Edith Sitwell I have in mind such poems as 'Still Falls the Rain', 'Lullaby', 'Romance' and 'Street Song'. But her constantly reiterated word is 'gold'. See *The Canticle of the Rose* (New York: Vanguard Press, 1949), *passim*.

3
Was R. S. Thomas an Atheist Manqué?

JOHN BARNIE

The answer to the question of my title seems obvious. Was R. S. Thomas not a priest all his working life? Did he not produce one of the great bodies of meditative religious verse of the twentieth century? He was and he did, of course, and most of the criticism of the poetry I have read takes for granted that he is writing from a Christian perspective, even when that perspective is one of sustained questioning and doubt involving, at times, theologically contradictory positions. If, however, one approaches the poetry from a position that might be described as scientific atheism, Thomas's questioning of God and the nature of reality can seem more like deep philosophical – and psychological – rifting which reveals a man struggling to retain a faith in God in the face of the evidence available to him from the material world. In his probing of the nature of God and of God's putative relation to humanity, he stumbled repeatedly against opposites he was unable to reconcile. Of course, Thomas never took that final step from belief to unbelief, and it is this position of indecision and indeterminacy which creates the powerful undertows and cross-currents of the poetry which reflect a far more troubled, fragmented and dis-harmonious vision than is sometimes allowed. It is some of these undertows, pulling towards doubt and the disintegration of faith, that I wish to discuss here.

The deepest of them relates to one of Thomas's abiding preoccupa-tions, the natural world. In his autobiography, *Neb*, he described how he was drawn as a child to the countryside, especially the sea and the coast near Holyhead where he grew up. All his adult life he was a keen birdwatcher and a meticulous observer of the processes of nature, as his prose diary *A Year in Llŷn* testifies. It is well known that nature was also his means of approach to God. More than once he observed that he could never have served as a priest in an inner-city parish; it was through nature that God called him.

It is a conviction expressed in that iconic poem from *Pietà* (1966), 'The Moor', where the expanse of moorland is likened to a church which the poet enters reverently 'on soft foot / Breath held like a cap in the hand'. The God of this church-in-nature is indeterminate – 'What God was there made himself felt, / Not listened to, in clean colours . . .' – but the experience bestows on the poet a momentary freedom from the turmoil of the intellect and the emotions. It is not a pantheistic moment exactly, but it encompasses a kind of blessing, nature itself fulfilling a sacramental role. 'I walked on,' the poem ends,

> Simple and poor, while the air crumbled
> And broke on me generously as bread.
>
> (*P*, 24)

'The Moor' is a very Wordsworthian poem, the broad brushstrokes of the landscape instilling in the poet a sense of reverence, an intimation of the creator-God who is reflected in his Creation. Such a position could be accepted without reservation two hundred years ago by Wordsworth, but it is not so simple for a modern Romantic such as Thomas since the shadow of *The Origin of Species* falls between us and the Lake poet.

One of the theories Charles Darwin's great book put paid to was the Argument from Design, as presented by natural theologians like William Paley (1743–1805). Paley had reasoned that the intricacy of design to be found everywhere in nature presupposes an intelligent designer. The classic instance he gave was the complexity of the human eye. Darwin showed, however, that given sufficient time the eye could evolve from simple photosensitive cells through the process of natural selection, and had done so in nature independently many times. All that was needed was immense periods of time for the processes of evolution to work themselves out, and time on this scale was coincidentally provided by geologists, like Darwin's older contemporary Charles Lyell (1797–1875), who in estimating factors like the depositional rate of sedimentary rocks realized that the Earth was older by several orders of magnitude than the few thousand years computed by theologians from the Old Testament. (The most influential of these was Archbishop Ussher (1581–1656) whose estimate of 4004 BC as the date of the Creation was still widely accepted in Christian circles in the mid-nineteenth century.) The current estimate of the age of the Earth is around 4.8 billion years.

Moreover, efforts by scientists to confirm or disprove Darwin's theory meant that nature was studied extensively as never before, revealing in the process the intense competition that occurs within and between species, as well as what appears to be the spendthrift waste inherent in the processes of nature – the millions of young of many species, for example, that are born only to be devoured in the food-chain and the impersonal, driven quality of so much instinctual behaviour. 'Terrifying are the attent sleek thrushes on the lawn,' writes the neo-Romantic Ted Hughes of the song thrush:

> More coiled steel than living – a poised
> Dark deadly eye, those delicate legs
> Triggered to stirrings beyond sense – with a start, a bounce, a stab
> Overtake the instant and drag out some writhing thing.
>
> ('Thrushes'; *Lupercal*, 1960)

The earlier Romantic sense of the grandeur and beauty of nature is not necessarily diminished by our new understanding of its processes (it is there in Hughes), but it must now be held in balance with what can seem to us to be nature's darker side – its subjugation to impersonal algorithmic processes devoid of any teleology, for example, which undermines that other Romantic belief in nature as a coherent *moral* phenomenon to be 'read' with benefit by humanity. Like the song of the skylark, it is 'incomprehensibly both ways', to quote another Hughes poem: 'Joy! Help! Joy! Help!' ('Skylarks'; *Wodwo*, 1967).

Strangely for someone with such an intense interest in natural history, Thomas's direct engagement with science (when he was not being hostile in a generally dismissive way) was with cosmology and the new physics, which he encountered through popularizations like Fritjof Capra's *The Tao of Physics* (1975). I know of no evidence that he read any evolutionary biology. He was aware in broad outline, however, of the neo-Darwinian synthesis of evolutionary theory with genetics that began to take shape after the Second World War and which provides such a powerful tool for our understanding of nature, and this certainly forms part of the background, at least, to his reflections on nature and God, especially in the three major collections of the 1970s, *H'm* (1972), *Laboratories of the Spirit* (1975) and *Frequencies* (1978).[1]

He was also aware of the disturbing implications of geological 'deep time' for a human sense of significance, as in this passage from *Neb* where he contemplates the Precambrian rocks of Braich y Pwll:

R. S. realised that he was in contact with something that had been there for a thousand million years. His head would spin. A timescale such as this raised all kinds of questions and problems. On seeing his shadow fall on such ancient rocks, he had to question himself in a different context and ask the same old question as before, 'Who am I?', and the answer now came more emphatically than ever before, 'No-one.'

(*Autobiographies*, 78)

This background radiation, as it were, from evolutionary biology and geology is particularly relevant when he confronts the beauty of nature and its apparent cruelty, and attempts to reconcile these apparent opposites with a benevolent creator-God.[2] It is something to which Thomas alludes in numerous contexts. Out birdwatching in January, he tells us in *A Year in Llŷn* how he comes across the remains of two blackheaded gulls, the prey of a peregrine falcon: 'The murderer has been round since last I visited Tŷ Mawr pool' (*Autobiographies*, 114). Rereading Nietzsche the same month, he reflects on the philosopher's assertion that eternal life can be justified only as an aesthetic phenomenon. That is how the poet feels when he looks on 'the impersonal, pitiless beauty of nature'. Birds of prey are beautiful, he adds in illustration, 'And yet they are killers.' That same day he sees a stoat, 'another beautiful killer' (*Autobiographies*, 118).

The word he uses here, *llofrudd* – 'murderer', 'killer' – is freighted with human assumptions about moral order, and to apply it in this way to raptors like the peregrine and other carnivores like the stoat is to imbue nature with ethical imperatives in a way that must have its origins deep in human prehistory. It has no validity in the world as described by evolutionary science, however, any more than the appellation 'pitiless'. Nature simply *is*, existing outside the bounds of any possible set of moral categories. Although he uses the old anthropomorphic idiom here, Thomas is nonetheless sufficiently aware of post-Darwinian biology to realize that nature cannot be addressed seriously in this way any more. It is anachronistic thinking which draws attention away from a question that is urgent and troubling for someone of a religious sensibility. For if nature is the result of the algorithmic processes of evolution by natural selection – processes that exclude moral categorization – what does this imply about the God Thomas assumes to have created it?

In the December entry in *A Year in Llŷn*, Thomas returns to the problem. He hears a sparrowhawk calling in a wood, 'as if it were sharpening its beak for the feast that will come its way in the new year'. He reflects that it is an ur-cry from long before the advent of man, an expression of non-human nature. But what is its significance?

That is nature. Is that God's economy? Life depends on the ability to obtain sufficient sustenance. The weak go to oblivion. In some ways, and at times, it is quite terrifying. Couldn't God have done better than to make the earth some giant mouth which devours, devours unceasingly in order to sustain itself?

Here, Thomas tries to stave off such a logical response: 'before placing the blame on God, let us ask ourselves whether we could have done better, or even half as well?' he flounders. The Creation can seem frightening, he repeats, 'and yet, on reflection, it is amazingly intricate and complex'. Moreover,

> on the whole it isn't nature but man that kicks over the traces. For millions of years, despite the killing and the devouring, the earth has kept the balance, and it is only in our period of history, and specifically towards the close of the present century, that we have started to see how man in his blindness and greed is endangering the earth's future.
>
> (*Autobiographies*, 170)

The non sequiturs in this passage are striking. Thomas first invokes the Argument from Design (nature is 'amazingly intricate and complex'), only to retreat to the Old Testament and a twist on the Fall (nature kept a balance for millions of years until the advent of man who is now destroying all before him). And the statement that 'the earth has kept the balance' is both true and not true: we are currently experiencing a human-induced mass extincion of species, as Thomas suggests, but the last five hundred and sixty million years are punctuated by at least five other extinction events.[3] Like a lapwing feigning injury, the poet leads the reader further and further from his starting point – the question of what nature might suggest about its putative creator – as he tries, none too subtly, to extricate God from this uncomfortable equation.

These issues find memorable expression in some of the poems of the 1970s, in which Thomas confronts the 'problem' of nature, not by addressing God in a poetic meditation or prayer as he often does, but by dramatically ventriloquizing him. The 'god' of these poems is a robust, peevish, vengeful deity in the manner of many religious folk tales and myths (Genesis not the least of them), and Thomas's portrait is clearly influenced by Ted Hughes's *Crow* (1970).

Such is the god of 'The Island' in *H'm* (1972), an unrhymed sonnet which echoes Genesis in its opening – 'And God said' – to reveal the 'motivations' of this trickster deity in his dealings with Creation:

> And God said, I will build a church here
> And cause this people to worship me,
> And afflict them with poverty and sickness
> In return for centuries of hard work
> And patience . . .

Made in this god's image, the people of this world are equally hard-hearted as they sit in their island-church before a priest whose words are 'drowned / By the wind's caterwauling'. 'All this I will do', God resolves, as the poem turns into the sestet,

> and watch the bitterness in their eyes
> Grow, and their lips suppurate with
> Their prayers. And their women shall bring forth
> On my altars, and I will choose the best
> Of them to be thrown back into the sea.
> (*H'm*, 20)

'And that', the sonnet ends, 'was only on one island.'

'The Island' evokes existence on the fringes of the British Isles – places such as Bardsey, St Kilda, Orkney and Shetland with their rocky shores, sparse grazing, tiny churches with narrow windows and, as the poem sees it, narrowly focused lives that have been ground down over the centuries. It is an exploration in pseudo-biblical, mythopoeic terms of the ground conditions for humanity. Like *Crow*, it takes the harshest substratum of human life on earth in order to explore what such conditions appear to say about the nature of a putative creator. In its bleakness, the poem is shocking, but no more so than Genesis where God tells Eve 'I will greatly multiply thy sorrow and thy conception; in sorrow thou shalt bring forth children' (3: 16), before turning his vengefulness on Adam:

> cursed is the ground for thy sake; in sorrow shalt thou eat of it all the days of thy life; Thorns also and thistles shall it bring forth to thee; and thou shalt eat the herb of the field; In the sweat of thy face shalt thou eat bread, till thou return unto the ground; for out of it wast thou taken: for dust thou art, and unto dust shalt thou return.
> (3: 17–19)

'The Island' is placed near the physical centre of *H'm* on a double-page spread opposite 'He'. (This juxtaposition is lost in *Collected Poems*, where the poems are on the recto and verso of the same page.) 'He', another unrhymed sonnet, considers things from the perspective of humanity rather than of God. The poem uses the same rhetorical narrative device from Genesis as 'The Island' – conjunction + substantive – but with a more savagely parodic effect:

> And the dogfish, spotted like God's face,
> Looks at him, and the seal's eye-
> Ball is cold.

Rejected by God, this unaccommodated human being, his hands 'calloused with the long failure / Of prayer', turns to nature, hoping for some kind of acceptance:

> Take my life, he says
> To the bleak sea, but the sea rejects him
> Like wrack.

No longer even a part of nature in any unequivocal way, he nonetheless 'dungs the earth / With his children' – an image which echoes the curse of God in Genesis but which also looks to the prolific wastefulness inherent in the evolutionary process, in which the many never reach maturity and only the few survive to breed. The implication is that, as an evolved species, humankind cannot escape these processes; at the same time, we are irrevocably alienated from full participation in nature. Humanity in these poems is thus doubly exiled, doubly rejected:

> Nothing he does, nothing he
> Says is accepted, and the thin dribble
> Of his poetry dries on the rocks
> Of a harsh landscape under an ailing sun.
> (*H'm*, 21)

In many of the poems in *H'm*, Thomas's vision becomes a vortex funnelling down to these perceptions, mixing motifs drawn from Old Testament mythology with the timescale and philosophical implications of evolutionary biology, as in 'Soliloquy', which begins:

> And God thought: Pray away,
> Creatures; I'm going to destroy
> It. The mistake's mine,
> If you like. I have blundered

> Before; the glaciers erased
> My error.

and ends with God invoking the virus as the instrument of his will:

> Within the churches
> You built me you genuflected
> To the machine. Where will it
> Take you from the invisible
> Viruses, the personnel
> Of the darkness that do my will?
> (*H'm*, 30)

In the corpus of R. S. Thomas's poetry Jesus is far less prominent than God. The poet's was not a Christ-centred faith, but one that dealt directly with the creator-God whose handiwork, nature, he found in almost equal measure appealing in its beauty and horrifying in its apparent savagery. Yet the question of love cannot of course be avoided by a poet-priest, even one who seems to have found the Old Testament more congenial in some ways than the New in that it corresponds more closely to the nature of things. The question is addressed directly in 'H'm', the title poem of the 1972 collection. 'and one said', the poem begins, 'speak to us of love',

> and the preacher opened
> his mouth and the word God
> fell out . . .

The congregation then ask about God,

> but the preacher
> was silent reaching
> his arms out but the little
> children the ones with
> big bellies and bow
> legs that were like
> a razor shell
> were too weak to come
> (*H'm*, 33)

The absence of punctuation adds to the pared-down, devastating effect of the priest's imitation of Christ in Matthew 19: 14: 'Suffer little children, and forbid them not, to come unto me: for of such is the kingdom of heaven'. But the starving children of the world in this poem are not 'suffered' to come to the priest's willing arms; they can only suffer and die. The priest, the would-be mediator of divine love, is powerless.[4] What does divine love mean under these conditions? It is a problem R. S. Thomas returns to in the poems without, I think, ever finding a satisfactory answer. 'Which', from *Laboratories of the Spirit* (1975), begins:

> And in the book I read:
> God is love. But lifting
> my head, I do not find it
> so . . .

What should he do? Is the truth between the lines of the book, where there is

> an air
> heavy with the scent
> of this one word?

Or should he trust

> only the blows that
> life gives me, wearing them
> like those red tokens with which
> an agreement is sealed?
>
> (*LS*, 54)

In a world where God is present only as an absence, it may be that he is absent in the more thoroughgoing sense of being non-existent. Looking about him at the world, Thomas sees no evidence that God is love – 'I do not find it / so'. Should he not, then, accept the 'blows of life' for what they are? Seal an agreement with material reality? The questions are raised but, typically, no attempt is made at an answer.

In 'Questions', Thomas returns to the problem of divine love, contrasting human love with the priest's search for its spiritual equivalent. A girl lies down with her lover, and

> enters the man's
> arms to be clasped between sheets
> against the un-love that is all around.

The priest too lies down,

> face to face with the darkness
> that is the nothing from which nothing
> comes.

In a harsh world, the lovers at least find brief comfort in each other's arms. As to the priest:

> 'Love' he protests, 'love'
> in spiritual copulation
> with a non-body, hearing the echoes
> dying away, languishing under the owl's curse.

The questions begged here are elusive of an answer, and perhaps there is no answer that could reconcile the material world as revealed by science – especially, here, evolutionary biology – with the desire of the religious for a coherent, transcendent meaning to our lives. The poem began as a question and ends as one:

> Tell me, then, after the night's toil
> of loving or praying, is there nothing
> to do but to rise tired and be made
> away with, yawning, into the day's dream?
>   (*EA*, 39)

For the one who yearns for divine love, rising to meet a new day devoid of such love makes reality seem like a dream. But what if it is no dream? What if the 'owl's curse' – the cry of unaccommodated nature – is the bedrock of reality? The question is raised, but once again, the implications are characteristically not followed through.

Nonetheless, we have come a long way in these poems from the church-in-nature of 'The Moor'. It is not that Thomas can no longer take pleasure in the beauty of nature; rather, it is harder for him to see its beauty in any simple sense as consolatory, as an affirmation of a benevolent deity. In 'Rough' from *Laboratories of the Spirit*, God ponders a distinctly post-Darwinian nature:

> God looked at the eagle that looked at
> the wolf that watched the jack-rabbit
> cropping the grass, green and curling

as God's beard. He stepped back;
it was perfect, a self-regulating machine
of blood and faeces.

In Thomas's retelling of the Creation myth, God creates man in his image
as in Genesis, but in this scenario humanity is governed, like the animals,
by the imperatives of evolution – with devastating effects:

It was not long
before the creature had the eagle, the wolf and
the jack-rabbit squealing for mercy.

This god is a kind of divine geneticist who takes 'a handful of small
germs, / sowing them in the smooth flesh', and then observes the progress
of his experiment dispassionately:

It was curious,
the harvest: the limbs modelled an obscene
question, the head swelled, out of the eyes came
tears of pus.

The poem ends like some divine, Frankensteinian *film noir*:

There was the sound
of thunder, the loud, uncontrollable laughter of
God, and in his side like an incurred stitch, Jesus.
(*LS*, 36)

What are we to make of the appearance of Jesus here? His presence in
God's side echoes the creation of Eve and also clearly presages the
Incarnation and the new dispensation of the New Testament which
superseded (as it incorporated) the Old. Yet it hardly seems convincing,
little more, in fact, than a deus ex machina, as Thomas tries to bolt
together the realms of the spiritual and the material. It is almost always
God the creator who is the poet's quarry, not Jesus the intermediary.

It is a hunt, however, which the poet knows will never reach a successful conclusion, because his is a very modern quest through a material
world where the best he can hope for is that the paradox that God's
absence is itself a kind of presence is true. He addresses the *deus
absconditus* again and again in the poems, as in 'The Absence' from
Frequencies (1978):

It is this great absence
that is like a presence, that compels
me to address it without hope
of a reply.

But nothing, it seems, can call God up, neither the rituals of religion nor the most intricate discoveries of the scientists. 'My equations fail / as my words do.' What remains, at the end of the poem, is a faith resting on something close to fear and desperation:

What resource have I
other than the emptiness without him of my whole
being, a vacuum he may not abhor?
(*F*, 48)

Another poem in *Frequencies*, 'The Porch', is symbolic of Thomas's dilemma. A man whose name is 'forgotten', who was 'like / anyone else, a man with ears / and eyes', is driven 'for no reason / he knew' to his knees in a church porch on a frosty winter evening:

The cold came at him;
his breath was carved angularly
as the tombstones; an owl screamed.

This man, however, 'had no power to pray'; he merely kneels there in the porch, which represents the interface between the spiritual world and the material world of nature:

His back turned on the interior
he looked out on a universe
that was without knowledge
of him and kept his place
there for an hour on that lean
threshold, neither outside nor in.
(*F*, 10)

The hunting owl recurs several times in the poetry as an emblem of everything that Thomas delights in yet fears in nature. The owl is at home in its world; its screams are those of a biological hunting machine, honed over millions of years of evolutionary development. The kneeling man understands this, but he can never belong in nature in this unequivocal way. The owl's behaviour is instinctual whereas consciousness in humans – itself a product of evolution – enables us to understand and to modify our behaviour. This function of the human brain is unique to our species in such a highly developed form, but it comes at a price: our dissociation from the instinctual world around us.

Consciousness can be seen as the fruit of the tree of knowledge of good and evil which only our species has eaten. Before the evolution of a fully developed modern consciousness, humankind did not know it was naked. It was not God but the exponential growth of the hominid brain, leading at some point in the past two million years to our kind of self-awareness, that expelled us from the Garden of Eden; that expulsion, however, created in us the need for God in order to make sense of what our eyes and ears appeared to tell us. There is no evidence for religious practice of any kind before about fifty thousand years ago, when there was a seismic shift in the cultural development of early modern humans that produced the first known art and the first indications of religious belief.

Concepts such as the soul and the spirit must have developed at this time too, as our ancestors tried to come to terms with their uniqueness. Such ideas are invoked in some animistic religions in an effort to integrate our humanity to a degree with nature, but in others, most notably the monotheistic religions of the Near East, there is instead a tendency towards dualism in which the material world is seen as 'fallen', in opposition to the spiritual. The problem for the modern Christian intellectual is that many of these beliefs are hard to take literally any more because they conflict with what we know about the universe from other sources – science most especially. It is sometimes said that religion and science are not in conflict because they operate in different realms, the spiritual and the material. Religion, however, has always claimed to offer its followers an understanding and interpretation of the material universe, and in the past four hundred years, faiths like Christianity have been forced into a long retreat as their dogma on these matters has come into conflict with the findings of science.

People respond to this in different ways, but among liberal humanist intellectuals there is often a determined hostility to the scientific enterprise, based on the argument that it is reductionist and materialist, that it deprives us of the 'spiritual' side of our lives and our sense of awe and wonder. It is the old objection of Keats to Newton, the response of a mind that would prefer to live in awe before a 'mystery' than to get at truth. This position is widespread. There is a flavour of it in Gillian Clarke's observation that 'atheism is like flat-earthism. It's so unimaginative.'[5] It is there too in

Thomas's comment that 'I have tried to maintain a slight understanding of scientific doctrines, as they evolve and change, remembering that he who marries the spirit of the age will be a widower tomorrow.'[6]

Liberal humanists often end up defending this kind of imprecise thinking when confronted by scientific ideas that question their own position. There is no reason why atheism should be regarded as unimaginative, except for the fact that the concept of the imagination (along with the 'spiritual') is the jealously guarded preserve of a certain kind of artist for whom it is a refuge beyond the questioning of reason. 'Mountains, old churches, or listening to Bach are spiritually rousing', Gillian Clarke adds by way of illustration. As to being married to the spirit of the age, Thomas has a point, but it is not one that can be levelled at science alone. What is the God of the Gaps, the untenanted cross, other than the theological fashion of the times?

From such a substantial body of work as the poetry of R. S. Thomas I am aware that it is possible to argue that, despite the torments of doubt, the poet always remained within a firmly Christian frame of reference. I concede that in some ways this is true, but I also believe that this was not an entirely frank position and that the poems discussed here point in another direction altogether. Atheism can be unimaginative, as Gillian Clarke asserts, but so can Christianity and New Age spirituality. Moreover, denial of the existence of a benevolent creator-God does not mean an automatic denial of imagination or of a sense of mystery and awe in the face of the universe. At one level, that sense is intensified when one removes the rivets of Christian theology. What I mean is well expressed by Thomas's contemporary, the Swedish poet Harry Martinson: 'For my kind of religiosity Buddhism is the most attractive: since I cannot be wholeheartedly religious I am forced to choose between an enigma and god. And of the two I choose the enigma – it is at least as overwhelming as any god.'[7] It should be added that Martinson is not opening the door here to New Age 'spirituality'; his sense of awe at the enigma of the universe is grounded in his love of nature, but substantiated by his broad knowledge of science and mathematics.

What might be called Thomas's unspoken position is in certain respects close to that of Martinson, with one crucial difference. Martinson was able to live without the baggage of theology yet satisfy his essentially religious sensibility in contemplating what he terms the enigma of the universe without the need for 'salvation' or any kind of ultimate answer. Thomas, judging from the poems, was unable to reconcile himself to such a position. His dilemma is expressed in the figure kneeling in the porch of the church who sees the great impersonal beauty of the universe for what it is, yet finds it hard to give up the consolation of religion. It is a consolation, however, which ironically fails to console, because the Christian religion has never been able to square itself with nature, and R. S. Thomas was too keen a thinker not to be aware of this. It was an impasse, but one that drove some of his finest poems.

Twenty years after 'The Moor' appeared in *Pietà*, Thomas published 'Moorland' in *Experimenting with an Amen*. It is an extension of the same meditation on God and nature, but with a considerable difference in emphasis. 'It is beautiful and still', the poem begins,

> the air rarefied
> as the interior of a cathedral
>
> expecting a presence.

These echoes of 'The Moor' are undercut, however, by the appearance of a harrier, that 'beautiful killer' of the upland moors,

> materialising from nothing, snow-
>
> soft, but with claws of fire,
>   quartering the bare earth
> for the prey that escapes it . . .

'The Moor' enacted the poet's intimation of the presence of God in nature, but, twenty years on, the religious image in the opening lines of 'Moorland' is almost incidental – the rarefied air is only *like* 'the interior of a cathedral // expecting a presence', and the image is not developed. The real presence on this moor is the bird of prey. And there is no epiphany for the poet who watches it:

> hovering over the incipient
>   scream, here a moment, then
> not here, like my belief in God.
>   (*EA*, 49)

Notes

[1] For a useful introduction to neo-Darwinism, see George C. Williams, *Plan and Purpose in Nature* (London: Weidenfeld & Nicolson, 1996). For a fuller discussion,

see Daniel C. Dennett, *Darwin's Dangerous Idea: Evolution and the Meanings of Life* (New York: Simon & Schuster, 1995).

[2] This is explored in Julian Gitzen's perceptive essay 'R. S. Thomas and the Vanishing God of Form and Number', *Miraculous Simplicity*, 170–81.

[3] See, for example, Niles Eldredge, *The Miner's Canary: Unraveling the Mysteries of Extinction* (New York: Prentice Hall, 1991).

[4] 'H'm' is surely indebted to 'Crow's First Lesson' in Ted Hughes's *Crow* (London: Faber & Faber, 1970).

[5] 'The Power of Absence', interview with Deryn Rees Jones, *Planet*, 144 (2000), 57.

[6] 'Probings', interview with Ned Thomas and John Barnie, *Miraculous Simplicity*, 36; the interview was originally published in *Planet*, 80 (April/May 1990).

[7] Quoted in Gunnar Tideström, *Ombord på Aniara: En Studie i Harry Martinsons Rymdepos* (Stockholm: Aldus, 1975), 153; my translation.

4

'The Curious Stars': R. S. Thomas and the Scientific Revolution

JOHN PIKOULIS

Prytherch and the Death of History

There they are – the 'curious' stars – right at the end of one of R. S. Thomas's earliest and best-known poems, 'A Peasant' (*SF*, 14), part of the apparently incidental background to the animal-like Iago Prytherch. At a stroke, the nature of the poem alters. Where before it offered a portrait of a man and a culture, now it embraces the universe. As a result, man and farm are queered and have to operate on several planes. These stars have something of Yeats's 'Babylonian mathematical starlight' about them (though we can appreciate that only with the benefit of hindsight), an intellectual power that eventually forces Iago out of the poetry. In this essay, I want to examine how this happens and why.

The stars carry a personal reference for one who was over six feet tall. In his youth, Thomas felt 'the mind's weight / Kept me bent, as I grew tall' (*BT*, 12). In both senses of the word, he looked down on the world, particularly when he arrived at Manafon. It is he who finds the stars 'curious'; the word introduces him formally into the poem and is related to the condescension he shows Prytherch, who does not himself have the inclination or the need to notice the stars. Nor can the stars feel anything for the human condition – that would be rank anthropomorphism. Though appearing briefly at the end, they are Thomas's epiphenomenon in the poem, his true subject.

Both man and stars have reached the end of history. They belong to a crisis of the grand narrative of Creation. Now, the stars shine on enigmatically, 'curious' in the eyes of that portion of Creation from which they have become alienated. In the same way, Prytherch is the diminished survivor of the crisis of the micro-narrative of Wales.

Where there were once princes, there is now only the peasant farmer. As God dwindles to stars in the sky, so the Welsh have dwindled to Prytherch. This twinning of man (be he peasant, priest, sailor or poet) and stars is a constant in Thomas's poetry: in 'A Priest to his People', the hill farmers live 'In a crude tapestry under the jealous heavens / To affront, bewilder, yet compel my gaze' (SF, 30); in 'The Airy Tomb', Twm from Bwlch contemplates life with 'the shrill rabble of stars / Crowding his shoulders' (SF, 46); in 'The Labourer', a hill farmer is 'blind with tears / Of sweat to the bright star that draws you on' (AL, 32). The stellar subject gathers such momentum that it eventually becomes Thomas's primary theme by force of utterance. What began as an incidental feature is foregrounded until it lends his work a structural unity it might not otherwise possess. As has often been noted, Thomas's poetry divides into two: from The Stones of the Field (1946) to Not That He Brought Flowers (1968), it dwells on Prytherch; from then on, it turns to God and the machine. First and last, however, there are the stars, originally as highly wrought ornament (another sense of 'curious', of course), then as a field force that generates a flood of images which constitute the super-arching theme of the poetry.

In 1972, it must have seemed a truism to say that Thomas's poetry was founded on 'three articles of faith: the Christian view of man, the human necessity for a life close to the soil, and the national cause in Wales'.[1] As late as 1986, John Barnie could claim that 'The idea of a Wales, rural, Welsh-speaking, Christian, is a fundamental, generative idea for R. S. Thomas'.[2] It did not turn out to be that way. The poet himself believed his work explored Wales, nature and the tension between time and eternity, reason and the emotions.[3] Now that his career can be seen whole, it is clear that, far from asserting 'articles of faith', the poetry problematizes them, in the process unpicking the very notion of faith. The poet is not in control of his poetry; he is driven by it. Where he wants to write about Prytherch, the poem – only at the last moment but then with considerable ingenuity – writes about the stars. He inscribes, it effaces.

Perhaps, as Thomas suggested, the idea of Wales dwindled in his work because it had been wrung dry. More likely, it disappeared because it was superseded by other ideas – first, the Creator (another 'curious' entity), then the universe of which he and the stars are part (though in a radically redefined sense). This essay traces the emergence of stars and space-time as Thomas's principal theme.

The concept of space-time was familiar in the 1920s (when Thomas was a child) as one aspect of the excited response to Einstein's theory of relativity. (Einstein himself encouraged the hyphenization.) 'Revolution in

Science – New Theory of the Universe – Newton's Ideas Overthrown', the headlines in *The Times* proclaimed in 1919. Around the same time, Lawrence's attack on the 'machine' also became well known, along with Freud's notion of the self, defined as a fractured entity riven with tensions arising from repressed aspects of the psyche – a notion given free rein in Thomas's autobiographical writings: 'Was it a slight gift of Keats's negative capability that made it often so difficult for me to believe in my separate, individual existence? Certainly it has come to me many times with a catch in the breath that I don't know who I am'[4] (and this in his seventies!).

It was the 1920s, too, that lent currency to concepts like calculus, radiation and particle matter, along with Heisenberg's Uncertainty Principle. Thomas's engagement with these ideas, therefore, argues not just an adult's cultivated interest encouraged by popularizers of science like Fritjof Capra and Paul Davies but the promptings of his earliest imaginative life. After 1945, he could add space travel, TV satellites, cassette tapes, moon landings, computers, space shuttles, DNA, gene therapy and deep-field photography of space to the list of subjects feeding his poetry. What Thomas has to say about the stars accordingly outlines the history of the twentieth century; it also brims over with personal feeling, as is suggested by the role stars played in his father's profession – marine navigation. As much as Jack Kerouac or Saul Bellow's Augie March, Thomas the stargazer is in pursuit of the absent father.

Prytherch and the Death of the Future

Prytherch and the stars together prove that nothing lasts forever. A shattered nation – of which no better, and no more, can be said than that it has survived – together with the stars cooling in the sky (Keats's diminished 'material sublime') are all that remain of once mighty forces. At first, Thomas is drawn to Prytherch but he eventually turns to wider themes. With the mention of stars in the last line of 'A Peasant', he alights on a subject that is already 'curious' but is about to grow a great deal curiouser.

In 'Taliesin 1952' (*SYT*, 105), Glyndŵr scans the stars 'for propitious omen' while the women of Wales lament their dead. As Glyndŵr's descendant and Thomas's own prototype, Prytherch shares in this historical calamity, being a 'winner of wars' in a different and highly ambiguous sense. He labours beneath the stars which are the auguries of his and Wales's fate; they are also magi's stars drawing Thomas on to a new nativity. Nearly forty years later, he wrote:

'Come,' life said
leading me on a journey
as long as that
of the wise men to the cradle,

where, in place of the child
it had brought forth,
there lay grinning the lubricated
changeling of the machine.

('Bleak Liturgies'; *MHT,* 60)

Where Prytherch docked mangels, Cynddylan drives his tractor, his 'grinning' repeating Prytherch's 'spittled mirth' and 'half-witted grin'. Where there was once 'a chaste // cradle with a star / over it' (*MHT*, 70) – in theological terms 'that illuminated citadel / that truth keeps' (*NTF,* 59) or Arnold's 'high, white star of Truth' offering us salvation – now there is only 'the sky's empty stare' (*MHT*, 59) and the mechanical 'churning [of] the crude earth'. Suddenly, the universe has gone unfriendly. Endurance offers hope of a kind, but it is not much. Even before God disappeared, therefore, Thomas's poems register an absence, being what Vimala Herman calls an 'exposition of the impassed', a 'writing of limitation'.[5]

With the end of history comes the death of the future. The landscape becomes a trope of existential agony – bald, lean, harsh, rough, bitter, 'pain's landscape' (*NBF,* 33). This Beckettian idea is repeated in *The Echoes Return Slow* (1988): 'Pain's climate. The weather unstable' (p. 2). In those five snap-shut words, Thomas defines the modern age. The barely human Prytherch is Thomas's Caliban-like imago, a projection of his damaged instinctual self. The poet is drawn in guilty sympathy to his uncouth persona but is then free to deny him before making his peace with him and eventually abandoning him altogether.

Thomas sucked in anguish and isolation with his mother's 'infected milk' (*WW,* 12). The effects may be gauged in images like 'the sky's emptiness' (*F,* 34) and 'the slow chemistry of the soil' (*F,* 51). 'Chemistry' is an interesting word in this connection, suggesting the wider context of geology, evolution, universal red-shift, subatomic particles and quantum mechanics that revolutionized astronomy at the turn of the twentieth century. History has narrowed to this end: a present that is also a history. Such historicity never leaves Thomas.

Remember him, then, for he, too, is a winner of wars,
Enduring like a tree under the curious stars.

The 'tree' echoes the Crucifixion and humanity's salvation from the consequences of eating the fruit of the tree of knowledge, but it is a dying echo.

At the end of history, Thomas grasps that reality is not 'given' but constructed. The aspirational, Anglo, middle-class respectability into which he was born offered him one version of it, but it was soon replaced by another – Welsh, rural, church, pacifist. The contrast is important but signifies less than the habit of creating worlds which it inspired in him. Reality was always provisional for Thomas. He was to perform the trick a third time when he turned space traveller in order to pursue twentieth-century astrophysics.

Coldness, Fate and the Stars: Poems after 'A Peasant'

Were the stars in 'A Peasant' born to satisfy a rhyme? Were they the only thing that could rhyme with 'wars'? But then 'star wars' was an idea current at the time, another way in which the stars had grown 'curious'. Prytherch's brutish existence reflects this new scientism, a further aspect of the revolution following the discovery that human beings were engaged in a struggle for existence. Prytherch is Darwinian man as well as a labourer who triumphs over hardship in an indifferent universe.

He and the stars thus mirror each other, though the idea is as yet undeveloped. The misprint (or is it correction?) of the phrase 'a stiff sea of clods' from 'A Peasant' as 'a stiff sea of clouds' in the *Collected Poems* repeats the mirror theme ('clods'/'clouds'). In 'Country Child' (*SF*, 16), Thomas writes of an 'orchard of stars in the night's unscaleable boughs'. We are in Minkowski's space-time again, earth and sky belonging to a continuum that operates in unresolved ways. Are the stars simply an incidental part of Prytherch's story, or are they its prime cause? Are there two dramas in the poem – terrestrial and celestial – or merely one? And what are we to make of the poet, who is unannounced in 'A Peasant' and ambiguously located within it? The only thing missing from this deep structure of Thomas's poetry is birds. Man, stars, birds (or as 'Sonata in X' puts it: 'Man . . . / Kestrel . . . / Rock . . .'; *MHT*, p. 85): this is the kernel of his imagination.

Here, we should not forget the influence of Alun Lewis, the only other Welsh–English poet to share Thomas's philosophic reach and power of utterance (he was the subject of an early elegy by Thomas). In 'The Jungle', Lewis describes how

> aloneness, swinging slowly
> Down the cold orbit of an older world
> Than any they predicted in the schools,
> Stirs the cold forest with a starry wind . . .
> . . .
> The night is shrill with crickets, cold with space.[6]

This, in brief, is Thomas's 'vacant' universe. Lewis counterpoints stellar loneliness with the kingfisher, quail and teal, as we might expect of a poet who employed avian and stellar imagery widely in his work, notably in 'Post-Script: for Gweno' and 'Threnody for a Starry Night', where the 'Imperishable stars' are 'Night's orchards' – as we have seen, an allusion duly picked up by Thomas in 'Country Child'.

The 'schools' who failed to predict the cold orbit of an older world are those of the medieval scholastic philosophers Thomas studied in his college days and whose diminished inheritor he is. Implicit in 'A Peasant', therefore, is the poet himself as spectator-preacher-philosopher at a watershed in his life, one who has to confront the *mysterium tremendum et fascinans* of the twentieth century. 'Curious' is itself a curious word, denoting a desire for knowledge, intriguing patterning and an interest in the rare. The second meaning implies Thomas's presence in 'A Peasant' as the poem's expert shaper. Without the stars, he could never have imagined such height, width, breadth, duration, density, distance, entity, interval – or coldness. In 'Lowri Dafydd' he writes:

> stars were out
> Over my roof, the door fallen
> About its hinges, and on the hearth
> A cold wind blowing for ever.
>
> (*PS*, 20)

These lines memorably conjoin coldness, fate and the stars. He was to pursue them in an adventure that is every bit as thrilling as any written by that other famous possessor of double initials, H. G. Wells, whose *The Chronic Argonauts* (a draft of *The Time Machine*) describes the mad scientist, Dr Nebogipfel, fashioning his travelling machine in a Welsh village – as our Dr Neb was shortly to do.

Thomas's voyage into space began in Chirk and continued in Hanmer, Manafon, Eglwys-fach, Aberdaron and elsewhere in north-west Wales. Had he not lived in these rural parishes, he would not have had such access to the night sky or to men like Prytherch, who practise their traditional skills under the stars. But then 'under the stars' is where all Thomas's characters live; it is where Buddug and Job Davies copulate in *The Minister* (1953) and where 'time's attrition' exposes death and men's vows as skeletal reality.

In 'Here' (*T*, 43), an important development occurs with Thomas's reference to 'the swift satellites' measuring the 'clock' of the protagonist's existence. Such satellites may be planetary bodies but they are also the manned and unmanned space vehicles that were beginning to circle the earth at that time. Suddenly, space fills up with machines in a development of the earlier technology of the clock. In 'Wallace Stevens', Thomas states that his favourite American poet was drawn to

> The deep spaces between stars,
> Fathomless as the cold shadow
> His mind cast.
>
> (*BT*, 25)

Coldness is identified with the star-like poetic imagination, as in Lewis's 'The Jungle'. Sky and earth are now reversed: whereas people once looked up at stars, now they look down on earth as they voyage through space. Thomas repeated this Kierkegaardian notion several times in images of marine travel and shipwreck in space. We no longer have any fixed points and things recede from us according to determinate laws. Starlight itself has been queered.

The same shadowy, interstellar cosmic space appears in 'Via Negativa' (*H'm*, 16), where it is internalized as the 'empty silence / Within' where God lingers in 'the interstices of our knowledge'. The darkness 'between stars' becomes another site of metaphysical anxiety which demands further exploration. Prytherch himself was wedded to dumbness and 'old silence' (*SF*, 19), having a dry mouth, bird-like tongue and cracked lips; the 'embryo music' is 'dead in his throat' ('The Welsh Hill Country'; *AL*, 7). In 'Peasant Greeting' (*SF*, 27), he offers 'no speech', only a raised hand in compensation for 'the mute tongue and the unmoistened lips'. Such silence – a portion of the cosmic silence – reinforces the 'shackle on the tongue' (*AL*, 11) imposed on him by the English language, which obliges the Welsh to remain dumb in their own language. (In 'Eviction', Thomas defines English as 'that cold language that is the frost / On all our nation' (*BT*, 13).) Even supposing, then, that Prytherch had any thoughts, he could not successfully articulate them. Indeed, Thomas himself felt that he had failed to communicate with his parishioners and that God, in turn, kept his distance from him.

Together with silence come footsteps that betray our brief tenure of space-time, whether Robinson Crusoe's, Neil Armstrong's or the departing Creator's:

Man leaves his footprints
Momentarily on a vast shore.
                    ('Young and Old'; YO, 7)

These lines have something about them of the Victorian crisis of faith. The boundless universe, symbolized by starlight, is inhabited by random beings thrown up by evolution and set on their 'journey to annihilation' (SF, 43). Such ideas are daunting but compelling; it is as if Thomas's mental purchase of them outweighs any repugnance he feels for them.

Yeats's mechanical birds of Byzantium could not have borne stranger – 'curiouser' – fruit. Into this universe now throng grey curlews, ravens, rooks, sparrows, hawks, kestrels; metonymic claws, wings and feathers; herons, robins, warblers, buzzards; God's choir, Rhiannon's birds and Yeats's birds; eagles, ouzels, little owls, barn owls, finches, thrushes, falcons, gulls, nightjars, larks, blackbirds, bitterns, starlings, shags, herring gulls, linnets, wild geese, dunnocks, jays, swallows, cranes, gnats, moths, hens, cocks, bats.

There is no solving the problem
They pose, that had millions of years
Behind it, when the first thinker
Looked at them.
                    Sometimes they meet
In the high air; what is engendered
At contact? I am learning to bring
Only my wonder to the contemplation
Of the geometry of their dark wings.
                    ('Swifts'; P, 9)

This is the herald of a new annunciation. Interestingly, the charm and precision of the birds are figured in terms of geometry and engineering (of which the 'first thinker' is the suitably unspecific personification). 'Engender' – a powerfully Yeatsian word – both captures the copulation of birds in mid-flight and intimates the birth of a new age, after Yeats's 'Leda and the Swan'. Such are the new metaphysics of nature.

When Thomas wrote 'Swifts', he was a fifty-year-old unsmiling public man who was about to enter the crisis of his life. Twenty years after 'A Peasant', he decided, like Yeats, to walk – in his case, fly – naked. That is why his subject matter changed. Frustrated by the continuing obduracy, not to say venality and selfishness, of his parishioners, despairing of prayer, sexually repressed and preternaturally aged (in 'The Dance' (*P*, 38), he asks a young child to take his hand and ignore 'its sly pressure, / The dry rut of age' so that he can 'smell / [His] youth again in [her] hair'), he had nowhere to go but up – to the birds, stars and the geometry of the mind. In such harsh conditions he found fertile soil for his poetry. Proleptically, Prytherch had shown the way.

Geometry, of course, is a threat as well as a promise, producing bombs as well as birds. To these we should add nature's subversive agents: molecules, viruses, microscopic organisms. They, too, now enter the poetry with an insistence that virtually fashions a new vocabulary. Prytherch may have seemed formidable when viewed as the rump of humanity that endures between the solstices harboured by the planets – themselves fortresses to his fortress, never to be stormed – but the 'influence' of the planets (in the medieval sense of sidereal emanations capable of shaping our lives) is clearly felt, destabilizing him and the poetry. Deep structure determines new directions.

Deus in Machina: 1968–75

The change in subject matter in Thomas's poetry was accompanied by a technical decision not to capitalize each new line of verse. This eased the flow of the poems but was accompanied by a more important decision to enjamb lines in ways that flexed and ironized them, offering something less impeded and impeding. Such enjambments suited the 'blank indifference' and 'neutrality' of 'These grey skies, these wet fields' and 'the wind's winding-sheet' (*NBF*, 44); the hesitations and elisions they generated seemed to mimic 'the mind's scansion' (*PS*, 31) in unpredictable conditions. Rowan Williams has written of 'a diffusion of sense beyond syntactical structure', 'an effort to pre-empt the temptations of formal closure at the level of prepositional order and intelligibility'.[7]

Here is the old style at something like its best:

> And endlessly the days go on
> With their business. Lovers make their appearance
> And vanish. The germ finds its way
> From the grass to the snail to the liver to the grass.
> The shadow of the tree falls
> On our acres like a crucifixion,
> With a bird singing in the branches

What its shrill species has always sung,
Hammering its notes home
One by one into our brief flesh.
('That'; NBF, 44)

These pithy lines conflate the Eden and Crucifixion stories. A bird – even now a messenger of fate – announces the cycle of existence that goes from grass to snail to liver and back to grass again. All flesh is grass, all love a biological imperative determined by nature's laws: creation, survival and dissolution. The logic of the species enters the poetry, and new forms of expression were needed to explore it. In 'The Place' (NBF, 45), Thomas describes a 'Spray of martins' but 'not as a man vowed / To science' – in other words, by counting their returns, sifting their droppings and recording the 'wave-length' of their screams. He seems unusually knowledgeable about the procedures he says he wants to avoid. Gradually, however, such procedures exercised their pressure on him and revealed that nuclear weapons and similar 'gifts that destroy' (H'm, 18) belonged with all the thefts, murders, rapes and illnesses he was asked to accept as part of God's providential plan. God's 'thin dribble' of poetry dries 'on the rocks / Of a harsh landscape under an ailing sun' (H'm, 21) and Thomas is drawn to some rough new Bethlehem.

God has failed his creation (or been rejected by it – it scarcely matters which) and leaves behind him the viruses that will infect it.

I have no name for today
But itself. Long ago
I lost count of the days.
Castaways have no mirror
But the sea, that leaves its wrinkles
On themselves, too. Every morning
I see how the sun comes up
Unpublicised; there are no news
On this beach. What I do
Neither the tall birds on the shore,
Nor the animals in the bush
Care about. They have all time
And no time, each one about
Its business, foraging, breeding.
I thought that they had respect
For a human. Here there are creatures
That jostle me, others that crawl
On my loved flesh. I am the food

> They were born for, endlessly shrilling
> Their praises. I have seen the bones
> In the jungle, that are the cradle
> We came from and go back to.
>
> ('Castaway'; YO, 27)

These enthralling lines measure the new cosmos. They are alert to the perceived danger and crackle with tension; they slip, slide, will not stay in place. Speech rhythms and line rhythms are syncopated, as if in reaction to the discovery of how vulnerable life now is: 'I thought that they had respect / For a human', Thomas cries. His poem is written in a new kind of English marked by unprecedented locutions – 'my loved flesh', 'there are no news', 'the sun comes up / Unpublicised', 'the sea, that leaves its wrinkles / On themselves'.

We can now see that Thomas's poetry was a poetry of beginnings constantly revised, an exploration of origins, of the birth-pangs of consciousness. In 'Castaway', we find him stranded, Crusoe-like, in space-time, 'foraging, breeding'. The human has been decentred and takes up habitation in a 'curious' universe where everything preys on everything else. 'The Sea' (YO, 28) repeats the same revelation: the ocean 'chews rocks / To sand'; 'bones, / Wrecks, continents are digested' and its embraces 'Leave you without breath'. As castaways in this destructive element, we have reached 'bone', Thomas's term for distilled truth. The 'praises' heard towards the end of 'Castaway' offer no hosannahs to the highest but testify to the birds' and beasts' success in the struggle for existence.

Twenty years later, Thomas revisited the same subject:

> Shipwrecked upon an island
> in a universe whose tides
> are the winds, they began multiplying
> without joy. They cut down the trees
> to have room to make money.
>
> The one who is without name,
> but all-powerful, sowed intelligence
> in them like a virus. As living room
> became scarce, as rain became acid,
> they became conscious there were other islands
>
> all round, garlands hung up
> at the festivities of science,

waiting to be colonised not by
the imagination but in fact.

Utopia and dystopia clash to create a Foucaultian heterotopia. Walford
Davies has written of Thomas's syntax inducing 'elegant vertigo', a 'free
fall' which obliges us 'to "catch" the meaning. The poem so risks its own
form that we have to reconstitute the idiom . . . realign the syntax.'[8] The
lineation of 'A Species' is spectacularly ragged: 'in a universe whose
tides'; 'the imagination but in fact'. Such garbled scraps cannot be
construed until they have been realigned in a process that resembles log-
rolling. They defer resolution so repeatedly that, when it comes, it feels
brittle. Such are the delicate reconciliations of the 'festivities of science':
virus, acid rain, space exploration. Thomas reinvents the beginning of
things in the manner of Kipling explaining how the elephant got its trunk
in his *Just So* stories. He is afraid that human beings, having gained the
power to harm the earth, will now repeat the trick more widely through
the universe,

> making an archipelago
> of the stars, hurrying from one
> to another with their infection.
> There came a day when the one
> without name and whose signature
>
> is in cipher willed them to go back
> to their first home, destitute but wiser.
> They turned as to a familiar, seeing it
> for the first time, suspended in beauty,
> blue with cold, but waiting to be loved.
>
> ('A Species'; *NTF*, 43)

Despite its coldness, the image of space as a sea dotted with islands
is hauntingly beautiful. Darwinian science is crossed with Christian
fancy.

'A Species' warns against humanity's virus-like intelligence; both
Creator and firmament long to be loved by the reformed sinner. Yet the
appearance of the planet as an island in space, the tropical garlands,
stellar archipelago and shipwreck are pregnant with an allure that
qualifies the moralizing intent. Like Wallace Stevens, Thomas offers a
pure play of fancy that is every bit as discordant as Prytherch and the
stars once were. The poem unleashes all language's power of contradiction: where he pulls, it pushes, and the tension is exemplified in the

concluding image of earth as seen from outer space in the famous NASA photograph – the very perspective and enterprise he cautions against. The stars will have their way, it seems; they are the topos of the poem, a metasubject that carries all else before it. As so often, Thomas dresses anti-scientific sentiments in scientific language and in so doing alters them, as the following syllogism suggests: God is what Thomas wants to write about; science is how he writes about Him; therefore Thomas writes about science. As 'Astronauts' (*YO*, 14) observes, 'Godhead' is 'a fire / Extinguished' whose light continues to reach us – just like that of the stars.

God's 'illuminated city / of the imagination' now burns with fires 'extinguished before the eyes' lenses / formed' (*WI*, 16). They light up a fresh reality: not that of the city on the hill but that of technology and science. 'Emerging' (*LS*, 1), addressed to the 'God of form and number', defines prayer as leading from 'the adolescence of nature' to 'the adult geometry / of the mind':

> Circular as our way
> is, it leads not back to that snake-haunted
> garden, but onward to the tall city
> of glass that is the laboratory of the spirit.

Not even Wallace Stevens, who worked in a city of skyscrapers, thought of identifying them with the scientist's workbench. In another Genesis, Thomas declares the garden of Eden defunct and replaces it with a realm partly physical and partly spiritual – at once contemporary and historical. Science is no longer the 'other' but one of the ways in which God communicates with us.

> He is alone, it is Christmas.
> Up the hill go three trees, the three kings.
> There is a star also
> Over the dark manger. But where is the Child?
>
> Pity him. He has come far
> Like the trees, matching their patience
> With his. But the mind was before
> Him on the long road. The manger is empty.
>   ('Lost Christmas'; *YO*, 32)

The discovery is poignant but not unexpected.

Evidently, these years represent something of a revolution in Thomas's mind. As Incarnation and Crucifixion fade, they leave behind the problem of the absent Creator for him to resolve and, as usual, the clue comes to him in the star hanging in the void:

> And to one God says: Come
> to me by numbers and
> figures . . .

(a perfect piece of lineatory wit: without 'figures', 'numbers' might refer to a book of the Old Testament, metrical feet or hymns),

> see my beauty
> in the angles between
> stars, in the equations
> of my kingdom. Bring
> your lenses to the worship
> of my dimensions: far
> out and far in, there
> is always more of me
> in proportion.
>
> ('Mediations'; *LS*, 17)

'Proportion', 'dimension', 'equations', 'figures', 'numbers': Thomas fashions a new language to define a new deity. How authentic it sounds in comparison with the by now tired imagery in the same poem of the 'bush burning' and the 'body / of a man hung on a tall / tree'!

Even so, Thomas never lost his fear of the scientific. 'Lens', a favourite word to represent inquiry and discovery, suggests the dangers implicit in using the mind as a microscope ('Out There'; *LS*, 4). But that is the way with field forces: they go where they will, driving poet and God 'among / the dumb cogs and tireless camshafts' ('God's Story'; *LS*, 7). Such imagery, though full of trepidation, is irresistible. In 'Relay' (*LS*, 9), technological man pauses on the mountain of his enterprise 'for lack of the oxygen / of the spirit'. The Thomas of yore would never have thought of metamorphosing 'oxygen' in terms of 'spirit'; it is another consequence of the disappearance of God. Since nature abhors a vacuum, it fills it with swarming echoes and germs. The deus is no longer *ex* but *in* machina.

In 'Poste Restante', the earth turns 'from season to season like the wheel /' – of what? Here is another fine piece of lineatory wit – 'like the wheel / of a great foundry' (*LS*, 14). This is as surprising as discovering church altars made of steel ('God's Story'; *LS*, 7). The whole universe has been systematized. The eighteenth-century god of mathematics gives way to the geometrical god who presides over a fearsome universe. Supra-physical revelation is now to be found in laboratory conditions:

> As I had always known
> he would come, unannounced,
> remarkable merely for the absence
> of clamour. So truth must appear
> to the thinker; so, at a stage
> of the experiment, the answer
> must quietly emerge.
>
> ('Suddenly'; *LS*, 32)

By the time of *Laboratories of the Spirit*, spiritual truth and laboratory truth ('experiment') have become one; metaphorically speaking, God is that which calculation yields.

Theo-sci

'Rough' (*LS*, 36) offers yet another retelling of Genesis. God accepts responsibility for – or acknowledges – the cycle of existence represented by the eagle that feeds off the wolf that feeds off the jack-rabbit that feeds off the grass. As wolves roam through the forest, so seals, cormorants and mackerel move through the sea:

> He stepped back;
> it was perfect, a self-regulating machine
> of blood and faeces.

A striking moment. The eagle is not just a bird but part of a system from which God, Frankenstein-like, stands back proud-aghast, as at the end of his labours. At that point, he adds human beings, who promptly take charge of it, together with 'a handful of small germs' to keep them in check. Finally, with a laugh, he offers Jesus. Of such is the new mythos of earth.

In 'Ivan Karamazov' (*LS*, 39), God turns into 'a kind of impossible robot / you insert your prayers into / like tickets' and our lives become 'airports at which we touch / down and remain in too briefly' ('Somewhere'; *LS*, 46). The language of the machine is everywhere and is now articulated with relish. Language has taken possession of subject and delights in describing stars as 'sleepless conurbations' (*LS*, 51) – a mirror-image of what *homo faber* builds on earth. Perhaps this is what the novelist William Gibson had in mind when he coined the word 'cyberspace', detecting in the star image an immense network of computer programmes and databases:

> A graphic representation of data abstracted from the banks of every computer in the human system. Unthinkable complexity. Lines of light ranged in the nonspace of the mind, clusters and constellations of data. Like city lights, receding.[9]

In 'What Then?', Thomas doubts whether a crucifixion could save 'the astronauts / venturing in their air-conditioned / capsules':

> They are planning their new conurbations
> a little nearer the stars
> incinerated by day and by night
> glacial . . .

We baulk at the third line's suggestion of their burning by day and night until we realize they will burn by day and freeze by night; the enjambment doubles the distress.

> but will there be room there
> for a garden for the Judas
> of the future to make his way through
> to give you his irradiated kiss?

The lines offer a modern version of an ancient sin. The romance of space travel and the audacity of that 'irradiated kiss' confound the poet's scepticism; it is as if the astronauts' air-conditioned capsules constitute a novelty too thrilling for his reservations to make much headway against. The result strengthens humanity's ties with the machine, which lie at the heart of sci-fi:

> What prayers will they say
> upside down in their space-chambers?
> Are you prepared to reveal
> the nuclear brain and the asbestos
> countenance to deserve their worship?
> (*MHT*, 75)

By now, Thomas's poems have become intensely quizzical and quizzing and the interrogative his favourite mood. The questions above are addressed to the Creator and raise a fundamental doubt: is the god in the asbestos mask radiating electromagnetic waves also the god of the tree? By 'irradiated', Thomas apparently means 'polluted', though 'irradiated' products are those that have had their shelf-life extended; they may be available at a supermarket near you. He recoiled from the idea of conurbations yet, imaginatively speaking, lived nowhere else. His habitation of the Llŷn peninsula was neither here nor there; the critical emphasis placed on it is a tribute to the continuing power of the biographical fallacy. (As Einstein said, what matters in the life of the scientist is 'what he thinks and how he thinks, and not what he does or suffers'.) When Thomas stopped being the man Yeats describes sitting down to eat his eggs at breakfast in Aberdaron, he resided in sci-fi land. And it is from there that he wrote his poems. Secure in Llŷn, he ventured with confidence into unfamiliar territory (which is the same as saying that the unfamiliar took possession of him with confidence).

The theological god has by now become the biochemical one, the 'metabolism / of the being of love'. Despite possessing a word that has an endless 'fall-out', like strontium-90, the metaphysical deity falls 'silent' and 'dumb' before 'the new // linguists' (*WI*, 28) – a different explanation for his having gone *absconditus*. In the same way, the future becomes a 'cassette' (*WI*, 15). In 'Barn Owl', the bird's 'soft / feathers camouflaging a machine' betray

> the voice
> of God in the darkness cursing himself
> fiercely for his lack of love.
>   (*WI*, 25)

Whether totalizing systems like metabolisms and machines prise open an ambiguity that was latent in Thomas's metaphysical quest or whether they introduce ambiguities to it is a moot point. When the owl screams in 'The Porch', the poet, at prayer, turns his back on the interior to gaze at 'a universe / that was without knowledge / of him', 'on that lean / threshold, neither outside nor in' (*F*, 10). In this liminal position, between inner and outer space,

> I have heard the still, small voice
> and it was that of the bacteria

> demolishing my cosmos. I
> have lingered too long on
>
> this threshold but where can I go?
> ('Threshold'; *BHN*, 110)

The answer is: neither backwards nor forwards but 'into open space, / hoping for the reciprocating touch'. In terms of freshness of response and stimulating insight, the reference to Michelangelo's Adam is tame and hopelessly outdated in comparison with the image of the 'demolishing' bacteria.

The owl reappears in 'Raptor' (*NTF*, 52), 'fastening his talons' on the sinful. The poem begins – even at this late stage in Thomas's career – by denying the power of science yet continues to draw its energy from it. The word 'raptor' in the ornithological sense dates from 1823 and is part of the tide of inquiry that led to Darwin. The poem also alludes to Gerard Manley Hopkins's 'The Windhover', another poem that tries to assert the Christian while, in fact, accomplishing the opposite. Evidently, Thomas felt the bird's talons suggestively figured God's power over the believer, but who ever thought a bird of prey swooping on its victim was a suitable image for the operations of grace?[10] Hopkins's 'The Windhover' survives this contradiction because it enacts it rather than resolves it. Hopkins added a dedication to the poem, 'To Christ our Lord', which he insinuates into the text as a subtitle. Dedicating a poem to Christ, however, does not mean it is *about* Christ, and no one would think that it were had Hopkins not suggested as much. The poet has designs on his poem – designs which it successfully resists. What Hopkins's sonnet shows us is a Darwinian bird doing what Darwinian birds do best, despite its mystifying guise as a spiritual 'dauphin'.

If evolutionary process compelled Thomas, how much more compelling was radio astronomy:

> I am at the switchboard
> of the exchanges of the people
> of all time . . .
> ('Present'; *F*, 9)

God speaking, over and out. Commenting on the lines from 'Emerging' quoted earlier – 'the adult geometry / of the mind' – J. D. Vicary remarks that the conceit places Thomas 'in a tradition of meditative and speculative religious poetry',[11] as if the power of the image were merely

decorative. Similarly, William V. Davis says of the above lines from
'Present': 'The poet, at the point of "exchange" between powers, between
man and God, is like the prophet of an earlier age.'[12] But no prophet sat
at a telephone exchange; the language alters the conception. In any case,
prophets no longer exist; they have become facilitators, identified with
the function they serve; nowadays they would be internet servers or
search engines.

The 'cell's core', in all its materiality, is part of 'the equation / that
will not come out' (*F*, 7–8), and we have reached the limit of language. In his
youth, Thomas believed thought was a 'contagion' which conflicted with
his parents' anxiety to keep him 'scrubbed' clean (*WI*, 8). But he also had
an 'interior mind' to which nobody else had access, and it is this depth
that the poetry now sounds. What was unplumbable before is raided by
space's 'new explorers', for whom 'far out' is 'deep down' and 'fathoms'
'space' (*WI*, 28). Prayer is redefined in theo-sci terms.

At which point, a remarkable journey begins:

> We lean far out
> over ourselves and see the depths
> we could fall to.
>   ('Phew!'; *WI*, 29)

Luciferian pride blends with Kierkegaardian sailing, as the stars
promised. 'It was not / I who lived, but life rather / that lived me' ('In
Context'; *F*, 13): any sense of a providential 'larger pattern', a
'developing structure', is replaced by 'the changes / in the metabolism of a
body / greater than mine'; the cosmic self, which is not 'I', dismantles the
biographical self, in accordance with universal laws. God now sits at 'that
strange [for which read 'curious'] table / of Eddington's',

> nodes and molecules
> pushing against molecules
> and nodes; and he writes there
> in invisible handwriting the instructions
> the genes follow.

He has become a scientist *in excelsis*, an *über*-Gregor Mendel. (A. S.
Eddington, the first English exponent of relativity, was the author of *The
Nature of the Physical World* (1928), a book with which Thomas was
familiar.)

> But there will be
> no judgement other than the verdict
> of his calculations, that abstruse
> geometry that proceeds eternally
> in the silence beyond right and wrong.
>
> ('At It'; *F*, 15)

The laws of God and of science are one and the same, as encoded in chromosomes, cells and DNA; eschatology is merely 'the verdict of [God's] calculations'.

The stars are now subjected to major development:

> What they are saying is
> that there is life there, too;
> that the universe is the size it is
> to enable us to catch up.
>
> They have gone on from the human;
> that shining is a reflection
> of their intelligence. Godhead
> is the colonisation by mind
>
> of untenanted space.
>
> ('Night Sky'; *F*, 18)

Colonization, once a sign of man's pride, now reflects his intellectual freedom, and 'God' becomes the name we give to the mind's absorption of the galaxies (one of the senses in which we 'catch up' with space). The poem bristles with the vitality of the cosmos. The 'they' of the poem are the Einsteins and Eddingtons who expound the 'conceptual truth' of our existence. Thomas now embraces space exploration:

> I let the stars inject me
> with fire, silent as it is far,
> but certain in its cauterising
> of my despair.

Thomas is inoculated (or 'engendered') by the stars in a sci-fi exchange that is Kubla Khanish with wonder, space replacing the Khan's paradise gardens and the Aleph his sacred Alph. (His 'mighty' fountain may be the stellar 'fountain / of the imagination' mentioned in 'A Thicket in Lleyn' (*EA*, 45)). So enkindling are the stars that Thomas turns space traveller on his 'launching pad' of prayer (*ERS*, 39). He who has previously been acquainted with the Frostian night sky and has 'outwalked the furthest city light' discovers his despair has been 'cauterised'. The illumination of the stars thus compensated for Thomas's loss of faith. What he found reflected in space was a god who is an eidolon of gas and dust. Sometimes, he believed that opposition to the machine could coexist with admiration for those who conduct scientific research, but 'Night Sky' shows the distinction to be empty. Space travel *is* the machine – booster rockets, capsules, satellite communication, spacesuits and all. The sombre gravity of the poem, its limpid simplicity, blank with astonishment, its woozy belief in the enlightenment it so hauntingly contemplates lend its abstract language utter conviction. Radio-telescopy enters Thomas's poetry.

Tuning into the Universe

From now on, science spreads like a virus through the verse: germs, chromosomes, electrons, molecules, spermatozoa, surds and equations, missiles, scalpels, becquerels, decibels, cells, filaments, acid rain, cordite, Valium, leptons, quarks, thermometers, barometers, pulsars, quasars, calculus, radiation, the Doppler effect.

> Oh, I know it and don't
> care. I know there is nothing in me
> but cells and chromosomes
> waiting to beget chromosomes
> and cells.
>
> ('Bravo!'; *F*, 22)

Such lines are not without irony ('I accept I'm predictable, / that of the thousands of choices / open to me the computer can calculate / the one I'll make') but they are not only ironic. In 'Seventieth Birthday' (*BHN*, 94), Thomas declares he is 'Made of tissue and H_2O, / and activated by cells / firing'. In 'Pre-Cambrian' (*F*, 23), he asks: 'After Christ, what? The molecules / are without redemption'. Suspended on his 'bough of land between sea and sky . . . where he had crawled out, far as he could go' (*ERS*, 68), he submits to 'an unseen / power, whose sphere is the cell / and the electron' (*F*, 29):

> Look over the edge
> of the universe and you see
> your own face staring
> at you back, as it does
> in a pool.
>
> ('The Game'; *F*, 31)

He is

> leaning far out
> over an immense depth, letting
> [God's] name go and waiting,
> somewhere between faith and doubt . . .
>
> ('Waiting'; *F*, 32)

The last line suggests the impact of chemical knowledge on him – and the nausea it induced:

> There was a hope
> he was outside of, with no-one
> to ask him in, where he stood
> with such stars over him
> as were like love only
> in the velocity of their recession.
>
> (*ERS*, 49)

As Christian love fades, we are bathed by the light that reaches us from an expanding universe and what was latent in the poetry becomes manifest. At night,

> rising from his fused prayers,
> he faces the illuminated city
> above him: All that brightness, he thinks,
>
> and nobody there! I am nothing
> religious. All I have is a piece
> of the universal mind that reflects
> infinite darkness between points of light.
>
> ('The Possession'; *F*, 33)

God and man unite in the stratosphere, as Prytherch and the 'curious' stars promised.

In these poems, Thomas strikes the Narcissus-like pose which Alun Lewis adopted in 'The Jungle' as he gazed into a stagnant pool, there to discover that 'all fidelities and doubts dissolve'. (In *Mass for Hard Times*, 'a still pool' reflects 'the roundness of our world' (p. 34) and is related to the 'gene-pool' of cloning scientists (p. 38).) 'We are beginning to see / now it is matter is the scaffolding / of spirit', Thomas states (*F*, 41). Accordingly, he abandons the 'easier certainties' of faith and walks his plank over seventy thousand fathoms – maximum punishment for such piratical freedom of enquiry.

> Above and
> beyond there is the galaxies'
> violence, the meaningless wastage
> of force, the chaos . . .
>
> Is there a place
> here for the spirit? Is there time
> on this brief platform for anything
> other than mind's failure to explain itself?
>   ('Balance'; *F*, 49)

These lines suggest a radical hesitation induced by the boldness of his enterprise. Are we at the centre of nothingness, colonization's ultimate frontier? Certainly, no kings come bearing gifts here. Thomas continues his questioning:

> What is a galaxy's meaning?
> The stars relay to the waste
> places of the earth, as they do
> to the towns, but it is
> a cold message. There is randomness
> at the centre, agitation subsisting
> at the heart of what would be
> endless peace.
>   ('Senior'; *BHN*, 97)

The stars are as Lewis predicted – waste, cold, chaotic. The enjambment that carries 'randomness' to the middle of the next line emphasizes its centrality to the sentence and to the poem as a whole while the succeeding lines pointedly reverse and update Wordsworth's description of what the 'ear of faith' hears in the 'shell' of an active universe: 'ebb and flow, and ever-during power, / And central peace, subsisting at the heart / Of endless agitation' (*The Excursion*, IV, 1141–7).[13]

The poet turns rocket-scientist, sending his probes out into 'God-space', and becomes an 'astronaut / on impossible journeys / to the far side of the self' (*BHN*, 99), emitting signals on such frequencies as he commands to a station that never replies. Lost in space, he realizes that more than physics will be needed if he is to reach God – if, that is, God and physics are not already one:

> Nightly
> we explore the universe
> on our wave-lengths, picking up nothing
> but those acoustic ghosts
> that could as well be mineral
> signalling to mineral
> as immortal mind communicating with itself.
>
> ('The Tree'; *LP*, 187)

Such lines record a grave doubt. They are a scrambled form of communication that is barely scannable. The shadow of the old certainty that haunts lines two and seven contrasts with the grammatical wreckage that surrounds them. Occasionally, Thomas wrote as a Christian; more often, he wrote as a post-Christian; here, he writes as 'composer of the first / radio-active verses' (*ERS*, 75).

Evidently, radical disintegration lay at the root of his personality and it gave rise to all his conflicts and contradictions: Anglo/Welsh, church/chapel, faith/doubt, pacifism/militancy, rural/scientific, rooted/ exploratory. Gazing into the mirror of space, he found there the chaos of his own life. Denied the conditions for an integrated personality at birth, he tried to fashion one for himself (as much outside his poetry as in it) but gradually yielded to his shifting identities, discovering in them greater stimulation than he could ever have imagined.

> The poet scans the stars
> and the scientist his equations.
> Life, how often must I
> be brought round to confront
>
> my image in an oblique
> glass? The spirit revolves
> on itself and is without
> shadow, but behind

> the mirror is the twin helix
> where the dancing chromosomes
> pass one another back
> to back to a tune from the abyss.
> (*ERS*, 109)

The helix, of course, offers another form of mirror symmetry. In this poem, Thomas fashions a formal music only to dissolve it at the mention of the oblique glass with its twin images of axial and reflective revolution; then we return to the earlier formality with the dancing chromosomes as they pass 'back / to back', as if in some parodic gavotte or quadrille. Are the poet's scanning of the stars and the scientist's scanning of equations complementary or contrasting activities? Whatever the answer, the dancing chromosomes possess a unique spectral charm. Twenty-three pairs of chromosomes arranged according to the law of chemical compounds, DNA, each atom observing the equation that is locked in the chromosomal nucleus: such is life, and it can be observed only when the cell's chromosomes divide (or 'dance').

These chemical observations, fine as they are, are eclipsed by Thomas's radio-astronomical ones:

> Homo sapiens to the Creator:
> Greetings, on the mind's kilohertz.
> ('Publicity Inc.'; *LP*, 190)

Like all great poetry, this has the capacity to surprise us, all the more so for implying scepticism about its chosen medium while simultaneously lending credence to what it mocks – a form of pseudo-irony Thomas was fond of. He may ridicule the notion that the machine 'has outpaced / belief' (*BHN*, 81) yet he addresses God through the very machinery that spreads the virus of modernity and lends currency to applied science:

> Realising the sound
> returned to us from a flower's
> speaking-trumpet was an echo
> of our own voices, we have switched
> our praise, directing it rather
> at those mysterious sources
> of the imagination you yourself
> drink from, metabolising
> them instantly in space-time
> to become the ichor of your radiation.
> ('Publicity Inc.'; *LP*, 190)

The title of the poem is another example of Thomas's pseudo-irony. These lines are as strange an address to the Creator as can ever have been written; this is what happens when old-style prayer is rejected as self-address. Like the Creator, Thomas reaches for 'mysterious' sources that nourish 'space-time', mixing ichor with radiation, myth with physics. That, too, is how science works, capturing different points of view from mutually exclusive vantage points. God and the emission of particle energy are one.

As above, so below:

> I am my own
> geology, strata on strata
> of the imagination . . .
>
> ('Inside'; *LP*, 199)

Just as God has metamorphosed into genes and rocks (like the stars themselves), so Thomas has cooled to his present state. In yet another variant of the Creation motif, he, Noah-like, sends his vocabulary to perch on 'steel branches'; it returns with a 'metallic / gleam' in its bill ('Vocabulary'; *D*, 11). And so are our days spent in a non-providential universe, 'in the endless procession / that goes nowhere' ('West Coast'; *D*, 24).

'[V]oices superannuating / the Bible' encourage Thomas to believe 'in a presence / without existence':

> You are an occasion
> merely; an event synchronous
> with other events,
>   not caused by them.
>   . . . You have no address,
> says life, and your destination
> is where you began.
>
> (*ERS*, 33)

He says he prefers Christian 'love' to 'the truth embalming itself / in the second law of your Thermo-Dynamics' and yet his dramatizations are more convincing than his assertions, as his portrait in this poem of a 'dissolving / world' shows. In the arctic winter of post-Christianity, he describes a flag flying at half-mast with the emblazoned legend: $E=mc^2$. Such satire, though, lacks all power to correct, radiating the secret power that comes when one confronts the unmentionable.

Keeping Afloat in the Abyss

After this extraordinary stretch of poems, Thomas tried to row back, as
if astonished by his own temerity. But then poetry's liaison with the
'silicon angels' (*EA*, 2) and the microelectronic revolution was never
going to be easy. He retained his suspicion of space orbits and the fixing
of lenses on 'stars and microbes' and trod gingerly amongst flywheels,
pistons and lasers but discovered nonetheless that his hostility towards
them was diluted the more he wrote about them:

> What power shall minister to us
> at the closure of the century,
> of the millennia? The god,
> who was Janus-faced, is eclipsed
> totally by our planet, by the shadow
> cast on him by contemporary
> mind. Shall we continue worshipping
> that mind for its halo,
> its light the mirage of its radiation?
>
> ('AD 2000'; *EA*, 25)

The modern is interpreted as the (temporary?) 'eclipse' of God, but so
intense is the astral imagery that it takes precedence over the argument
between them. God becomes another source of radiation in a universe
awash with particle emissions, like the Van Allen belts that ring the earth
in a 'halo', trapped by gravity and sending out electromagnetic waves.

Part of Thomas longed for a return to Eden; part recoiled from existential freedom. Steadfastly, he contemplated 'nature, mechanism,
evolution':

> Must we
> draw back? Is there a far side
> to an abyss, and can our wings
> take us there? Or is man's
> meaning in the keeping of himself
> afloat over seventy thousand
> fathoms, tacking against winds
> coming from no direction,
> going in no direction?
>
> ('Strands'; *EA*, 32)

– a perfect definition of the 'absurd'. Out on his bough of land, he observes the harrier's 'claws of fire, / quartering the bare earth / for the prey that escapes it' (the windhover image again),

> hovering over the incipient
> scream, here a moment, then
> not here, like my belief in God.
> ('Moorland'; *EA*, 49)

Of such contradictions is he composed, 'Doubtful / of God, too pusillanimous / to deny him' (*EA*, 52). Scrupulously but generously, he 'give[s] these things that share / the world with us' tender recognition:

> Can molecules feel? There is the long sigh
> from the shore, the wave clearing
> its throat to address us, requiring
> no answer than the due
> we give these things that share
> the world with us, that compose
> the world: an ever-renewed
> symphony to be listened to
> admiringly, even as we perform
> it on whatever instruments
> the generations put into our hands.
> ('Andante'; *EA*, 61)

And with this we have come almost full circle:

> Do the molecules
> bow down? Before what cradle
> do the travellers from afar,
> strontium and plutonium, hold out
> their thin gifts? What
> is missing from the choruses
> of bolts and rivets, as they prepare
> for the working of their expensive
> miracle high in the clerestories
> of blind space? What anthem have our computers
> to insert into the vacuum caused
> by the break in transmission
> of the song upon Patmos?
> ('Reply'; *EA*, 65)

Here is another mordant version of the nativity story. Thomas once more alludes to Alun Lewis's 'The Jungle' with its description of 'The banyan's branching clerestories' and its alienation from the 'humming cultures' of the West. Perhaps the physical universe possesses its own guiding principle; Thomas blenches, however, at the thought of a breach with St John's 'song upon Patmos'. Surely computers belittle the spirit? Yet he has juxtaposed soul and science so insistently that his understanding of them in terms of each other exceeds his grasp of either.

Ad Astra

The Echoes Return Slow (1988) opens with a passage in which Thomas relives his birth, which appears to have been an experience for him like any other, consciously suffered. It is harrowingly etched on his mind. He refers to himself as 'trash' – one unworthy of the pain he caused his mother. In 'Alma Mater' (*WA*, 36), he describes how she 'relieved herself / of me', as if he were voided matter. Perhaps this accounts for his attraction to the theme of beginnings; it certainly explains his anguish and instability. *Neb* portrays his bad birth thus: 'Augmenting the pain of the world, a girl cries, then a baby howls, and continues to howl for a long time . . . The photographs show a child only half-sane.'[14] Half-sane? The old fear of meningitis, contracted shortly afterwards, gives rise to the pseudo-ironic suggestion that his birth scarred him for life. Mentally or spiritually, perhaps. Is this what Prytherch was meant to gesture at all those years ago?

Thomas's infantine punishment of his mother was repaid by the 'hard love' of her 'small breasts' (*LP*, 161). Abandoned at birth to disturbance and fragmentation, he grew up to believe his parents were ill-sorted and unloving, wrong-headed, proud individuals. Truly, he was ill-starred: conceived in a sham marriage, he fetched up in the 'fake nation' (*ERS*, 4) of Wales rather than anywhere else and was reared in a sham society with sham values to match. The Thomases' lives were marked by cultural neglect and linguistic shame, both of which he sought to correct, but it would have been better had he had different parents and a different beginning – a 'slut' for a mother, for one thing, who might have encouraged in him a freer attitude towards women and a more pressing grasp of reality (see 'Welsh'; *BT*, 15–16).

He was thus forced to live life on two levels – one external, where he was the dutiful son, a not-especially industrious student and an uxorious husband, the other internal, where he remained restless, attracted to girls from a distance and nursing resentment against his ever-complaining mother, perhaps as a form of inverted guilt. This suggests considerable frustration, a surplus of aggression which he converted into writing. Moreover, it may account for his male cast of mind; no poet ever wrote with less of a sense of the female.

Yet he never became the rebel, preferring instead to exploit his ability to 'lie sideways' (*ERS*, 59). Outwardly, he remained conventional; inwardly he was furtively lustful. In due course, he arrived in the pulpit without any sense of vocation, as the following prose passage suggests: 'At the funeral of the collier's child, when his eye should have been on the book, he saw, with raised eyes, the wild drake mallard winging skyward to disappear into a neutral sky' (*ERS*, 16). 'Neutral' makes such cold sentiments colder. The blankness of the sky is what ensues when insecurity deepens into the scientific abyss, though the casual reader might be forgiven for thinking that the drake mallard's flight represented the flight of the child's soul to heaven. In fact, it is our friend the windhover again – nature's bird rejecting the spurious consolations of faith. Thomas contrasts its naturalness with the service he is conducting, the Church being 'renowned for its pianissimo' in conducting funeral performances of the 'shabby orchestra of sniffs and tears'.

Some might find this moment hypocritical; that the occasion should be a child's death – and a *collier*'s child at that – compounds the offence. Yet no man ever set himself more flintily against the comforts of emotion and none more urgently needed escape from the circumstances of his life via the winging beat of a bird, past praise or blame. The amount of white space that surrounds the text in *The Echoes Return Slow* resonates with emptiness, as if ventilated by a cold draught. Once more, but now with unparalleled astringency, Thomas sounds the tonic of

> Around you the bunched soil;
> above you the empty sky . . .
> (*ERS*, 27)

Teleology vanishes and all tenses are synchronized. While this does not necessarily exclude the Argument from Design, it admits it only in its modern guise of physical periodicity:

> What listener
> is this, who is always awake
> and says nothing? His breathing
> is the rising and falling of oceans on remote
> stars.
>   . . . I lift my face
> to a face, its features dissolving
> in the radiation out of a black hole.
> (*ERS*, 39)

An enthralling moment. The stars fall into a body so dense that no radiation can escape from it. Thomas believed that humanity would be punished for its presumption in pursuing nature's laws – 'What will come forth / to wreak its vengeance on us / for the disturbance?' – but naughty boys will persist, as he proves when he articulates his apprehensions in terms of the very same presumption. In the process, he directs Alun Lewis's image of the dissolving jungle pool outwards into deep space in the form of a black hole. The poem is full of a trepidation indistinguishable from mute exhilaration. It is luminous with its own horror.

Perhaps such mental feats justified his kind of priestly existence. Thanks to his modest demeanour and docility, he was left to explore his thoughts and slipped through life without experiencing the Byronic extremes of joy or woe. As he gazed into the ocean, the heavens or the Precambrian rocks, he experienced again the primal vertigo. Lying awake 'in the lean hours', he heard the waves rising and falling and in that *haecceitas* – and in no other – confronted the 'other being' on whom prayer falls throughout eternity. Spiritual absence is immanent in physical presence.

Sleepless in Llŷn, Thomas discovered his vocation as a voyager in a universe constituted by one action, imperium, gyre, pulse or evolutionary phase after another:

> What matter
> for grief? The stars are as dew
> in [the planet's] world, punctuating
> an unending story. It is the spirit-
> level which, if love cannot
> disturb, neither can evil.
>
> (*ERS*, 81)

Here is the 'neutral' universe, one that sustains as it undermines. Truly, we exist between love and evil; at no time are we asked to choose between them. 'Spirit-level' is Thomas's pun for this idea and it is balanced across two lines, suggesting what *homo faber* uses to build with as well as the equanimity we shall need if we are to survive the 'unending story'. (Consider the effect here had Thomas written 'eternity'.) As in Yeats's 'A Prayer for my Daughter', a storm brews in the mid-Atlantic presaging the end of custom and ceremony. Using a Yeatsian locution but without Yeatsian panache, Thomas cries: 'What matter?' With Yeatsian tragic gaiety, he salutes the new age, eschewing tragedy in favour of detachment.

When God created the world, he broke the primeval silence and became 'architect of our failure', one who gave us language, reflection and, in due course, 'genes / and experiments' (C, 20). He is everything that has happened to us:

> Lord of the molecule and the atom
> are you Lord of the gene, too?
> (C, 51)

And back the answer comes:

> Nothing is outside
> God. We have attributed
> violence to him. Why not
> implicate him in injections?
> (C, 55)

– as Thomas himself had been injected by the stars. The process was analogous to a 'photosynthesis / of an inward light', which Thomas explores in another example of pseudo-irony:

> Tricyano-aminopropene –
> it is our new form
> of prayer, with biological
> changes as an Amen.
> (C, 55)

All is changed, changed utterly. The divine is not *in* the universe; he *is* the universe – black holes, atomic weights and all. In his negativity, he is more convincing than the being of the theology schools.

> And his coming testified
> to not by one star
> arrested temporarily
> over a Judaic manger,
> but by constellations innumerable
> as dew upon surfaces
> he has passed over time
> and again, taking to himself
> the first-born of the imagination
> but without the age-old requirement of blood.
> (C, 33)

The Incarnation is not a unique event but as frequent as the stars, captivating 'the first-born of the imagination' – poets and scientists – with a Pharaonic power but without the bloodlust of the god of Exodus. At such a moment, Thomas contemplates a male birth free from the pain – or necessity – of a mother.

It would be difficult in the volume *Counterpoint* to say what was quotation and what original poetry, though all of it is novel to the highest degree:

> $x + y^2 = y + x^2$?
> it does not balance.
> What has algebra to do
> with a garden?
>
> (*C*, 39)

But Thomas cannot resist mathematics; humanity must bend to universal laws: 'We are used by the bacteria' (*C*, 51). Did science precede Creation or was it produced by it? For 'over twenty centuries' Christ's face – like a curious star – has 'stared, from unfathomable / darkness into unfathomable light' (*C*, 40).

> From the stars that are but as dew
> and the viruses outnumbering the star clusters,
>
>   Gloria.
>
> From those waiting at the foot of the helix
> for the rope-trick performer to come down,
>
>   Gloria.
>
> (*MHT*, 11)

Blessings to all that is. God, 'like light itself, now / in waves from a great distance, / now in the intimacy of our corpuscles' (*MHT*, 58), is a particle of matter in motion.

> Quantum mechanics
> restores freedom to the cowed
> mind that, winking at matter,
> causes it to wink back.
>
> (*MHT*, 62)

However terrible our position, understanding it allows us to wink at the universe, which winks back at us, star-fashion – a bleak yet not uncheerful conclusion.

And all the while, the God of the Hebrews retreats:

> We have captured position
> after position, and his white flag
>
> is a star receding from us
> at light's speed.
>
> (*MHT*, 63)

Astrophysics articulates the Christian recession. Thomas regrets what has happened but accepts it, taking his cue from stars ('time's fires' (*C*, 36)) that died before Christ was lifted from the cross:

> There was something I was near
> and never attained: a pattern,
> an explanation. Why did I address it
> in person? The evolutionists told
> me I was wrong. My premises,
> the philosophers assured me,
> were incorrect. Perpendicular
> I agreed, but on my knees
> looking up, cap in hand,
> at the night sky I laid astronomy
> on one side. These were the spiritual
> conurbations illuminated always
> by love's breath; a colonising
> of the far side of the mind
> without loss of the openness of its spaces.
>
> ('Sonata in X'; *MHT*, 82)

Mistakenly, he pursued meaning in a 'person' (God); now, with newfound tenderness, he takes up his position among the stars' 'spiritual / conurbations' and the colonial image sanctions the shift. All the while, he protests:

> I believe in God
> the Father . . .
> Rid, therefore
> (if there are not too many
> of them), my intestine

of the viruses that against
(in accordance with? Ah, horror!)
your will are in occupation
of its defences.

('Mass for Hard Times'; *MHT*, 12)

It is what the substructure of his poems has been telling him: the spiritual
and microbiological are one, as he proves again when he likens the
ringing of a nightjar in the ferns to 'an electric bell / whose battery had
not run down / millions of years' (*NTF*, 40). The image marries nature to
the machine with outstanding beauty.

Beyond
the stars are more stars where love, perhaps,
or intellect or the anonymous is busy.

('The Promise'; *NTF*, 59)

A poem that makes synonyms of 'love' and 'anonymous' measures how
far we have come. We exist in a process that is beyond our imagining, for
good or ill (and both are implicit in these lines). He whose image was
once graven

gives now
before mind's groping
after him among germs,
galaxies.

('Anybody's Alphabet'; *NTF*, 89)

Thus Thomas, unlike his great predecessors, Coleridge and Hopkins,
can be said to have healed his schizogenetic existence by submitting
his Christian self to the biochemical visionariness of his mythopagan
'Unleavened Self'.[15]

Notes

[1] Randal Jenkins, 'R. S. Thomas: Occasional Prose', *Critical Writings*, 47.
[2] *Critical Writings*, 153.
[3] See *Selected Prose*, 84.
[4] 'Autobiographical Essay', *Miraculous Simplicity*, 20.
[5] *Miraculous Simplicity*, 148 and 149. I avoid the term *deus absconditus* here,
which I think ought to refer to a god who comes and goes; Thomas's god, however, is

permanently AWOL and may be detected only in his absence. This represents a state of affairs far graver than is comprehended by a phrase like *deus absconditus*.

⁶ Alun Lewis, *Collected Poems*, ed. Cary Archard (Bridgend: Seren, 1994), 157.

⁷ *Page's Drift*, 92. For further comments on Thomas's verse form, see R. G. Thomas, *Critical Writings*, 27, and James A. Davies, *Critical Writings*, 133. Donald Davie has some interesting remarks about Thomas's use of enjambment in *Miraculous Simplicity*, 127–39.

⁸ *Page's Drift*, 204.

⁹ From Gibson's *Neuromancer* (1984) quoted in M. Keith Booker, *The Dystopian Impulse in Modern Literature: Fiction as Social Criticism* (Westport, Conn., and London: Greenwood Press, 1994), 147.

¹⁰ In *Neb*, Thomas remarks: 'Anyone who has seen a peregrine falcon falling like lightning on its prey is sure to experience a certain thrill that makes him feel quite humble. These are the masters of the world of nature. One of the unfailing rules of that world is that life has to die in the cause of life. If there is any other way on this earth, God has not seen fit to follow it' (*Autobiographies*, 95). Ah, but which god?

¹¹ *Miraculous Simplicity*, 90–1.

¹² *Miraculous Simplicity*, 113.

¹³ I owe this reference to the editor of this volume.

¹⁴ I quote Justin Wintle's translation in *Furious Interiors: Wales, R. S. Thomas and God* (London: HarperCollins, 1996), 86; see also *Autobiographies*, 27.

¹⁵ See *A Choice of Coleridge's Verse*, ed. Ted Hughes (London: Faber & Faber, 1996), 1–97.

5

'Blessings, Stevens':
R. S. Thomas and Wallace Stevens

TONY BROWN

For Stevens fictions
were as familiar
as facts and if far-
fetched preferable.
Forfeiting for faith
fable, he feasted on it.

('Anybody's Alphabet'; *NTF*, 89)

At the close of an interview he gave in the early 1980s, R. S. Thomas
regretted what he saw as the lack of a 'great new voice' on the poetry
scene in England: 'I can't honestly say there's one about . . . I think
Wallace Stevens comes nearest to expressing the situation, in poetry'.[1]
Thomas was referring to our 'situation', our condition, in a modern,
unpoetic world. This is of course far from being the only reference R. S.
Thomas made, directly or indirectly, to the work of Wallace Stevens. For
instance, in his 1990 interview with John Barnie and Ned Thomas, he
quotes some lines from Stevens's 'Chocorua to Its Neighbor' and in a
BBC radio programme recorded a year before he died, in which he was
asked to choose passages of literature which had given him pleasure, he
included Stevens's 'Peter Parasol'.[2] When interviewed by the *Daily
Telegraph* the previous year, he had noted that 'Wallace Stevens once said
that poems should resist intelligence'; what he is remembering is Stevens's
comment in his *Adagia* (a set of brief *obiter dicta* on poetry) that 'Poetry
must resist the intelligence almost successfully' – 'intelligence' here, of
course, meaning rationality alone, what Wordsworth called 'that false
secondary power'.[3] While a number of commentators have mentioned
Thomas's response to the work of Wallace Stevens (almost always in a list

alongside Yeats and Eliot), the extent and nature of that response has yet to be examined in any detail; the present essay seeks to begin that examination.

In fact, Thomas the Welsh poet-priest had by the time of the above comments been aware of Stevens the American poet and insurance company executive for many years.[4] Indeed, Thomas had written a poem about him in 1962, included the following year in his collection *The Bread of Truth*:

Wallace Stevens

1

On New Year's night after a party
His father lay down and made him
In the flesh of a girl out of Holland.
The baby was dropped at the first fall
Of the leaf, wanting the safe bough
He came from, and was for years dumb,
Mumbling the dry crust
Of poetry, until the teeth grew,
Ivory of a strange piano.

Yet it was not those that he played.
They were too white; he preferred black,
The deep spaces between stars,
Fathomless as the cold shadow
His mind cast. In the bleak autumn
Of real time here I remember
Without eloquence his birth.

2

How like him to bleed at last
Inwardly, but to the death,
Who all his life from the white page
Infected us chiefly with fear
Of the veins' dryness. Words he shed
Were dry leaves of a dry mind,
Crackling as the wind blew
From mortuaries of the cold heart.

There was no spring in his world.
His one season was late fall;
The self ripe, but without taste.

Yet painfully on the poem's crutch
He limped on, taking despair
As a new antidote for love.[5]

Clearly, by this point Thomas knew not only Stevens's poetry but something of his life (possibly from the first chapter of Frank Kermode's study, published in 1960 – the first substantial, and one of the few appreciative, studies of Stevens's work to be published in Britain up to that date[6]): Stevens's mother was indeed of Pennsylvania Dutch extraction, and he was born in the autumn (in October 1879), though Thomas has evidently built on the facts that could have been available to him, portraying the birth in the cheerless terms in which birth is frequently described in his work.[7] The baby is born into a world in which secure beliefs are fading, the leaf's fall leading into the allusion to the breaking bough of 'Rockabye baby'. (Stevens's family ancestors – 'the safe bough / He came from' – were staunch Lutherans.[8]) Thomas's poem manifestly sees Stevens as a bleak, grim poet, born 'In the bleak autumn' and associated with the 'dry leaves' of that season. (Thomas's reference to 'The deep spaces between stars' surely recalls Robert Frost's 'Desert Places': 'They cannot scare me with their empty spaces / Between stars – on stars where no human race is. / I have it in me so much nearer home / To scare myself with my own desert places'.[9]) What Thomas seems to admire in Stevens is his bleak courage, which enabled him to struggle on in a dark world: 'Yet painfully on the poem's crutch / He limped on, taking despair / As a new antidote for love'.

But what is striking, of course, is how partial – and how ultimately inadequate – an account of Stevens this is. 'His one season was late fall': that is demonstrably not true. The cycle of the seasons is there in Stevens's poetry, and, indeed, has particular imaginative significance for him, as the present discussion will indicate. More remarkably, what Thomas's account of Stevens strikingly ignores is the colour, the ludic exoticism that is present in *Harmonium* (1923), which occupies over a hundred pages of the *Collected Poems*:

In Yucatan, the Maya sonneteers
Of the Caribbean amphitheatre,
In spite of hawk and falcon, green toucan
And jay, still to the night-bird made their plea,
As if raspberry tanagers in palms,
High up in orange air, were barbarous.
('The Comedian as the Letter C'; *WS*, 30)

In that November off Tehuantepec,
The slopping of the sea grew still one night
And in the morning summer hued the deck

And made one think of rosy chocolate
And gilt umbrellas.

('Sea Surface Full of Clouds', *WS*; 98–9)

This is the poet whose use of words like 'girandoles' 'daiphanes', 'cantiline', 'peignoir' and 'pannicles' and of titles like 'Homunculus et La Belle Étoile', 'The Apostrophe to Vincentine' and 'Hymn from a Watermelon Pavilion' caused early critics to accuse him of mere aestheticism and of 'attenuated preciosity'.[10] There is no sign of this kind of sensual gaiety in the Stevens that Thomas portrays in his poem. Indeed, it is difficult to imagine the creator of Iago Prytherch responding to many of these poems. The Stevens with whom Thomas engages (not just in this poem) is the poet of, for instance, 'Sunday Morning', 'To the One of Fictive Music', 'The Man Whose Pharynx Was Bad' and 'Le Monocle de Mon Oncle' – poems which, though not always solemn, are ultimately deeply serious in their contemplation of the modern world and the place of transient humans in it, works which contain moments of sensuously apprehended meditation in gently modulated blank verse:

Like a dull scholar, I behold, in love,
An ancient aspect touching a new mind.
It comes, it blooms, it bears fruit and dies.
This trivial trope reveals a way of truth.
Our bloom is gone. We are the fruit thereof.
Two golden gourds distended on our vines,
Into the autumn weather, splashed with frost . . .

('Le Monocle de Mon Oncle'; *WS*, 16)

'Wallace Stevens', then, seems to tell us rather more about Thomas at this point in his imaginative career than it does about Stevens. By 1962, Thomas had left Manafon and the hill country of Montgomeryshire and was vicar at Eglwys-fach, near Aberystwyth. To judge from the poems alone, this seems to have been a period of considerable personal anguish. There seems to be an acute sense of isolation and insecurity, imaginatively and emotionally.[11] That echo of Frost's 'Desert Places' is surely revealing and far from coincidental. A sense of spiritual loneliness seems to haunt the poems of this period, especially those in *The Bread of*

Truth (the volume in which 'Wallace Stevens' was collected). In 'This', Thomas writes:

> Keeping my own
> Company now, I have forsaken
> All but this bare basement of bone,
> Where the one dry flame is awake.
> (*BT*, 42)

('Dry flame' seems to echo the 'dry leaves' of the poem to Wallace Stevens.) The bone image is present again in 'Truth' (*BT*, 38) where the only truth, it seems, is to be found 'In this bare bone of life that I pick'. 'A Country' opens grimly:

> At fifty he was still trying to deceive
> Himself. He went out at night,
> Imagining the dark country
> Between the border and the coast
> Was still Wales . . .
> (*BT*, 30)

Thomas regards the country as lying 'like a bone / Thrown aside and of no use / For anything except shame to gnaw'. Here, the particular issue of Welsh identity gives focus to the spiritual bleakness we find elsewhere. Again in 'Welsh Border' (*BT*, 9), 'It is a dark night'; the poem ends: 'The real fight goes on / In the mind; protect me, / Spirits, from myself'. 'Spirits', we notice, not 'God'; Thomas is surely very much aware of the resonance of the phrase 'a dark night': in 'Pietà' and 'In Church', both from *Pietà,* the volume which followed *The Bread of Truth,* the cross is 'untenanted' (*P*, 14, 44).

So we can perhaps see why Thomas in the early 1960s finds his own Stevens in that poem, limping 'painfully' in the dark of autumn. And of course there *is* bleakness in Stevens, and an ennui comparable to that of Eliot's Prufrock:

> The time of year has grown indifferent.
> Mildew of summer and the deepening snow
> Are both alike in the routine I know.
> I am too dumbly in my being pent.
> ('The Man Whose Pharynx Was Bad'; *WS*, 96)

There is isolation and spiritual emptiness, and it is to this mood that Thomas would evidently have responded:

in the sound of the wind,
In the sound of a few leaves,

Which is the sound of the land
Full of the same wind
That is blowing in the same bare place

For the listener, who listens in the snow,
And, nothing himself, beholds
Nothing that is not there and the nothing that is.

('The Snow Man'; *WS*, 10)

What Thomas found in Stevens was a poet who placed the highest possible value on the power of the poetic imagination, on individual intellectual creativity, in a world which, for Stevens, was otherwise empty of secure meaning. There is no God in Stevens's world; God, as much as the gods which preceded Him, was merely a construction of the human imagination, necessary to make sense of human existence. 'Sunday Morning', from *Harmonium*, is about not going to church:

She hears, upon that water without sound,
A voice that cries, 'The tomb in Palestine
Is not the porch of spirits lingering.
It is the grave of Jesus, where he lay.'
We live in an old chaos of the sun,
Or old dependency of day and night,
Or island solitude, unsponsored, free,
Of that wide water, inescapable.

(*WS*, 70)

Thus, 'To sing jubilas at exact, accustomed times . . . /. . . is a facile exercise' ('Notes Toward a Supreme Fiction'; *WS*, 398). In such a world, though, songs of the human imagination still have a crucial role: 'After one has abandoned a belief in god, poetry is that essence which takes its place as life's redemption' (*Adagia*; *OP*, 158). Human beings cannot live in a world devoid of meaning and values; they need myths and patterns to satisfy the basic human longing for meaning, that human 'rage for order' ('The Idea of Order at Key West'; *WS*, 130). For Stevens, only the imagination can supply such patterns, some moral or aesthetic order, however temporarily. As Frank Lentricchia summarizes: 'Spirit in Stevens is not soul but imagination, and his hymns are not the poetry of the soul in praise of God and paradise, but constructions of the imagination'.[12]

Thus the artist – the truly imaginative individual capable of providing such consoling constructions – is for Stevens a key figure. The action of the imagination is frequently seen in terms of music, but it is the poet who is pre-eminent:

Poetry

Exceeding music must take the place
Of empty heaven and its hymns . . .

('The Man with the Blue Guitar'; *WS*, 167)

What the poet constructs, however, must for Stevens be formed in and from the world around us: 'In poetry at least the imagination must not detach itself from reality' (*Adagia*; *OP*, 161). Stevens's poetry insists on the world's reality, in all its physicality. The task of the imagination is to interact with that reality, to discover, not impose, meanings: 'The imagination is the power of the mind over the possibilities of things'; 'like light, it adds nothing, except itself'.[13] Such terminology strongly signals that Stevens's thinking about the imagination has its roots in Romanticism, especially in the work of Coleridge ('we receive but what we give, / And in our life alone does Nature live . . . / . . . Ah! from the soul itself must issue forth / A light, a glory, a fair luminous cloud / Enveloping the Earth' ('Dejection: An Ode')). Indeed, when the capacity of the creative imagination to contend with the pressure of reality fails, when the poet is faced with imaginative 'poverty' (a word Stevens repeatedly uses for such states and a mood we glimpsed in 'The Man Whose Pharynx Was Bad'), he is, as Kermode points out, in a state similar to that of Coleridge's 'Dejection': we 'see, not feel' how beautiful the world is.[14] Thomas also draws on Coleridge, of course, when discussing the operation and central importance of the creative imagination. Speaking in 1972 of the Resurrection and the Incarnation as a 'metaphorical use of language', he stated:

> People, no doubt, are worried by the use of the word imagination, because imagination to many people has a fictional connotation . . . Of course I'm using the word imagination in its Coleridgean sense, which is the highest means known to the human psyche of getting into contact with the ultimate reality; imaginative truth is the most immediate way of presenting ultimate reality to a human being . . . The ultimate reality is what we call God, and this again is the use of human language in its search for contact with that reality.[15]

Even as we register the common ancestry of thought, however, the ultimate difference between Thomas and Stevens is immediately evident. For Thomas, God is no mere constructed fiction; however hard His presence in the world may be to detect, God has a real – indeed is ultimate – existence. But in his long search in the poetry of the 1970s and 1980s for the elusive God, as well as in the dark period I have suggested Thomas experienced in the early 1960s, the world Stevens inhabited was frequently a recognizable one: 'The trouble is . . . that men in general do not create in light and warmth alone. They create in darkness and coldness. They create when they are hopeless, in the midst of antagonisms' ('Two or Three Ideas'; *OP*, 210). Kermode writes at one point of Stevens's expressing 'Romantic regret in a voice chastened by irony';[16] it is a phrase which might equally describe tones frequently heard in R. S. Thomas.

Stevens's poetry insists that the world to which the imagination responds is mutable, subject to time and to the movement of the seasons. The notion of natural process, the tension between the human longing for permanence and the painful awareness that to be human is inescapably to be transient, is as fundamental to Stevens as it is to Keats. Equally, the transience of the natural world is inseparable from its beauty: Stevens's 'Death is the mother of beauty' (*WS*, 69) echoes Keats's awareness of a 'Beauty that must die' ('Ode on Melancholy'). Thus, far from there being 'no spring in his world', Stevens's world is in constant and sensuous movement between seasons, a movement, indeed, which becomes an analogue in his writing for the activity of the imagination itself. While his icy winters (one thinks in particular of a poem like 'The Snow Man') represent, in Kermode's words, 'pure abstracted reality, a bare icy outline purged clean of all the accretions brought by the human mind to make it possible for us to conceive of reality and live our lives',[17] the arrival of spring is the analogue of the imagination's clothing of the hard, bare body of reality, producing 'what will suffice' (Stevens's phrase)[18] to console us in this world and give us pleasure. Summer is the season when the creative imagination discovers, however briefly and vulnerably, harmony and meaning:

> Now in midsummer come and all fools slaughtered
> And spring's infuriations over and a long way
> To the first autumnal inhalations, young broods
> Are in the grass, the roses are heavy with a weight
> Of fragrance and the mind lays by its trouble.
>
> ('Credences of Summer'; *WS*, 372)

It is possible that Thomas's 'There was no spring in his world' was a half-recollection of Stevens's 'No spring can follow past meridian' in 'Le Monocle de Mon Oncle',[19] a poem very much about natural process, about growing old and the gradual decline of human passion:

IV

This luscious and impeccable fruit of life
Falls, it appears, of its own weight to earth.
When you were Eve, its acrid juice was sweet,
Untasted, in its heavenly, orchard air.
An apple serves as well as any skull
To be the book in which to read a round,
And is as excellent, in that it is composed
Of what, like skulls, comes rotting back to ground.
But it excels in this, that as the fruit
Of love, it is a book too mad to read
Before one merely reads to pass the time.

. . .

VI

If men at forty will be painting lakes
The ephemeral blues must merge for them in one,
The basic slate, the universal hue.

(*WS*, 14, 15)

At Eglwys-fach, Thomas also seems to have reflected on the passing of the years ('At fifty he was still trying to deceive / Himself), and in 'Winter Starlings', published in *Tares*, the volume which preceded *The Bread of Truth*, he reflects directly and sombrely on these issues:

In the evening starlings come from the fields
To circle the wood; they will roost here;
The wood will be an orchard of starlings.

This is an image out of the mind,
Thrown off as it weighs heavier things:
The death of love, the growth of evil,
The inexorable passing of time.

But the starlings fly round and around,
An amorphous mass, whose dark ingredients
Are delicate nodes of joy and fear.[20]

(*T*, 36)

John Powell Ward shrewdly suggests that the poem contains 'a very strong echo' of Wallace Stevens, adding recently that the opening two lines of the second stanza are for him 'pure Stevens'.[21] One might now take the connection further and suggest that the reflective, meditative tones of such poems as 'Le Monocle de Mon Oncle' and 'Sunday Morning' were very much in Thomas's mind as he wrote. Given the similarity of mood, it was perhaps the recollection of the sensuous images of 'luscious' fruit in the 'orchard air' that at some level caused Thomas's mind to 'throw off' the striking image of 'an orchard of starlings'. Stevens's poem refers to 'the fruit / Of love' and 'the intensity of love' ('measure, also, of the verve of earth'), but its ultimate theme is the decay of love resulting from the 'inexorable passing of time'. Stevens's poem does not refer to 'the growth of evil', but for Thomas, the reference to 'Eve' in such a context would be a powerful trigger. At the end of 'Le Monocle de Mon Oncle', the poet looks up and sees not starlings but pigeons, though their movement is precisely echoed by Thomas's birds:

> A blue pigeon it is, that circles the blue sky,
> On sidelong wing, *around and round* and round.
> A white pigeon it is, that flutters to the ground,
> Grown tired of flight.
>
> (WS, 17; my emphasis)

Pigeons appear in a number of Stevens's poems, usually as emblems of natural vitality. They appear most memorably at the beautifully modulated ending of 'Sunday Morning', one of his finest poems. The old beliefs have gone, but the natural world endures:

> Deer walk upon our mountains, and the quail
> Whistle about us their spontaneous cries;
> Sweet berries ripen in the wilderness;
> And, in the isolation of the sky,
> At evening, casual flocks of pigeons make
> Ambiguous undulations as they sink,
> Downward to darkness, on extended wings.
>
> (WS, 70)

Ultimately, it is perhaps Stevens's general mood and a sense of the quiet persistence of the natural world which Thomas is recalling rather than particular poems, but the echoes are suggestive.

Something rather similar seems to happen in a poem collected in *The Bread of Truth*, the volume in which 'Wallace Stevens' appeared. In two of Stevens's poems, the creative power of the imagination is associated with the feminine. In 'To the One of Fictive Music' (*WS*, 87–8), this power is invoked as 'Sister and mother and diviner love':

> Now, of the music summoned by the birth
> That separates us from the wind and sea . . .
>   . . . none
> Gives motion to perfection more serene
> Than yours, out of our imperfections wrought,
> Most rare, or ever of more kindred air
> In the laborious weaving that you wear.
> . . .
>
>   On your pale head wear
> A band entwining, set with fatal stones.
> Unreal, give back to us what once you gave:
> The imagination that we spurned and crave.

In 'The Idea of Order at Key West' (*WS*, 128–30), the young woman is less 'unreal' as she walks by the sea. But for the poet she takes on emblematic significance:

> She sang beyond the genius of the sea.
>   . . .
>
> If it was only the dark voice of the sea
> That rose, or even colored by many waves;
> If it was only the outer voice of sky
> And cloud, of the sunken coral water-walled,
> However clear, it would have been deep air,
> The heaving speech of air, a summer sound
> Repeated in a summer without end
> And sound alone. But it was more than that . . .
>
>   It was her voice that made
> The sky acutest at its vanishing.
> She measured to the hour its solitude.
> She was the single artificer of the world
> In which she sang. And when she sang, the sea,
> Whatever self it had, became the self
> That was her song, for she was the maker.

There is one poem in Thomas's *The Bread of Truth* that is utterly different from the other dark poems in that volume. It was first published seven years earlier in 1954 (when Thomas was still at Manafon) as 'Afternoon at the Sea' and collected as 'Mrs Li' (itself a rather more Stevens-like title):

> Mrs Li, whose person I adore,
> Said to me once, walking on the shore,
> The wind's voices whispering at the ear's
> Innocent portal: Love is like the sea's
> Wandering blossom; we are the waves,
> Who wear it wreathed a moment in our hair.
>
> But I replied, toying with the sand
> That was the colour of her carved hand,
> Though warmer, veined more freely with the sun's
> Tropical gold: No, love is like the sea's
> Measureless music; we are the shells,
> Whose lips transpose it to a brief despair.
>
> <div align="right">(<i>BT</i>, 21)</div>

It seems to me a remarkable piece. It is not in *Collected Poems*; in fact, one would barely recognize it as a poem by R. S. Thomas, and it has received hardly any sustained critical attention. The exception is again John Powell Ward who, in his study of Thomas, sees it as 'an antiphonal poem' to Stevens's 'To the One of Fictive Music'.[22] Like Thomas's Mrs Li, the woman in Stevens's poem walks on the windy seashore, and the opening stanzas of both poems end on the same rhyming word, 'hair'. However, one might contend that 'Mrs Li' owes at least as much to the 'Key West' poem, in which the female figure is again present and the sea with its 'grinding water' is more prominent. There is also one incidental echo: in Thomas we have 'The wind's voices whispering at the ear's / Innocent portal'; at the end of 'Key West', the 'words of the sea' are 'Words of the fragrant portals'. ('Portal' in fact occurs at a number of points in Stevens's writing, in poetry and prose; in another early Stevens poem, 'Peter Quince at the Clavier' (*WS*, 91), for instance, 'Beauty is momentary in the mind – / The fitful tracing of a portal'.)

Given the scene, the Stevens-like title, the way the syntax runs across the line-breaks and the sensuous tones, it is tempting to assume that echoes of Stevens's poetry were again in Thomas's head. However, while there are similarities of mood, especially with regard to 'The Idea of Order at Key West', the subject matter of 'Mrs Li' is ultimately different from that of the Stevens poems. If Stevens's subject is the solace and beauty the imagination can bring, then Thomas's is love. Mrs Li sees herself and her companion as (albeit momentarily) at one with the sea ('Love is like the sea's / Wandering blossom; we are the waves, / Who wear it wreathed a moment in our hair'); the narrator, however, sees love as less attainable, something from which humans, as 'transposers' of some purer love, are perhaps more detached ('No, love is like the sea's / Measureless music; we are the shells, / Whose lips transpose it to a brief despair' – despair, presumably, at being unable to attain it fully or render it permanent). Despite the difference in subject-matter, however, there is in Thomas's uncharacteristic lyric a poignant suggestion of human incapacity which is also present, as we have seen, in Stevens on numerous occasions.

As is clear from Thomas's references in interviews later in his career, Stevens continued to be an important presence for him beyond the 1950s and 1960s. In 1978 Thomas published 'Thirteen Blackbirds Look at a Man' – clearly a direct response to Stevens's 'Thirteen Ways of Looking at a Blackbird'.[23] Thomas's sequence was collected in *Later Poems* and is the product of a period of experimentation with longer poems such as 'Salt' and with sequences – 'Plas Difancoll', 'Covenanters' and 'Perspectives' – which consider a topic or theme from a variety of angles.[24] In Stevens's sequence, Thomas had a ready-made model. Famously, Stevens called 'Thirteen Ways of Looking at a Blackbird' a collection of sensations rather than of epigrams or ideas, though other comments on it suggest a more intellectual reading, including the view that the last section was intended to express despair.[25] The sequence is set in winter, Stevens's season of hard, unmodified reality. The poems, syntactically simple and taut, set up sharp contrasts between the snow and the blackbird; this is far from a lush evening scene in summer with gently descending pigeons. It is the bleak world of 'The Snow Man'. The sequence concerns our relation to the universe around us and our perceptions of it. The blackbird focuses those perceptions, or rather, given the ambiguity of its brooding presence, shadows the moods of the speaker:

> VI
> Icicles filled the long window
> With barbaric glass.
> The shadow of the blackbird
> Crossed it, to and fro.
> The mood
> Traced in the shadow
> An indecipherable cause.

At the same time, the poet again insists, the perceiver must engage the realities of this world of life and movement, not escape into the perspectives of a wholly mythical one:

> VII
> O thin men of Haddam,
> Why do you imagine golden birds?
> Do you not see how the blackbird
> Walks around the feet
> Of the women about you?

Thomas's sequence follows the thirteen-part structure but, characteristically, prefers the perspective of the birds, which he spent so much of his life observing, to that of the human. Ultimately, Thomas's sequence lacks the austerity and tautness of Stevens's, having perhaps a rather narrower range of perspectives. But it similarly concerns fundamentals, dealing not with the issue of how man will survive in an inimical world but with the question of how the world will survive his coming. As William V. Davis has noted, the sequence presents 'an alternative myth of beginnings',[26] and in this Thomas is revisiting a technique used most notably in *H'm* but also as early as 'Becoming' in *The Bread of Truth* ('After the silence / Sound, / Sound of the wild birds, / And movement . . . / . . . But over the sunlight / Shadow / Of the first man' (*BT*, 14)). The garden the blackbirds inhabit is, evidently, Eden ('In the cool / of the day' in section 9 alludes to Genesis 3: 8):

> 1
> It is calm.
> It is as though
> we lived in a garden
> that had not yet arrived
> at the knowledge of
> good and evil.
> But there is a man in it.

Unlike the empty world of the Stevens sequence, that of 'Thirteen Blackbirds Look at a Man' is immediately given a theological context, although God makes no appearance in the poem. Man has been given free rein and we know what the consequences will be:

5
After we have stopped
singing, the garden is disturbed
by echoes; it is
the man whistling, expecting
everything to come to him.

Man is already acquisitive and self-orientated; his whistle of demand
contrasts with the song of the birds. And already, man's desires are setting
him on the path to temptation and the Fall:

10
To us there are
eggs and there are
blackbirds. But there is the man,
too, trying without feathers
to incubate a solution.

The sequence concludes at summer's end, but here is no lush Stevensian
autumn:

13
Summer is
at an end. The migrants
depart. When they return
in spring to the garden,
will there be a man among them?

Though more overtly ominous than Stevens's poem, Thomas's is less
intellectually exploratory and perhaps less immediately disturbing.

Given Thomas's long engagement with the poetry of Wallace Stevens,
it is appropriate that in the final volume Thomas published, *No Truce
with the Furies* (1995), he included 'Homage to Wallace Stevens':

I turn now
not to the Bible
but to Wallace Stevens.
Insured against
everything but the muse
what has the word-wizard
to say? His adjectives

are the wand he waves
so language gets up
and dances under
a fastidious moon.
We walk a void world,
he implies for which
in the absence of the imagination,
there is no hope. Verbal bank-clerk,
acrobat walking a rhythmic tight-rope,
trapeze artist of the language
his was a kind of double-entry
poetics. He kept two columns
of thought going, balancing meaning
against his finances. His poetry
was his church and in it
curious marriages were conducted.
He burned his metaphors like incense,
so his syntax was as high
as his religion.
                    Blessings, Stevens;
I stand with my back to grammar
at an altar you never aspired
to, celebrating the sacrament
of the imagination whose high-priest
notwithstanding you are.

(NTF, 62)

Here, clearly, is a very different poem from the early 'Wallace Stevens'. The poem itself feels altogether more assured than the earlier one, more at ease with itself. Thomas still registers the 'void world' which exists without the imagination, but he now also registers Stevens's sensuality: 'his metaphors like incense'. He notes Stevens's fastidiousness and formality as well as his sense of imaginative play. There is also the punning on 'insured' and on 'balance', which picks up on the tightrope image; Thomas is surely referring not just to the insurance executive's word-conjuring but to the kind of tightrope of the imagination he sees Stevens as walking over the void world.

This gives us a further clue as to what in Stevens continued to draw Thomas to the American poet's work. A repeated image in Thomas's later poetry is that of the lonely individual searching in a dark world for a God who seems to have absented Himself, the lonely believer struggling to keep his faith and maintain his spiritual footing in a world which gives little or no reassurance. In 'Revision' the speaker walks

                              a rope
                        over an unfathomable
            abyss, which goes on and on
            never arriving.

                                (*EA*, 22)

while in 'Balance' 'there is a plank / to walk over seventy thousand
fathoms' (*F*, 49). The specific reference here of course is not to Stevens
but, explicitly, to Kierkegaard ('The Christian . . . has to renounce the
comfort of calm assurance bolstered upon objective proofs . . . He
constantly lies over a depth of seventy thousand fathoms'[27]), but one
should also recall those lines in the earlier poem to Stevens: 'fathomless
as the cold shadow / His mind cast'.

Having quoted Stevens's comment in a letter that 'The things that we
build or grow or do are so little when compared to the things that we
suggest or believe or desire', Helen Vendler comments that 'the true
function of poetry, for [Stevens], was a reaching to those long projections
of suggestion, belief, and desire that stretch to the grand, the sublime,
and the unnam[e]able'.[28] The comment – especially the reference to
Stevens's reaching for 'the unnam[e]able' – is also suggestive when
applied to Thomas. Thomas's search finds a local habitation in Wales,
the central myth of the later work being Abercuawg, a pure and
transfigured Wales – that 'place of trees and fields and flowers and bright
unpolluted streams, where the cuckoos continue to sing'.[29] It is not an
actual place, of course, since its value and significance reside in its being
a spiritual aspiration:

> [Man] is always on the verge of comprehending God, but insomuch as he is
> a mortal creature, he never will. Nor will he ever see Abercuawg. But
> through striving to see it, through longing for it, through refusing to accept
> some second-hand substitute, he will succeed in preserving it as an eternal
> possibility.[30]

But again, Thomas is ultimately sure of the transcendent reality which
the myth of Abercuawg signifies, that 'something unnameable',[31] the
ultimate reality; there *is* a God at whose altar Thomas stands. For
Stevens, as we have seen, the myths created by the imagination are merely
necessary, and temporary, enabling fictions: 'The final belief is to believe
in a fiction, which you know to be a fiction, there being nothing else. The
exquisite truth is to know that it is a fiction and that you believe in it
willingly' (*OP*, 163). For both writers, though, the role of the poet was

crucial, a source of imaginative vitality in the human world. In this, again for both, the poet was a heroic, though often isolated, figure. One of the works in which Stevens portrays this figure ('where / He is, the air changes and grows fresh to breathe') is 'Chocorua to Its Neighbor' (WS, 296–302) – the poem Thomas quoted in his 1990 interview when discussing the significance of literature:

> It is the communication of thought and emotion at the highest and most articulate level. It is the supreme human statement. You remember Wallace Stevens's stanza in 'Chocorua to Its Neighbor':
>
> > To say more than human things with human voice,
> > That cannot be; to say human things with more
> > Than human voice, that, also, cannot be;
> > To speak humanly from the height or from the depth
> > Of human things, that is acutest speech.
>
> We must remain articulate to the end . . . [32]

Notes

[1] 'R. S. Thomas talks to J. B. Lethbridge', *Anglo-Welsh Review*, 74 (1983), 56.

[2] 'Probings: An Interview with R. S. Thomas', *Miraculous Simplicity*, 34; the interview was originally published in *Planet*, 80 (April/May 1990). The radio programme was *With Great Pleasure*, broadcast on BBC Radio 4 in 2000. 'Peter Parasol' appears in Wallace Stevens, *Opus Posthumous*, ed. Samuel French Morse (New York: Knopf, 1957), 20; hereafter, *OP*.

[3] *Daily Telegraph*, 4 December 1999; Wordsworth, *The Prelude* (1805), II, 221. The passage from Stevens's *Adagia* appears in *OP*, 171.

[4] While it is impossible to know exactly when he first read Stevens, Thomas seems to have been reading widely in American poetry by the late 1950s and early 1960s. For instance, 'On a Line in Sandburg' was published in *Poetry for Supper* (1958) and Thomas quotes Marianne Moore in the W. D. Thomas Memorial Lecture, *Words and the Poet* (1964) – see *Selected Prose*, 58 and 60. Thomas included Stevens's 'Common Soldier' alongside poems by Robert Frost, Robinson Jeffers, John Crowe Ransom and Walt Whitman in his anthology *The Penguin Book of Religious Verse* (Harmondsworth: Penguin, 1963). Stevens's *Collected Poems* was first published in London by Faber in 1955 and his *Opus Posthumous* in 1959.

[5] *BT*, 25. The poem had originally appeared in the magazine *Listen* in 1962, where it began at line 17 of the *BT* version.

[6] Frank Kermode, *Wallace Stevens* (Edinburgh: Oliver & Boyd, 1960).

[7] See, for example, 'Country Child' (*SF*, 16), and *ERS*, 2.

[8] See Kermode, *Wallace Stevens*, 1–3, which quotes at length Stevens's account of visiting his ancestors' home and their graveyard, and also his poems 'Dutch Graves in Bucks County' and 'The Bed of Old John Zeller', in *The Collected Poems of Wallace Stevens* (New York: Knopf, 1973), 290 and 326; hereafter, *WS*.

[9] *The Poetry of Robert Frost*, ed. Edward Connery Lathem (New York: Holt Rinehart & Winston, 1969), 296.

[10] Louis Untermeyer, quoted in *Wallace Stevens: A Critical Anthology*, ed. Irvin Ehrenpreis (Harmondsworth: Penguin, 1972), 36.

[11] One contributory factor may have been the strained relations between Thomas and some of his Eglwys-fach parishioners, who had retired to the area after careers in the armed services and whose values were markedly different from those of their Welsh, pacifist vicar. See *Autobiographies*, 74–5, and *ERS*, 47 and 52–3. The poem on p. 59 of *ERS* – one of the uncompromising self-portraits which Thomas wrote at several points in his career – shows the poet recollecting his state of mind and sense of futility in this period: 'A will of iron, perforated / by indecision . . . / . . . Voyeur / of truth because of an ability / to lie sideways . . . / A man with principles so / high as to be out of sight / of his fellows, wrestling / in the small hours with the angel / over the irresponsibility / for life's evil to which / both of them laid claim'.

[12] In 'Wallace Stevens: The Ironic Eye', in Ehrenpreis, *Wallace Stevens*, 283.

[13] 'Imagination as Value' and 'The Figure of the Youth as Virile Poet', in Wallace Stevens, *The Necessary Angel: Essays on Reality and the Imagination* (London: Faber, 1960), 136, 61.

[14] Kermode, *Wallace Stevens*, 25.

[15] 'R. S. Thomas: Priest and Poet', *Poetry Wales*, 7:4 (Spring 1972), 53–4.

[16] Kermode, *Wallace Stevens*, 53.

[17] Ibid., 34.

[18] See, for example, 'Of Modern Poetry', *WS*, 239–40. Versions of the phrase recur in other poems in *Parts of a World* (1942).

[19] I am grateful to Jon Dressel for pointing out to me this possible echo when a preliminary version of this essay was delivered at the conference of the North American Association for the Study of Welsh Culure and History at Le Moyne College, Syracuse, New York, June 2002.

[20] The poem does not appear in *Selected Poems, 1946–1968* nor in *Collected Poems, 1945–1990*.

[21] John Powell Ward, *The Poetry of R. S. Thomas* (2nd edn; Bridgend: Seren, 2001), 74, and letter to present writer, 8 June 2002. I am most grateful to John Ward for his suggestions regarding the links between Thomas and Stevens.

[22] Ward, *Poetry of R. S. Thomas*, 74. In a letter to me of 8 June 2002, Ward draws attention to 'The Conductor', published in *Tares* (1961), as possibly owing something to Stevens. This seems a very shrewd suggestion: the poem certainly shares something of the tranquillity of poems like 'The Idea of Order at Key West'; it is set on the shore 'at the end of the day' and, as in the Stevens poem, the person makes (or in this case imagines) music in a natural landscape.

[23] *LP*, 174–6; the poem was originally published in *Encounter* in 1978. Stevens's 'Thirteen Ways of Looking at a Blackbird' is in *WS*, 92–5.

[24] See *LP*, 159–73.

[25] See *Letters of Wallace Stevens*, ed. Holly Stevens (New York: Knopf, 1966), 240 and 251, and Helen Vendler, *On Extended Wings: Wallace Stevens' Longer Poems* (Cambridge, Mass: Harvard University Press, 1969), 76.

[26] William V. Davis, ' "An Abstraction Blooded": Wallace Stevens and R. S. Thomas on Blackbirds and Men', *The Wallace Stevens Journal*, 8:2 (1984), 79–82.

[27] *Concluding Unscientific Postscript,* trans. David F. Swenson and Walter Lowrie (Princeton, NJ: Princeton University Press, 1941), xviii; Lowrie's summary.

[28] Helen Vendler, 'Wallace Stevens: The False and True Sublime', in Ehrenpreis, *Wallace Stevens*, 294.

[29] *Selected Prose*, 125.

[30] *Selected Prose*, 131.

[31] *The Mountains*, *Selected Prose*, 82.

[32] *Miraculous Simplicity*, 34. The mountain in Vermont to which Stevens is referring is called Chocoru; see Kermode, *Wallace Stevens*, 78.

6

Mirror Games: Self and M(O)ther in the Poetry of R. S. Thomas

KATIE GRAMICH

Narcissism starts from mirrors – from the mirroring mother . . .
We are all fascinated by mirrors . . .[1]

The Quarrel with the Self

R. S. Thomas's poems are characteristically dialectical in form. They dramatize a protracted argument that reminds us of W. B. Yeats's well-known dictum that 'we make out of the quarrel with others, rhetoric; but of our quarrel with ourselves, poetry',[2] to which Thomas refers ruefully in *The Echoes Return Slow*: 'A man who had refrained from quarrelling with his parishioners for fear of rhetoric, over what poetry could he be said to preside from his quarrel with himself?' (*ERS*, 112). In Thomas's earlier work, this quarrel is often dramatized by means of antagonistic characters such as the priest and the peasant, but gradually the dialectic becomes less externalized, so that the later work is often quite overtly a first-person self-interrogation, the only antagonist being the image staring out of the mirror.

Self and Other

Although the image of the self gazing into its reflection in a pool or glass replaces the dialectic between self and other found in the earlier poems, it succeeds in retaining that uneasy combination of strangeness and familiarity with which the relationship between priest and peasant had been presented. As the self gazes at its reflection, it appears to recognize itself, and yet the recognition is actually a misrecognition, since the image is not actually the self, but a strange, other entity. Thus, the reflection tends to convey feelings of alienation and solitude, rather than of solace and reassurance.

As Marie-Thérèse Castay has observed,[3] mirror imagery is relatively rare in Thomas's early work, although images of water representing the unconscious or collective memory are certainly present, as in 'The Ancients of the World': 'The salmon lying in the depths of Llyn Llifon, / Secretly as a thought in a dark mind' (*AL*, 13). However, it is not until *Tares* (1961) that Thomas begins to explore what will become, according to William V. Davis, 'in the second half of Thomas's career, his insistent thesis, his dominant theme.'[4] *Tares* begins with 'The Dark Well', which functions as an image of Iago Prytherch's heart, 'From which to draw, / drop after drop / The terrible poetry of his kind' (*T*, 9). The well is full of 'gulped tears', indicating both repression and suffering. 'Judgment Day' in the same collection is a more developed expression of the mirror image. Written in the first person, it takes the form of a prayer:

> Lord, breathe once more
> On that sad mirror,
> Let me be lost
> In mist for ever
> Rather than own
> Such bleak reflections.
>
> (*T*, 20)

The poem is a grim expression of self-disgust – of a desire to escape from the tyranny of selfhood and be remade in God's image. Thomas is also clearly entranced by the ambiguities contained in the word *reflection* (his punning tendencies are explored fully elsewhere in this collection). In poem after poem, he plays on the double meaning of *reflection* as introspective thought and mirroring representation of reality. We see this in 'Judgment Day', in many later poems such as 'Retirement' and 'Reflections' from *Experimenting with an Amen* (1986) and in his auto-biographical work, *The Echoes Return Slow* (1988).

In addition to mirrors, windows recur in Thomas's poetry, but it is important to differentiate between these two similar images, since they appear to represent contrasting concepts for the poet. The mirror is frequently used as an image of the inescapable ego, the self that is always in the way, whereas the window affords a possible escape from that self, a view of the Other, whether that be another place or another being.

Nevertheless, the mirror can appear teasingly like a window, posing the eternal question: is there something on the other side of the looking-glass?

It seems always that Thomas's speakers wish to penetrate beyond that surface reflection in order to see what lies on the other side of the mirror or beneath the surface of the pool. In 'Retirement' from *Experimenting with an Amen*, the phantom Other lurks behind the speaker, misting the mirror with its breath, tantalizingly close, yet always out of reach:

>   Must
> I console myself
> with reflections? There are
>
> times even the mirror
> is misted as by one breathing
> over my shoulder.
>
>   (*EA*, 38)

The image may be taken as one of Thomas's representations of the hidden god, that creator of the human in his own image. Similarly, in 'The Presence' from *Between Here and Now* (1981):

> There is nothing I can do
> but fill myself with my own
>   silence, hoping it will approach
>   like a wild creature to drink
> there, or perhaps like Narcissus
> to linger a moment over its transparent face.
>
>   (*BHN*, 107)

The Mirroring Pool

Often, as in these two poems, the mirror is the surface of a pool of water, and the poet seems mesmerized by the pool's troublingly reflective surface and its mysterious depths in equal measure. Despite Thomas's own resistance to psychological readings of human life[5] – he was drawn rather to the philosophical and, to a lesser extent, the theological – it is clear that he uses the pool/mirror image frequently to represent the depths of the human mind, particularly the unconscious. Often, Thomas seems to exploit these possibilities in quasi-Lacanian terms, regarding the hidden depths of the waters as the human unconscious, containing all kinds of repressed emotions, monsters of the deep. Sigmund Freud was himself prone to using images of pools of water to represent the hidden impulses of the mind; for example, he speaks of 'that great reservoir from which the libido that is destined for objects flows out and into which it flows back from those objects.'[6] Similarly, R. S. Thomas draws time and time again on the image of the unconscious as a reservoir from whose depths memories and poems can be – perhaps must be – dredged up:

> The creative mind usually has a poor memory. It will forget the things that are on the surface of life, but unbeknown to the poet other things sink into his subconscious to form there a matrix or pool from which he can draw at some time in the future. It is in this way that so many successful poems come into being.[7]

Gendered Reflections

The idea of the contemplative poet at the water's edge brings to mind Yeats's 'The Fisherman',[8] but not all of Thomas's mirror poems are couched in these serene terms. Some, like 'Looking Glass', have about them a grim, Borgesian playfulness:

> There is a game I play
> with a mirror, approaching
> it when I am not there,
> as though to take by surprise
>
> the self that is my familiar. It
> is in vain. Like one eternally
> in ambush, fast or slow
> as I may raise my head, it raises
>
> its own, catching me in the act,
> disarming me by acquaintance,
> looking full into my face as often
> as I try looking at it askance.
>
> (*EA*, 40)

The speaker plays a game with the mirror, and yet the effect is far from light-hearted, since it is a game he knows he can never win. There is a strong sense of self-alienation here. Thomas also delights in semantic play, with 'familiar' in the second stanza suggesting membership of a family, a family resemblance, the familiarity of custom, the contempt bred by familiarity and also, of course, the sinister creature accompanying a witch or warlock. There is an overtone of the diabolical Other here: the self in the mirror is not the protagonist but an antagonist whom the speaker must constantly attempt to outwit. The poem is about the individual's inability to avoid the constant terror and challenge of existence. The other self constantly apes the subject, imitating and mocking his every movement in an act of self-parody. The image of a life spent 'in ambush' suggests an eternity of futile waiting and perhaps a forlorn hope for a life of authenticity far removed from this continual game.

In considering the various and complex meanings of Thomas's mirror poems, it is illuminating briefly to take a comparative perspective. As already mentioned, images of the mirror begin to appear regularly in Thomas's work in the early 1960s, the period when Sylvia Plath's best-known, posthumous volume, *Ariel*, first appeared. It seems to me that both poets are similarly obsessed with the mirror as an image of the reflective mind and of the human capacity for self-questioning and despair. If we look for example at Plath's poem 'Mirror' and Thomas's 'Looking Glass' side by side, interesting similarities and intriguing, perhaps gender-determined, differences appear. Here is Plath's 'Mirror':

> I am silver and exact. I have no preconceptions.
> Whatever I see I swallow immediately
> Just as it is, unmisted by love or dislike.
> I am not cruel, only truthful –
> The eye of a little god, four-cornered.
> Most of the time I meditate on the opposite wall.
> It is pink, with speckles. I have looked at it so long
> I think it is a part of my heart. But it flickers.
> Faces and darkness separate us over and over.
>
> Now I am a lake. A woman bends over me,
> Searching my reaches for what she really is.
> Then she turns to those liars, the candles or the moon.
> I see her back, and reflect it faithfully.
> She rewards me with tears and an agitation of hands.
> I am important to her. She comes and goes.
> Each morning it is her face that replaces the darkness.
> In me she has drowned a young girl, and in me an old woman
> Rises toward her day after day, like a terrible fish.[9]

On the face of it, Plath's poem is more chilling than Thomas's deceptively playful 'Looking Glass' since it is spoken from the apparently objective point of view of the mirror itself. As Thomas observes in the poem 'Reflections', 'A mirror's temperature / is always at zero' (*NTF*, 31). Plath's mirror becomes disturbingly *humanized*: it possesses a 'heart' and 'the eye of a little god'. The woman who bends over the mirror's pool-like surface is observed solely from the point of view of the unmoved 'little god': her human distress is seen in a reflection, at one remove. The perspective is unnerving; it is as if we are looking, powerless, through glass at another's intense anguish. The poem offers an interesting reversal of what we find in Thomas: although there is a constant suspicion that a mirror god exists, we never hear the god's voice speak.

Plath's poem also contrasts with Thomas's in that it is, specifically, a woman who gazes into the mirror. In this regard, Plath is following in a tradition of women's writing where the trope of the mirror is commonly used to signify the woman's search for identity. She seeks confirmation of her youth and beauty, which amounts to a legitimization of her right to exist in a man's world, where her decorative appearance is held to be of primary importance. This is why old age – 'the terrible fish' which is about to swallow her – is so threatening. This dimension appears absent from Thomas's poem: unlike Yeats, Thomas does not rail at physical decrepitude; his male speaker's obsession appears wholly metaphysical. Indeed, in many of Thomas's love poems, there is a tender regard for the signs of age in the *woman's* face: 'The wrinkles will come upon her / calm though her brow be / under time's blowing' ('Remembering'; *NTF*, 78). Yet in Plath's poem, the woman is not a passive victim of time; she comes to the mirror with a petrifying earnestness, a murderous intent. She has actively 'drowned a young girl' (her younger self) in its depths already; what more terrible deed will now result from the 'tears and agitation of hands'? If Thomas's multivalent 'familiar' suggested, among other things, being part of a rather sinister family, Plath's image of an older woman drowning a young girl contains a distinctly discomfiting hint of murderous maternity. I suggest, then, that both poets, despite gender differences, use mirror images not only to interrogate notions of personal identity but to explore repressed familial tensions, particularly between mother and child.

But to return for the present to the metaphysical dimension of Thomas's poems: in a number of places, he speaks of the 'turning aside' from quotidian concerns in order to catch a glimpse of another kingdom, as for instance in 'Aside':

> Progress
> is not with the machine;
> it is a turning aside,
> a bending over a still pool,
> where the bubbles arise
> from unseen depths, as from truth
> breathing, showing us by their roundness
> the roundness of our world.
>
> (*MHT*, 34)

In this context, the 'looking askance' in 'Looking Glass' may be seen as the frustrated quest for a divine Other. The suggestion is that a glimpse of the Other can be gained only when the reflection of the self is not obscuring the view. And yet the harrying reflection is always there, and is inescapable. 'Looking Glass' acknowledges both the lack of fulfilment inherent in the quest and the necessity of continuing with the game. The poem is couched in the present tense, and the game goes on.

Ambivalent Narcissus

Not surprisingly, given the recurrence of the image of gazing into mirrored pools and Thomas's own early education in the Classics, the poems often allude to the myth of Narcissus, as we have already observed in 'The Presence'. Ovid in the *Metamorphoses* recounts how the beautiful youth Narcissus cruelly rejects the many suitors, male and female, who fall in love with him. One nymph, Echo, pines away from unrequited love until she is reduced to nothing but an echoing voice. As a punishment, the gods cause Narcissus to fall in love with his own reflection glimpsed in a pool of water, and he, too, pines away – from unrequited *self*-love in his case – until he is transformed by the gods into a narcissus flower, growing on the margins of the pool. The gods' punishment of this hard-hearted male was apt: Narcissus falls in love with the only person who is unable physically to reciprocate his love: himself, viewed as a reflection. It is a myth which has fascinated artists throughout the ages – one which can be interpreted as a moral tale about the folly of self-love or the deceptive nature of surface and appearance. Nor is Thomas the only contemporary poet who has been drawn to the myth; as Jeremy Holmes reminds us: 'Seamus Heaney's poem "Personal Helicon" . . . describes his fascination with wells as a child, into which, "big-eyed Narcissus", he would stare endlessly. He compares this with his adult activity as a poet in which: "I rhyme / To see myself, to set the darkness echoing".[10] Clearly, both Heaney and Thomas are attracted to Narcissus as a positive image of poetic contemplation, but their engagement with the figure also suggests a measure of self-criticism in that the image implies self-absorption.

Elaine Shepherd sees Thomas in 'The Presence' taking the 'negatively charged image' of Narcissus and 'daringly chang[ing] it into a positive one' in the context of his search for the absent god. Shepherd remarks that 'It is a Miltonic device which effectively demonstrates the superiority of the Christian view over the classical.'[11] However, poems such as 'Aside' and 'Wrong?' demonstrate that the introspective, contemplative stance of Narcissus is in fact attractive to the poet because it is, essentially, the attitude of the artist and the philosopher. The rapt gaze of Narcissus becomes a way of figuring a retreat from the world of humans and the machine, a turning aside to embrace an idealistic quest for spiritual truth and beauty. In 'Wrong?', for example, 'we' are figured as having taken a wrong turning, missing the way to what should have been our destination:

> you are at our shoulder, whispering
> of the still pool we could sit down
> by; of the tree of quietness
> that is at hand; cautioning us
> to prepare not for the breathless journeys
> into confusion, but for the stepping
> aside through the invisible
> veil that is about us into a state
> not place of innocence and delight.
>
> (*NTF,* 26)

The mirror is also connected with art and the processes of artistic creation, as suggested in Heaney's 'Personal Helicon' and in Thomas's own 'Return':

> Art
> is not life. It is not the river
>
> carrying us away, but the motionless
> image of itself on a fast-
> running surface with which life
> tries constantly to keep up.
>
> (*BHN,* 109)

And yet the speaker can also upbraid himself for his attraction to narcissism and to the dangerous misrecognition of the self that narcissism involves. In 'Hark', for instance, he baldly states:

> You were wrong, Narcissus.
> The replica of the self
> is to be avoided. Echo
> was right, warning you against
>
> the malevolence of mirrors.
> Yet the scientist still bends
> over his cloning, call as she may,
> irrefutable beside the gene-pool.
>
> (*MHT*, 38)

Unusually here, it is the scientist and not the poet who bends over the pool, searching for answers. The image is negative, since the scientist is trying literally to replicate himself by cloning, usurping God's role as creator of man in his own image. The poem becomes a critique of the scientist's egotism and of applied science's dereliction of its social and ethical responsibilities. *Laboratories of the Spirit* (1975) contains numerous mirror images, focused mainly on the hard, probing gaze of the scientist into his lenses. In 'The Gap', for example, the human mind stares into 'the emptiness of the interiors / of the mirror that life holds up / to itself' (*LS*, 37) while 'Probing' concludes with the reflection that 'we never awaken / from the compulsiveness of the mind's / stare into the lenses' furious interiors' (*LS*, 24). In 'Gone', the needy gaze finds that 'the mirror [is] empty' (*LS*, 55).

But it is not only the scientist who is criticized for this kind of narcissism. 'Present' is a reminder of social responsibilities, including those of the poet and the priest. Despite the individual's yearning to stand aside, to abstain from involvement, and his desire to 'be the mirror / of a mirror, effortlessly repeating / [his] reflections' (*F*, 9), the cries of those who wish to communicate with him cannot be ignored. Their fear and need connect him with others. In this clamorous world, his conscience places him

> at the switchboard
> of the exchanges of the people
> of all time, receiving their messages
> whether I will or no.
>
> (*F*, 9)

Such a poem indicates the reluctance of the narcissistically-inclined priest ('I engage with philosophy / in the morning, with the garden / in the afternoon . . . / . . . It is enough, / this') to answer the shrill and urgent demands of his flock and of the wider world. Yet Marie-Thérèse Castay's analysis of Thomas's mirror imagery suggests that these poems present a parable of the Christian way: 'in the same way as Christ was prepared to go to "the back of love's looking glass", that is to die for the love of mankind, so too must man attempt to do the same: not to shatter the looking glass (that would mean suicide), but to go behind it, that is to sacrifice himself, to die to himself for the love of God'.[12]

In 'Pardon', the first-person speaker is a poet and praise-giver. But can he bring himself to praise Man?

> And homo sapiens, that cracked mirror,
> mending himself again and again like a pool?
>
> Who threw the stone? I forgave him his surface
> in the name of the unseen troubler of his depths.
>
> (*EA*, 29)

The image of Man as a 'cracked mirror' suggests that it is only in this imperfect, distorted surface that one may glimpse an image of God. The constant 'mending' suggests hope, but the ripples in the pool caused by the stone produce an image that is difficult to decipher, impossible to fix. As ever, Thomas's punning resonances radiate from individual words such as 'cracked', containing ripples of secondary meanings, including madness and ill-omen.

The Narcissistic Wound

Thomas is also writing with an inevitable awareness of the way in which the Narcissus myth was taken up by Freud and used as a fable to explain pathological conditions of self-obsession and self-love. Freud identified 'primary narcissism' as a normal stage in infant development, differentiating it from 'secondary narcissism', a pathological state afflicting adults who are unable to form attachments or loving relationships with others and who therefore remain obsessed with themselves: 'The solution to [secondary] narcissism is to love another.'[13] In a number of poems and autobiographical pieces, Thomas expresses his regret at not being able fully to express love towards another. In the poem entitled 'A Life' in

Experimenting with an Amen, for example, the speaker, reviewing his life, brands himself 'Bottom . . . / of his class' in 'love's school.' He goes on to describe himself as both 'the unwanted / third' and 'a Narcissus tortured / by the whisperers behind / the mirror' (*EA*, 52). Again, the suggestion is that this particular Narcissus is obsessed not so much with the beauty of his own image as with what is going on behind that image. One can imagine Narcissus bending down over the water, closer and closer to its surface, attending to the mysterious susurrations under the water. The poem offers a tantalizingly contradictory image: that of a self-obsessed speaker obsessed with trying to escape from the self. It may not be too far-fetched to argue that the tormented solipsism of Narcissus may have seemed to the poet-priest an apt emblem of his own soul.

Later psychoanalytical theorists have variously contested and elaborated upon Freud's theories of narcissism. One of the most interesting developments here is the theory of 'negative narcissism', propounded by Karl Abraham in the 1920s. In negative narcissism, 'paradoxically, sufferers are not so much irredeemably pleased with themselves but, rather, are in a constant state of anxious self-dissatisfaction'.[14] This certainly seems to be the case with Thomas's often anguished and self-lacerating personae. Psychoanalysts who subscribe to this theory believe that negative narcissism has its origins in 'a harsh superego, internalised from parental strictures . . . Narcissistic rage . . . seems to provide a measure of security for the narcissist who is fundamentally . . . lonely and deprived of a secure base . . . Beneath the narcissistic rage lies . . . "the narcissistic wound".'[15]

I am not suggesting that Thomas's exploration of the Narcissus myth should simply be read in a quasi-diagnostic manner, as evidence of some supposed negative narcissism on the part of the poet. Nevertheless, the elements identified in psychoanalytic theory – namely, the inability to love another, the anxious self-dissatisfaction, the internalization of and revolt against parental strictures, and the frequent expression of rage – all point suggestively to the presence of a narcissistic wound from which the poems may spring. Since narcissism is from the outset, according to Freud and others, connected with the infant's relationship to his mother, I think it is possible to read Thomas's Narcissus poems as painful reflections on the frequently problematic bond between mother and son. I believe the poems contain both a specific biographical resonance and a more general psychological truth.

Jacques Lacan has identified a 'mirror phase' in a child's development – the stage at which the infant, before learning to speak, identifies with the image of itself reflected in the mirror. The child has to negotiate the recognition of its own separate identity, primarily its separation from the mother's body. 'According to Lacan, this phase forms the basis on which the ego develops, and it is called the mirror phase because it is evidenced by the infant's jubilant response to its own mirror reflection, with which it is believed to identify.'[16] Lacan would claim that the mirror phase is the first stage in the human being's gaining an illusory sense of control, since the child observes that it is able to control the reflected image and initially perceives no split between the self who watches and the self who is watched. This is what Lacan calls the 'imaginary' phase. Only later, when the child begins to gain mastery of language, does this stage give way to what Lacan terms the 'symbolic order', which is ruled not by the mother but by the Law of the Father.

Focusing on the so-called phallogocentricity of the patriarchal world in which we live, feminist appropriations of Lacanian theory by theorists such as Julia Kristeva juxtapose the restrictive symbolic order with the more free-flowing semiotic stage preceding the advent of language.[17] However, a feminist approach to Thomas's work reveals that the usual Lacanian or Kristevan contrast between a free semiotic stage associated with the maternal body and a restrictive symbolic stage associated with the paternal is precisely reversed. We find that in Thomas's poetry the paternal – often associated with fluid sea-imagery – is almost always positive, while maternal imagery, connected with restriction and limitation, is negative. In the poem entitled 'It Hurts Him to Think', for example, from *What is a Welshman?* (1974), we are presented with an unsettling image of the infant's primary relationship with the mother being poisoned:

> The
> industrialists came, burrowing
>   in the corpse of a nation
> for its congealed blood. I was
>   born into the squalor of
> their feeding and sucked their speech
>   in with my mother's
> infected milk, so that whatever
>   I throw up now is still theirs.
>   (WW, 12)

Milk is identified with language, so that the categories of semiotic (pre-Oedipal) and symbolic (post-Oedipal) are confused. Language is not associated with the Law of the Father but is a kind of disease ingested from the mother in the fluid, semiotic stage of life. Neither Lacan nor

Kristeva have anything to say on the specific language which the infant acquires, but it is clear that Thomas is referring here to the English language, associated with the 'industrialists' who came to transform Wales and taint his mother's milk with their alien tongue. The representation of orality in this poem is alarming: a mother suckles her baby and imparts not nourishment but infection. The feeding imagery is also explicitly connected with death (necrophiliac industrialists feeding off a corpse), figuring the death of the Welsh language and the Welsh nation in grotesquely physical terms. Given also the iconic nature of the image of the Madonna and child in Christian symbolism, in which the Virgin Mary is frequently depicted giving suck to the Christ child, the poem presents a startlingly unorthodox vision of the mother–child relationship.

Self and Mother

Thomas's references to his mother in his writings have been less than kind. He seems to blame his mother for his own Anglicized upbringing, suggesting that her social aspirations led to her mollycoddling her only child and encouraging him to aspire towards respectable middle-class goals. Poems in *Welsh Airs* (1987) such as 'Alma Mater' and the savage 'Welsh' –

> I was born late;
> She claimed me,
> Brought me up nice,
> No hardship;
> Only the one loss,
> I can't speak my own
> Language – Iesu,
> All those good words;
> And I outside them . . .
>
> (WA, 19)

– articulate Thomas's deep-rooted resentment. Similarly, in an interview published in 1990, Thomas stated: 'Because my father was often at sea and because my mother was of a domineering nature I was ruled mainly by her. And being an only child I was the centre of her attention for good or ill'.[18] In 'The Boy's Tale', an indication of the relationship between mother and father is given in the line 'Her tongue ruled his tides' (BT,

36). In 'Mother and Son', the speaker is the oppressed son who bemoans the restrictive respectability imposed on him by his mother. He expresses an impassioned desire to escape the confines of her world:

> let me go
> Beyond the front garden without you
> To find glasses unstained by tears,
> To find mirrors that do not reproach
> My smooth face . . .
>
> (*T*, 37)

Nearly thirty years later in the 1990 interview, Thomas expressed a similar sentiment when he confessed, 'My background was culturally *borné*.'[19]

There are indications, however, that these feelings may have been problematized by guilt and the need for forgiveness. At the end of the autobiographical volume *The Echoes Return Slow*, the speaker suggests that his own inability to love may be redeemed by the fact that he has *been* loved by two women, presumably his wife and his mother: 'nothing to hope for but that for the love of both of them he would be forgiven' (*ERS*, 120). Thomas clearly tends to romanticize his sailor father, presenting him as a passionate, frustrated, aspiring figure, while his references to his mother are either unflattering or suppressed; these relationships have recently been explored in two illuminating articles by Tony Brown.[20] The furies, however, lurk in all his mirrors, reminding him of his guilt and, significantly, of the mother who ultimately cannot be repressed.

Returning again to Thomas's poem 'Looking Glass', it is tempting to see the ludic attitude of the speaker as being almost child-like, reflective of the kind of peep-bo games that children find eternally fascinating. And yet the attitude of the speaker towards the reflected image is hardly childlike: instead of the satisfaction and the illusion of control that the child, according to the Lacanian model, gains in the 'imaginary phase', this mirror-gazer is constantly unsettled and disturbed, even outwitted, by his image. The speaker here is a nostalgic adult, fully incorporated into the inescapable tyranny of the symbolic order, seeking in vain for that illusory sense of wholeness experienced in infancy. One might go further and suggest that there is here a futile desire to return to the mother, to go beyond even the 'mirror stage', and plunge back into the primal wholeness. Equally, if one accepts the idea of a frustrated search for the lost mother, one might interpret the image of the 'one breathing'

over the speaker's shoulder in the poem 'Retirement' not as the hidden
god, but as the absent female creator or life-giver.

The Furies' Address

In the poetry of his final years, Thomas identifies the mirror as the hiding
place of the furies. Again, as with the myth of Narcissus, he is drawing
on his early education in the Classics in order to flesh out his own
personal demons. Commentators have already drawn attention to the
possible significance of the furies lurking in Thomas's looking-glass: they
may be identified as a set of personal torments and nagging preoccupa-
tions that have pursued him throughout a career of iconoclastic
questioning and self-scrutiny. Probing the origins of the classical allusion
reveals even more layers of meaning in Thomas's image. The Furies were
female deities renowned particularly for hounding to death those who
had committed matricide, as in the case of Orestes, who murdered his
mother, Clytaemestra. In Aeschylus' *Oresteia* we witness how these
ancient female deities are finally placated and tamed. Some commentators have interpreted the plays as representations of the shift from a
matriarchal social structure based on worship of ancient, female earth-
goddesses to a patriarchal structure based around the sun-god Apollo
and associated with ratiocination and the law. Why, then, should the first-
person speaker of Thomas's poems feel himself to be, Orestes-like,
pursued by the furies? If we interpret the poems from a psychological
perspective, it is possible to see the speaker of these late poems as
someone who regards himself as a disloyal son, a haunted figure who has,
symbolically, been guilty of his mother's murder.

In the last poem I wish to refer to – 'Patterns' – Thomas again suggestively draws on classical mythology in his reference to the Greek hero
Perseus, the slayer of the Gorgon Medusa. Medusa had the capacity to
turn anyone to stone with her terrible gaze; Perseus managed to outwit
her by looking only at her reflection in his polished shield and was thus
able to cut off her snaky head. It is interesting that in Thomas's use of the
myth, the monstrous Other beheld in the hero's shield is described simply
as an 'anonymous face', leaving the poem open to several interpretations:

> the hero stands
> sword drawn at the looking-glass
> of his mind, aiming at that
> anonymous face over his shoulder.
> (*BHN*, 106)

The Medusa might be a repressed or hidden aspect of the hero himself. Equally, the anonymous face might be seen as that of the hidden God, feared yet hunted down. Finally, the decapitated Medusa, whose laugh has become the emblem of the repressed female voice in modern feminist theory,[21] might be seen as the lost mother, always present, gazing with the implacable stare of the (over-)concerned parent, inescapable, terrible, yet always lacked. The poem ends with a tableau of arrested movement, the hero standing poised with his sword drawn. Time stands still. Has Perseus been turned to stone by the Medusa's gaze after all?

Both Narcissus and the Furies experience a metamorphosis in the classical myths, while Perseus experiences an apotheosis into the figure of epic hero. Narcissus is transformed into a flower, reunited with nature and presumably released finally from his self-torment. Similarly, the Furies are transformed into the Eumenides, the 'Kindly Ones', who are complacent, beneficent figures, no longer agents of vengeance and pursuit. In contrast to the classical hero, however, Thomas's Perseus-figure experiences no apotheosis but rather a continuing quest, known from the outset to be futile. Thomas consistently stops short of effecting closure – be it metamorphosis or apotheosis – which would provide an ending for his borrowed myths. His Narcissus remains endlessly tormented, and there is to be no truce with *his* furies.

Notes

[1] Jeremy Holmes, 'Narcissism', *On a Darkling Plain: Journeys into the Unconscious*, ed. Ivan Ward (Cambridge: Icon, 2002), 173.

[2] W. B. Yeats, 'Per Amica Silentia Lunae' (1917), *Mythologies* (London: Macmillan, 1959), 331.

[3] See Marie-Thérèse Castay, 'The Self and the Other: The Autobiographical Element in the Poetry of R. S. Thomas', *Page's Drift*, 144–7.

[4] William V. Davis, 'The Presence of Absence: Mirrors and Mirror Imagery in the Poetry of R. S. Thomas', *Analecta Husserliana*, 73 (2001), 349.

[5] Marie-Thérèse Castay notes that *Neb* resorts very little to psychological terminology or analysis; her explanation for this is that 'the subconscious workings of the psyche tend to magnify man out of all proportion, while, on the contrary, R. S. Thomas's aim is precisely to show how unimportant and puny he is'; *Page's Drift*, 126.

[6] Sigmund Freud, *The Ego and the Id*, trans. Joan Rivière, ed. James Strachey (London: The Hogarth Press, 1962), 53.

[7] *Autobiographies*, 71.

[8] See W. B. Yeats, 'The Fisherman', *Collected Poems* (London: Macmillan, 1979), 166–7.

[9] Sylvia Plath, 'Mirror', *Collected Poems* (London: Faber and Faber, 1981), 173–4.

[10] Holmes, 'Narcissism', 186. For Heaney's poem 'Personal Helicon', see *Opened Ground: Poems 1966–1996* (London: Faber and Faber, 1998), 15.

[11] Elaine Shepherd, *R. S. Thomas: Conceding an Absence – Images of God Explored* (Basingstoke: Macmillan, 1996), 143.

[12] *Page's Drift*, 146.

[13] Holmes, 'Narcissism', 183.

[14] Ibid., 178.

[15] Ibid., 179.

[16] Andrew M. Colman, *The Oxford Dictionary of Psychology* (Oxford: Oxford University Press, 2001), 453.

[17] A useful summary of Kristeva's appropriation of Lacan is provided in Sara Mills, Lynne Pearce, Sue Spaull and Elaine Millard, *Feminist Readings/Feminists Reading* (Hemel Hempstead: Harvester Wheatsheaf, 1989), 154–62, and in Toril Moi, *Sexual/Textual Politics: Feminist Literary Theory* (London: Routledge, 1989), 150–73.

[18] 'Probings: An Interview with R. S. Thomas', *Miraculous Simplicity*, 22; the interview was originally published in *Planet*, 80 (April/May 1990).

[19] *Miraculous Simplicity*, 23.

[20] Tony Brown, ' "Over Seventy Thousand Fathoms": The Sea and Self-Definition in the Poetry of R. S. Thomas', *Page's Drift*, 148–71, and ' "Eve's Ruse": Identity and Gender in the Poetry of R. S. Thomas', *English*, 49:195 (Autumn 2000), 229–50.

[21] See Hélène Cixous, 'The Laugh of the Medusa' in *New French Feminisms*, ed. Elaine Marks and Isabelle de Courtivron (Hemel Hempstead: Harvester Wheatsheaf, 1981), 245–64.

7

'Double-entry Poetics': R. S. Thomas – Punster

DAMIAN WALFORD DAVIES

'[T]he word like a sword / turning both ways / to keep the gate of vocabulary' (*MHT*, 25): so many of R. S. Thomas's words cut both ways that even a cursory reading of his work reveals him to be an inveterate and mordant punster who 'fed / full on the ambivalences' (*MHT*, 67). Philip Larkin nastily referred to him as 'Arse Thomas' (after he had won the Heinemann Award) and as 'Arsewipe Thomas'[1] (after their first meeting) – a good example of what Derrida has identified as the 'monumental, derisory transformation of one's name, a rebus, into a thing or name of a thing'.[2] Despite the irreverence of Larkin's pun, the Reverend Thomas would have been fundamentally (as it were) tickled by such verbal larkin',[3] recognising that he had himself a habit of equivocation (a tic, a mannerism) that amounts to an exploratory tool, indeed a whole cognitive method.

Thomas's punning can be seen as an inscription of the dualities and tensions at the heart of his cultural, linguistic and religious experience. Puns – those Janus words – and the phenomenon of 'hearing double', of having simultaneous 'second thoughts',[4] are part of his wider obsession with echoes, reflections, mirror images, narcissistic doubles and the Janus-faced god. William V. Davis remarks that 'R. S. Thomas has grown accustomed, and has accustomed his readers, to seeing things in terms of mirrors and mirror images'.[5] Puns are similarly employed by Thomas as a way of interrogating the world, of balancing the competing claims of the physical and spiritual, faith and doubt, absence and presence, sincerity and irony, the private and the public (brilliantly caught in the pun 'navel engagement' (*MHT*, 82)), even first and second wives, and of throwing into relief 'discordant ideological positions or values'.[6] What Thomas said of Wallace Stevens is true also of his own method: 'his was a kind of double-entry / poetics. He kept two columns / of thought going' (*NTF*, 62). His constant deployment of the connotative vigour of the pun is part of his protracted deconstructive tussle with unitary meaning, single truths, easy pieties and cultural shibboleths. Molly Mahood says of Shakespeare that 'his imagination works through puns' and that 'puns help to clarify the particular view of life that he seeks to present in a particular play',[7] and the same is true of the particular play of Thomas's puns. Though Thomas's wit is far from 'mirthless laughter / at the beloved irony / at his side' (*C*, 36), the pun is for him a means of *serio ludere*, of focusing an intellectual or spiritual crux (pun intended – Thomas always has a *crux* to *bare*) and of dramatizing his own fraught identity. *Neb*, his most famous pun on the self, constructs him simultaneously as 'no one' and 'someone'.

'Parsimonious', 'spare', 'austerely chiselled', 'astringent', 'notoriously attenuated', 'laconic', 'Calvinistic' (an interesting one, that): such phrases have been endlessly recycled by critics to characterize Thomas's verse, especially the later work. His punning is both an aspect of this 'spareness' – a pun is language on an economy drive – and, given the polyvocality and 'antiphonal music // in infinite counterpoint' (*MHT*, 82) of the pun, its very opposite; a pun is both frugal and fugued, laconic and Lacanian. 'What I've tried to do, in my own sort of simple way as I've got older', Thomas said in 1983, 'is to try to operate on more than one level, to try to bring ambivalence and so on into the phrases'.[8] In the same interview, he lamented the way in which the tonal nuances he so relished in the work of Geoffrey Hill (whom he refers to as an 'ironic' poet) were lost when the univocality of speech displaced the suggestiveness of the written word as Hill read the poems aloud.[9] With the exception of a few brief discussions, attention to the workings and significance of Thomas's punning method has been surprisingly desultory, though critics have stressed that the pared-down quality of the poetry belies a ludic, mischievous energy whose apotheosis is the verbal inventiveness of late tours de force such as 'Words' (*NTF*, 85), 'Play' (*NTF*, 86), 'Anybody's Alphabet' (*NTF*, 88) and 'Aye! There's the rub' (*R*, 29): 'To seem at once lean and sensuous, transparent and deeply crimsoned, is part of his distinction'[10] (Calvin Bedient); 'R. S. Thomas is full of tricksiness, and a good deal of his poetry occupies a *Through the Looking-Glass* world'[11] (Tony Conran); 'like Borges, Thomas is an (unrecognised) humorist . . . for this poet the price of serious pursuit of a chronically deviant and devious deity is eternal levity'[12] (M. Wynn Thomas). Vimala Herman and Peter Abbs see Thomas constantly employing 'contraries', 'troubling ambivalence of statement', 'instabilities of tone', paradox and dialectic –

all of which 'enter into the organization of meaning . . . by exceeding, transforming, defeating, contradicting, any "primary" or "literal" level of meaning' which then appears only 'in relational terms'.[13]

Moreover, Elaine Shepherd and M. Wynn Thomas have offered valuable discussions of Thomas's 'preferred mode of irony' which, like the poet's punning strategies (to which it is of course closely related), constitutes a whole epistemological and spiritual methodology – 'ironic ratiocination',[14] as Patrick Crotty terms it. Shepherd refers to the poems' 'Simultaneous sounding of two or more melodies', their 'contrapuntal schema' (a good description of a pun); witness Thomas's parenthetical sabotaging of his 'Credo': 'I believe in God / the Father (Is he married?)' (MHT, 12).[15] M. Wynn Thomas characterizes Thomas's simplicity as 'the innocent face of profoundly duplicitous ironies', and his important article on the 'radical doubleness' of Thomas's discourse and the operations in the poetry of a Kierkegaardian/Socratic 'maieutic irony' (which serves to vouchsafe precious 'revelations' of meaning, bringing the reader to a 'revaluation' and a 'full consciousness' of the poem) is one of the few discussions that locate Thomas's puns as part of a wider intellectual programme rather than as mere local frissons.[16]

The terms of the critical discourse sampled above implicitly locate Thomas's poetry within the context of a post-structuralist concern to pluralize and destabilize meaning and the certainties of faith, and that is precisely where this essay locates Thomas's use of puns. As Dirk Delabastita reminds us, a deconstructive view of language as an endless chain of signification and web of fluid intertextual relationships sees the pun as characteristic of all language – 'the rule rather than the exception'.[17] Ben Astley's recent deconstructionist critique of Thomas's religious poetry from H'm to Between Here and Now is alive to a number of destabilizing, relativizing puns. Astley relates the radical indeterminacy of the poetry and its 'loosening of restrictive presence' to Thomas's interest in quantum physics, arguing that his 'ambiguous or unstable diction' and his delight in thwarting 'grammatical expectations' have the effect of wresting meaning 'away from any grounding centre'.[18] Comparing what he regards as the 'essentialist rhetoric' of Thomas's identity politics with Oliver Reynolds's punning 'distrust of essentialism', Chris Wigginton in the same journal is, by contrast, strangely reticent regarding the subversive effects of Thomas's puns and his suspicion of 'totalizing notions of words and meanings' and of complacent myths of national identity. Witness, as an obvious example, the way in which 'A Welsh Testament' – 'All right, I was Welsh. Does it matter?' – ironically inflects an earlier 'essentialist' poem like 'Welsh History' – 'We were a people . . .'. Trumpeting Reynolds's puns, Wigginton fails to acknowledge what Reynolds's technique, and indeed some of the *specific* examples cited, owe directly to Thomas.[19]

The Cultural Politics and Ontology of the Pun

In *Wales: A Problem of Translation*, Thomas views the pun as a specific site of resistance to the colonizer: the untranslatability of a pun in Welsh marks the untranslatability of Wales itself as a cultural entity. The insistence that 'all words and phrases, proverbs and idioms' be 'patient of translation into the speech of the conqueror'[20] (an interesting pun there on 'patient' – 'capable of', but also, significantly, 'enduring' or 'suffering') results, Thomas remarks, only in distortion. (Rather disingenuously, however, Thomas has experimented deftly in the poetry with the translatability of Welsh idioms and with interlingual puns.[21]) Had he been able to write poetry in Welsh that satisfied him – and it pained him that he could not – it is tempting to suppose that the pun would have appealed to him as a 'site / Inviolate' (*NBF*, 45) which the translator-colonizer could not traduce (which means 'translate', too, of course, with *traductio* in Rhetoric being a term for a pun). As the speaker of the poem 'Welcome' emphasizes, 'You can come a long way; / . . . But you won't be inside' (*BT*, 24).

As it is, we have a body of work written in a language Thomas often lamented having to use. Can one, then, account for Thomas's obsessive deployment of puns, which increase in number in the later poetry – as, significantly, do those poems which take language and vocabulary as theme? What needs did the pun satisfy, and what tensions did it enact and perhaps assuage? Thomas's statements about his divided cultural identity offer an interesting context in which to locate his fascination with puns – a context which reflects back in illuminating ways on the ontology of the pun itself.

'[T]he pun, with its inherent shiftiness, is probably the best way to symbolize a state of mind torn by contradictions, yet desiring unity', remarks Conor Cruise O'Brien.[22] Might not a pun be seen as an inscription of an 'Anglo-Welsh' cultural predicament, a divided allegiance? 'I am not the first to have noticed a large element of schizophrenia in the Welsh psyche', Thomas remarks; 'Gerallt Gymro . . . was already aware of fissiparous tendencies among us'; 'Hyphenisation is betrayal':[23] a pun is on one level (but then puns are always multi-stor(e)y) a schizophrenic word in which allegiances are divided and different meanings jostle for the same phonemic space – a site of contention and cultural angst where two or more signifieds seek to possess one signifier. For Thomas, 'An Anglo-Welsh writer is neither one thing nor the other':

> He subsists in a no-man's-land between two cultures . . . Who is wounded, and am I not wounded? For I bear in my body the marks of this battle. Who in fact is this wretched Anglo-Welshman, except one who knows that he is Welsh, or wishes to think of himself as such, but who is continually conscious that he speaks a foreign language?[24]

The doubleness and 'fissiparousness' of the pun may hold a mirror up to Thomas's fractured, hyphenated cultural self and psyche – for him a state of painful division, as the discourse of physical wounding employed here (characteristic of other writers' and critics' explorations of Anglo-Welsh identity[25]) makes plain. It is a double identity to which double-speak is appropriate; the pun is precisely 'the rhetoric of the split // mind' (*Fr*, 13). Jonathan Swift has a piece entitled 'God's Revenge on Punning'. The pun might be Thomas's revenge on English – a way of ambushing the colonizer by means of his own troublingly 'pliable' and 'flexible'[26] (Thomas's terms) language. As befits a colonizer's language – which English emphatically is for Thomas[27] – it speaks in the poems in a forked tongue. But, as also befits a pun, there are two conflicting ontologies of the figure. A view of the pun as representing duplicitous division, schizophrenic duality and cultural bifurcation should be supplemented by a more positive interpretation. A pun is also a site of syzygy and plenitude; it is a yoking, bridging, catholic device that establishes relationships between unrelated concepts. Certainly, Thomas can find the very arbitrariness of language that makes puns possible intellectually troubling, and he confronts the paradoxes involved in a disarmingly direct way as he 'meditat[es] upon gold' in *Experimenting with an Amen*: 'Explain to me / why we use the same word // for the place that we store our money in, / and that other place where the gorse blows' (*EA*, 21; the 'word' in question, by the way, is given in the title of the poem: 'The Bank'). And yet, a pun can make linguistic arbitrariness – the ' "accidental" or external relationship between signifiers',[28] 'arbitrary quirk[s] of the specific language system'[29] – seem providential. Fortuitous likeness becomes meaningful coincidence. A pun is not, as the tortured Thomas portrays himself, 'in between'; it is in a 'straddle position', and can be seen as a cosmopolitan hybrid, not as a split of the tongue (pun intended). In 'The Creative Writer's Suicide', Thomas inveighs against the 'diabolical bilingualism' of his country: 'Oh, I know about all the arguments in its favour: how it enriches the personality, sharpens the mind, enables one to have the best of both worlds, and so on.'[30] A pun, however, represents a kind of positive bilingualism which allows the poet to have 'the best of both worlds'. For Thomas, then, the pun may also be redemptive, a *compensation* for 'the split in the Welshman's soul',[31] his cultural wound, as well as an inscription of it.

Scepticism and the Theology of the Pun

Wordplay often functions as a successful tool 'in the deconstruction of fixed concepts'.[32] Located 'somewhere between faith and doubt' (*LP*, 111), Thomas's poetry works doggedly against dogma to celebrate the contingent, the heterodox, the heretical even, and the pun for Thomas is an agent of lateral, latitudinarian thinking. 'From my reading', Thomas remarked, 'I continue to see that the present is the age of relativism . . . Woe to the people in days gone by who claimed that this is how things were meant to be, and that such and such was the fundamental truth.'[33] The pun is one mode in which an acknowledgement of 'relativism' operates. For M. Wynn Thomas, 'the very possibility of faith' is questioned by Thomas 'from the sceptical viewpoint of the enlightened humanist and the worldly-wisdom of the relativist'.[34] His poetry is 'a record of the endlessly unstable, mutating terms' on which a Kierkegaardian selfhood 'understands ultimate existence'.[35] Discussing Thomas's debt to gnostic and dualistic concepts, Christine Meilicke refers to Thomas's 'imaginative theodicy of protest feeding on religious scepticism'; his poetry 'refus[es] easy solutions', conditioning us to reject unitary truth and 'endure unresolved tensions and paradoxes'.[36] Viewed in these terms, the pun in Thomas's work resonates with a sense of Kierkegaardian risk and struggle. For Rowan Williams, Thomas's poems are characterized by a clear determination '*not* to arrive at a point of mastery and closure'.[37] When 'truth' is glimpsed in the poetry, it is often seen double – 'Between two truths / there is only the mind to fly with' (*EA*, 45) – or as being in motion between fixities – 'the tide's pendulum truth' (*NTF*, 42). With Thomas, one might usefully speak of the pun's pendulum truth. His puns emphasize how mendacious an apparent truth can be: ' "The answer is at the back / of the mirror", says Alice, "where truth *lies*" ' (*R*, 15; my emphasis).

As we shall see, a great deal of Thomas's punning wit is generated by the disconcerting enjambments and subversive lineation which have characterized the verse since the late 1960s.[38] '[L]ine-endings can be a type or symbol or emblem of what the poet values, as well as the instrument by which his values are expressed',[39] Christopher Ricks remarks of Wordsworth's suggestive lineation, and Thomas's line-endings represent another destabilizing strategy which resists closure, 'relativis[es] the claim of any particular sentence',[40] 'prolongs the speculation'[41] and sets up subversive cross-currents of meaning. One must be wary of being taken in by the illusions generated by Thomas's line-endings:

> Fifty-two years,
> most of them *taken in*
> growing or in the
> illusion of it . . .
>
> (*NBF*, 7; my emphasis)

'The worship of the word must be pagan and polytheistic. It cannot endure one god.'[42] What are the implications of being a religious poet and a punster/puntheist? Is a play on words appropriate to a belief in the Word? For the Milton of *Paradise Lost*, the pun (that 'wild coupling without priest' in Jean Paul Richter's memorable phrase[43]) is an ulterior mode, a figure for our fallen condition – essentially a sign of sin since it marks a moment of confusion and duplicity and a fall from Adamic, Edenic clarity.[44] As Walter Savage Landor dryly observed of Satan's tendency to pun: 'It appears . . . that the first overt crime of the refractory angels was punning: they fell rapidly after that.'[45] (Landor is himself punning: one meaning of 'refractory' is 'able to withstand extreme heat' – useful on hell's burning marl.) According to this view, one *commits* a pun (as, in Thomas's work, one *'perpetrate[s]* / a marriage' (*NTF*, 44; my emphasis)). Clearly, there was a part of the divided Thomas that craved the certainty of unitary, unambiguous, transcendent meaning: 'Divided / mind, the message is always / in two parts' (another good description of a pun), 'Must it be / on a cross it is made one?' (*BHN*, 91); 'Are we sure we can bend / the Absolute to our meaning?' (*MHT*, 36). As a religious poet he was all too aware of the 'compromised' nature of 'mortal utterance'[46] with its attendant tricks, deferrals and failures, from which there is 'no redress' (*LS*, 43): 'We have been victims / of vocabulary for too long' (*MHT*, 42); 'vocabulary has on a soft collar / but the tamed words are not to be trusted' (*NTF*, 63); 'Syntax is words' // way of shackling / the spirit (*R*, 69); 'The duplicity / of language, that could name / what was not there' (*BHN*, 98) – God, for instance. Yet he could see the transcendent Word itself in terms of the frustrations of labile language, saying of himself that 'The simplicity of the Sacrament absolved him from the complexities of the Word' (*ERS*, 68). He called Jesus a poet.[47] And it was in terms of the double-speak of metaphor and the symbolic nature of language (which, he emphasized, can only give us 'something in terms of something else') that Thomas said he understood the Resurrection.[48] Moreover, the Church he served was institutionalized on a pun (a 'rocky foundation'[49] indeed, as Thomas demonstrates in a sacrilegiously parodic pun in *The Way of It*: 'The Church, as promised, / was petrified' (*WI*, 7)). And at the very heart of his faith is that mysterious pun yoking matter and spirit (and 'spiritual' can mean 'witty'): Incarnation. M. Wynn Thomas rightly states that 'Thomas's theology may be inscribed in every aspect and at every level of his writing – from lexicon and syntax to formal patterning . . . we need constantly to be aware of the theology of his style',[50] and one should add the pun to the list. Puns are marshalled by Thomas to deconstruct 'traditional theological metanarrative';[51] their doubleness catches the modalities of a universe now random, absurd and pitiless, now providential and ordered – 'In the beginning was the pun', says Beckett[52] – as well as the duality of a now present, now absent ludic deity ('Mild and dire, / now and absent, like us but / wholly other – which side / of you am I to believe?' (*C*, 53)). By inscribing *multiple* presence, the pun also refuses to 'conced[e] / An absence' (*H'm*, 4) and hints, as Rowan Williams has put it, at the co-presence of God and world,[53] at the hidden patterns of Creation. It offers more than a mere echo to the amen – it articulates a reply. Thomas might have been speaking not only of the mitching god but of the pun when he wrote:

> Imagine rather how it would be
> in its absence: a relationship
> broken; the possibility of a listener
> removed; soliloquy replacing
> a dialogue between two minds.
>   (*R*, 65)

The pun is also an approximation of the divine – an act both pious and presumptuous – in that, as Shoaf remarks of Milton's puns, 'the simultaneity (of meanings) in a pun is time's version of eternity's instantaneity of knowing'.[54] And for one increasingly conscious of the perils of narcissistic selfhood (what is narcissism but a pernicious and illusory pun on the self?) and of the falsifying simplicity of mere objective thought, the pun, as a window onto difference, relationship and copia, offers an escape from 'the malevolence of mirrors' (*MHT*, 38). It offers a means of cultivating a Kierkegaardian 'double reflection' on the Christian self that is 'continually in the process of becoming'. A pun shows the subjective thinker to be, in Kierkegaard's terms again, 'aware of the dialectic of communication' and 'essentially interested in his own thinking';[55] one might say that a verbal quibble puns consciousness into self-consciousness.

Though fully in agreement with the view that Thomas's career, from the bleak Prytherch pastorals and the Welsh airs of nationalist valency to the poems of spiritual questing and the late love lyrics and elegies, is all of a piece (John Pikoulis's chapter in this volume offers a stellar take on this),[56] I have chosen to take advantage of some of these admittedly well-worn critical groupings to get a purchase on Thomas's ubiquitous puns (only a fraction of which can be explored here). First, however, four puns deserve to be identified as good examples of bad puns in Thomas. Each, for me at least, is 'a pistol let off at the ear; not a feather to tickle the intellect', as Charles Lamb described the pun;[57] each, in William Empson's words, 'jumps out of its setting, yapping, and bites the Master in the ankles'.[58] They serve to emphasize what Thomas's puns – the great majority of which are tickling feathers, not yapping shih-tzus – usually succeed in avoiding. Describing Holocaust victims in 'Beacons', Thomas writes: 'Their flesh was dough for the hot / ovens. Some of them rose / to the occasion' (*BHN*, 100) – an outrageous pun which, crucially and despite the irony, trivializes rather than emphasizes the outrage. (Thomas himself was later to rise to the occasion with the plangent, and significantly pun-less, lines: 'That time / the queue winding towards / the gas chambers, and the nun / . . . to the girl / in tears: Don't cry. Look, / I will take your place' (*MHT*, 44).) The three other examples all lack the maieutic economy that makes the reader work for – and therefore deserve – the 'revelation' offered by less pat puns. 'The second stood up: He appeared to me / in church in a stained window. I saw through him' ('Testimonies'; *EA*, 4) – a transparent one, that; 'She who had decomposed // is composed again in her hymns' ('Fugue for Ann Griffiths'; *WA*, 51) – a dead one; and, on another Welsh worthy, Bishop William Morgan: 'If he was incumbent, / there was a responsibility also / incumbent upon him' ('R.I.P.'; *MHT*, 35) – a cumbersome one, in which the repetition is overkill since 'responsibility' is enough to suggest the pun.

Prytherch's World

Puns in Thomas's poetry begin in Prytherch country, in what *The Minister* describes as 'the marginal land where flesh meets spirit' (*M*, 9) –

an appropriate place for the pun (though, typically, the beginning of the next line – 'Only on Sundays . . .' – ironizes the statement, suggesting early on that this is a place where flesh is often at odds with or wholly divorced from spirit). The pun is adept at capturing that tension between distinct domains of knowledge and experience. 'Twm was a dunce at school' is the bald opening of the anti-pastoral 'The Airy Tomb'; forever looking up from his 'books and sums' at untamed nature outside, 'This was Twm . . . / *Subject* to nothing but the sky and the wind's *rule*' (*SF*, 42; my emphasis). They are modest puns, but 'subject' and 'rule' nicely contrast the elemental laws of nature and the harsh discipline of farm work (to which Twm's life is mortgaged) with the lessons and wooden rulers of the 'dull school'. Puns in a Thomas poem are often (re)activated remotely by other poems, and lines (with the same rhyme) from a related early piece, 'The Lonely Furrow', serve to emphasize the play in 'The Airy Tomb': 'When I was young, I went to school / With pencil and foot-rule / . . . Then who was it taught me back to go / To cattle and barrow, / Field and plough . . .?' (*AL*, 36). In 'Iago Prytherch' (clearly an ironic version of Kipling's 'If—' – one might say a pun on it), the speaker addresses the peasant with advice on how to survive in a world that is fast overtaking him:

> If you can till your fields *and stand to see*
> The world go by, a foolish tapestry
> Scrawled by the times . . .
>
> > . . . then you shall be
> The first man of the new community.
>
> > > (*SF*, 38; my emphasis)

Seldom in the poetry do we see Prytherch's back 'com[ing] straight / Like an old tree lightened of the snow's weight' (*SF*, 8): usually he is manifestly stooped (*SF*, 8), 'awry' (*SYT*, 109), 'crouched' (*PS*, 36) and moves with 'a beast's gait' (*SYT*, 113), his 'knees crumbl[ing] to the downward pull / Of the harsh earth (*SF*, 27), his 'deep eyes earthward' (*T*, 10); the poem 'Bent' (*BHN*, 102) is about precisely this bowed state. The pun in 'Iago Prytherch', however, offers an alternative portrait: 'If you can . . . stand to see' resonates not only with the primary sense of 'bear to see', but with the injunction to stand tall – in all senses. As a group, the Prytherch lyrics dramatize the poet-priest's ambiguous response to the peasant archetype who 'affront[s], bewilder[s] yet compel[s]' his gaze, and the pun in 'The Face' – 'I knew when / I first saw him that was the man / To turn the mind on' (*T*, 17) – captures succinctly the reality of Prytherch as both a curiosity on which to turn the mind dispassionately or harshly ('Consider this man in the field beneath'; *SF*, 20) and an inspiring phenomenon which turns the mind on. In 'Too Late', the speaker confronts Prytherch with his imminent demise in the face of harsh economic realities and the coming of the Machine:

> But look at yourself
> Now, a servant hired to flog
> The life out of the slow soil,
> Or come obediently as a dog
>
> To the pound's whistle.
>
> (*T*, 25)

Prytherch is also confronted here with the pun on 'pound' (dog-pound and sheepfold, but also cash) which emphasizes his hireling status. 'Can't you see . . .?', the line continues, as if alerting Prytherch to a quibble that represents the duplicities of a world he can no longer understand. Having criticized the tendency of Welsh-speaking businesses to forsake the language in order to secure English pounds in the later uncompromising polemic *Cymru or Wales?*, Thomas writes: 'All credit to the people of Eifionydd, who showed in the early days of the Butlin camp that they were not prepared to see the local railway halt of Penychain being changed by the jokey English into Penny Chain'.[59] Thomas would have been aware of the chance interlingual pun which emerges out of the horrendous Anglicization and which appropriately emphasizes the role the pound's whistle plays in the dilution of Welsh culture. Prytherch is on his way out, and puns correct the tendency to romanticize him: 'Watching the pattern of your slow *wake* / through seas of dew' (*AL*, 29; my emphasis) – he is a dead man walking, and this is his wake from which he won't be waking. The phrase 'slow wake', similarly nuanced, returns in *Tares* in the context of the death of the Welsh, those 'castaways on a sea / Of grass' whose 'slow wake / Through time bleeds for our sake' (*T*, 32).

'Gone?' from *Frequencies* is a late return to the dualities of Prytherch country in Thomas's career:

> Will they say on some future
> occasion, looking over the flogged acres
> of ploughland: This was Prytherch country?
>
> (*F*, 34)

The flogging of harsh acres reminds us of the earlier poem, 'Too Late', quoted above; the irresistible whistle of the pound in that poem, together with the reference later in 'Gone?' to 'financed hills', also alerts us to the pun on 'flogged': these acres are both beaten into meagre production and sold off cheaply ('Ah, but to whom?'; *NTF*, 83).[60]

Thomas's punning habit can make the reader over-zealous. One often expects him to deliver a play on horizon/orison (see, for example, *BHN*, 102; *NTF*, 66; and *R*, 35), but it never materializes. However, Thomas can play with the reader by constantly suggesting a pun without delivering it, only to supply it when our expectations have long been thwarted. The phrase 'ewes and wethers', of which he is fond in the early poems, is a case in point: 'Did you detect like an ewe or an ailing wether, / . . . My true heart wandering in a wood of lies?' (*SF*, 29); 'hands, / Shamed by the pen's awkwardness, toyed with the fleece / Of ewe and wether' (*SF*, 43; a pun perhaps on 'pen' here, but not on anything else); 'I passed knee-deep / In ewes and wethers' (*T*, 39). The potential pun on 'wether' is resisted in each of these poems, but Thomas finally yields to the suggestiveness of the word in 'Death of Peasant': 'Lonely as an *ewe* that is sick to lamb / In the hard *weather* of mid-March' (*AL*, 20; my emphasis) – interestingly, a play to which Dylan Thomas had also yielded in the second and third sonnets of the notoriously enigmatic 'Altarwise by Owl-light' sequence (published 1936): 'And hemlock-headed in the wood of weathers'; 'That Adam's wether in the flock of horns'; 'We rung our weathering changes on the ladder'.

'A People Tau(gh)t for War': Gwalia Traducta

If 'wethers' begs a pun, so does begging, fissiparous Wales as a cultural entity. Early on, Thomas sought to pun Wales into heightened awareness of its dualities, and the pun becomes one of the staple ingredients of the later nationalistic poetry. The 'river wended vales' of Dylan Thomas's 'A Winter's Tale' become in R. S. Thomas the rivers of a vended Wales.[61] 'A Welshman to Any Tourist' seeks to flog Wales to the English: 'We've nothing vast to offer you, no deserts / . . . No canyons'. But 'The hills are fine, of course',

> pocked with caverns,
> One being Arthur's dormitory;
> He and his knights are the bright ore
> That seams our history . . .
>   (*SYT*, 112)

The speaker of this poem has no illusions – he knows what he's selling – as the pun on 'seams' emphasizes. Romantic myth merely *seems* our history; in reality it is fake, and what 'seams' our 'real' and unromantic history is not gold but coal, not the Matter of Britain but the matter of industrial south Wales. '[T]he copper and gold / Seams in the wood are all unquarried', remarks the speaker of 'The Old Language' (*AL*, 11), as if stressing the point; 'Life is not hurrying // on to a receding future, nor hankering after / an imagined past', Thomas admits in 'The Bright Field' (*LS*, 60). 'Genealogy', patterned on the famous boast of the mythological Taliesin, offers various historical incarnations of a Welsh 'I', from 'the dweller in the long cave' to the soldier marching to Bosworth, ignorant of the consequences for his country of that victory, down to the inhabitant of the 'new town' and his 'purse of tears'. The poem ends:

> I stand now
> In the hard light of the brief day
> Without roots, but with many branches.
> (*T*, 16)

In the context of the portrait of the 'new town', one cannot resist hearing a pun on 'branches' – those of the high street banks and businesses against which Thomas inveighs in *Cymru or Wales?* (p. 25). This particular 'I' at the end of the poem is the 'I' that has been flogged, that has been sold and has sold out; the pun suggests that rather than being a compensation for lack of roots, having 'many branches' is at the root of Welsh cultural rootlessness. Puns queer Wales, and *The Minister* stresses that Wales is God's strange as well as particular dwelling-place – 'Wales in fact is [God's] peculiar home' (*M*, 10) – while the same pun in 'A Welsh Testament' reveals God's solicitude for Wales to be odd as well as exclusive: 'He was to have a peculiar care / For the Welsh people' (*T*, 39) – a hint there of the nature of the peculiar deity which Thomas's later poetry would explore.

Thomas's most savage and cynical puns occur in poems on the state of his nation (pun intended). Coleridge referred to puns as 'the language of resentment . . . of suppressed passion, especially of hardly smothered dislike',[62] and 'Welcome to Wales', not surprisingly, is shot through with them:

> No one lives
> In our villages, but they dream
> Of returning from the rigours
> Of the pound's climate.
> (*NBF*, 30)

In a poem about death ('Come to Wales / To be buried . . .'), 'No one lives' is a lineatory pun heightened by the pun on 'rigours' (they are also the stiffenings of rigor mortis). The puns continue as the Welsh undertaker drums up English business: 'Let us / Quote you; our terms / Are the lowest'. 'Quoting' the English language is the cause of Wales's cultural death, and the 'terms' of the indigenous language are indeed the 'lowest' for those seeking social and economic advancement. The poem is clinched – and 'clinch' was a seventeenth-century term for a pun[63] – with another quibble: Wales is 'a place where / It is lovely to lie'.

What is a Welshman? (1974) is Thomas's bleakest, most vituperative book. For J. P. Ward, the collection evinces 'a cynicism as sour as it is depressing'.[64] 'With their deliberate appeal to our less "cultured" instincts', Justin Wintle states, these poems are 'a kind of political pornography';[65] 'less of an albatross and more of a turkey' was Robert Minhinnick's punning appraisal.[66] 'To Pay for his Keep', a poem on the political stunt that was the 1969 Investiture at Caernarfon castle, spits puns out. The 'keep' of the title is both the Civil List and the castle keep, and in the light of the final lines of the poem, in which the prince fails to notice a vision of 'young people, young as himself', climbing a 'far hill', the title also suggests that he will have to forfeit something of real value ('pay for') in becoming thus institutionalized. Then there is the pun on the suffocating 'dead weight / of the past' and the reference to the 'fagged / clergy', whom the quibble identifies as both superannuated and the products of the public schools (*WW*, 5). The reference in 'His Con-descensions are Short-Lived' to 'the clapped ranks of / the peerage' (*WW*, 9) offers a mordant companion pun which captures the loyally applauding but clapped-out and gonorrhoeal Lords. 'To Pay for His Keep' had studiously avoided the vocabulary of homage – 'pavements filthy with / dog shit' – and R. S. is certainly not averse to arses in this scatological volume: 'He Agrees with Henry Ford' refers to Iolo Goch licking Owain Glyndŵr's arse 'for a doublet'. Sooner or later, we would have to negotiate a scatological pun:

> I have drawn the curtains
> on the raw sky where our history
> bleeds, where Cilgwri's ousel
> on my ramshackle aerial
> keeps the past's *goal*
> against the *balls* of to-morrow.
>   (*WW*, 11; my emphasis)

The metaphor of a football match, listened to or watched via the aerial, portrays the ouzel of Cilgwri (one of the ancients of the world in *Culhwch ac Olwen* and a feature of Thomas's early poetry – see *AL*, 8 and 13) as the lonely keeper of Wales's goal against the onslaught of English strikes. But for 'goal' one should also read 'ideal', and for 'balls', of course, the bullshit of modern life. (There's a whiff of the scatological about the ouzel's Latin name – *turdus torquatus* – which punster Thomas would certainly not have, in a manner of speaking, sniffed at.[67]) 'It Hurts Him to Think' disturbingly figures the depredation of English industrialists:

> I was
> born into the squalor of
> their feeding and sucked their speech
> in with my mother's
> infected milk, so that whatever
> I *throw up* now is still theirs.
> (WW, 12)

'Throw up' emphasizes Thomas's conviction that any poetry he might have to offer, being in English, is vomit, rejected matter, the product of the cultural 'gut's trouble' (*BT*, 15). Disturbingly, what should be loving contact with his mother results in infection, and the puns in 'He Lives Here' heighten Thomas's fraught, Swiftian relationship with the maternal: 'I said God *deliver* me / from the womb that is stubborn to *bear*' (*WW*, 1; my emphasis).

In *Welsh Airs* (1987), whose title puns on breezes, musical airs, cultural heirs and the airs and graces of such figures as Sir Gelli Meurig (all of which are central to the complex portrait of Wales constructed in the volume[68]), Thomas once again accuses the womb that bore him by means of a pun. Indeed, Thomas has a punning relationship with his mother in the poetry: linguistic equivocation enshrines his sense of being linguistically and culturally disenfranchised specifically by her, and the pun should be seen as the reflex response of an emotional and psychological neurosis. This could also surface in his speech, as it did in a 1989 Welsh interview in the form of a Freudian slip (often the site of puns) involving the words *bai* ('blame') and *baich* (burden'): Thomas explained that since his father was away for protracted periods at sea, *ar fy mam y syrthiodd y bai o ofalu amdanaf* – 'it was on my mother that the *blame* of raising me fell'. In the tumbling, unpunctuated 'Alma Mater', Thomas offers an unflattering picture of Anglicized Cardiff, his birthplace, which the ironic title identifies as his 'bounteous mother'. Cardiff, he says,

> to me is
> streets houses one
> where a girl relieved herself
> of me . . .
>
> (WA, 36)

It is a shocking lineatory pun: Thomas was excreted into the world, and the lines animate the pun on 'mater' in the title. ('Relieved' recurs as a pun in another harrowing account of Thomas's Caesarean birth in *The Echoes Return* Slow, which soon twitches with yet another pun: 'The woman was opened and sewed up, *relieved* of the trash that had accumulated nine months in the man's absence. Time would have its work *cut out* in smoothing the birth-marks of the flesh' (p. 2).) In 'The Parlour', addressed to English visitors who are served with 'polite tea' and 'the iced cake of translation', the Welsh soldiers of the Falklands conflict appear as 'framed casualties' in photographs on the shelves (WA, 40); the pun characterizes them also as gulled victims of an English imperialist set-up. And just as puns in the Prytherch poems correct the residual tendency towards romantic pastoral, so in the Welsh airs they sabotage Thomas's idealized portraits of a Welsh nation preserved from global capitalism, as in 'Afallon' (Avalon, another Abercuawg): 'In a world / oscillating between dollar / and yen our liquidities / are immaterial' (NTF, 25). The poem proudly announces that Wales's liquid assets ('liquidities') are those of the spirit ('immaterial'); but it is also emphasized that in a global context they are 'immaterial', insignificant, with 'liquidities' reminding us of English appropriation of the literally 'liquid' assets of Wales and of the drowning of Welsh valleys like Tryweryn – places that have become, in Thomas's iconic phrase, 'the subconscious / Of a people'. 'Imports, strontium in bulk; / Exports, H_2O, free', as Thomas puts it in an uncollected poem on Wales.[69] The subconscious of the pun allows us to see that behind 'Afallon' lies 'Reservoirs'.

'Plotting the Future': Science, Technology, The Machine

Phrases such as 'laboratory of the spirit' (note how the spiritual laboratory harbours an oratory), 'oxygen of the spirit', 'mineral poetry', 'transmitted prayers' and 'computed darkness' – all quintessential

Thomas, of course – have been criticized by some commentators for being formulaic ingredients too facilely and repetitively deployed, but a point often overlooked is that formulae are the very things that concern Thomas (in both senses) when he resorts to such formulations. These trademark coinages hold science, technology and faith in fraught balance, and, not surprisingly, Thomas also regularly employs puns to articulate his ambiguous response to applied science in particular – for him, a predominantly Anglo-American evil which puts humanity at the mercy of the old adversary, the machine.[70]

Addressing the deity in 'Earth', Thomas laments: 'the microscope / Is our sin . . . / . . . The machine replaces / The hand that fastened you / To the cross, but cannot absolve us' (*H'm*, 28). The pun emphasizes that modern science is interested only in 'solving' us as a positivist challenge. Solutions (both 'answers' and 'liquids', as in the laboratory context of 'Emerging' – 'There are questions we are the solution to' (*LS*, 1)) replace outmoded absolution. Indeed, medical science has made prayer redundant – 'Once I would have asked / healing. I go now to be doctored, / to drink sinlessly of the blood / of my brother' (*LS*, 1) – and the pun on 'doctored' allows us to see the modern miracle of blood transfusion as both healing and emasculating.

Thomas has God take the machine out of his side in a grim parody of the birth of Eve (indebted to Yeats, of course[71]); similarly, 'the scientists breach / themselves with their Caesarian / births, and we blame them for it' (*LP*, 82): the pun on 'breach' (which picks up on the earlier reference to the 'split mind') strengthens the poem's emphasis on 'unnatural' birth (as we have already seen, Caesarean births bode ill in Thomas's poetry – see also 'Obstetrics' (*D*, 12)). A pun used twice by Thomas reminds us that man's inventions, however basic, are not harmless commodities transferred from manufacturer to consumer; rather, they are impious incarnations: 'The immaculate conception/ preceding the *delivery* / of the first tool' (*LS*, 2; my emphasis; see also *MHT*, 39).

Science is corrupted into technology and becomes a threat. In 'The Hand', God sees 'cities / the hand would build, engines / that it would raze them with' (*LS*, 2): the pun captures succinctly the creative ('raise', which continues the sense of the previous line) and destructive ('raze') potential of modern technology. As a later poem, 'Almost', recapitulates (beginning with a pun): 'Had he a hand / in himself? He had two / that were not his: with one / he would build, with the other / he would knock down' (*WI*, 17). A lineatory pun in *Counterpoint* prompts the reader to make the link between technology and destruction, the tractor and the tank, as Satan

> harrow[s] the ground
> for the drumming of the *machine-*
> gun tears of the rich that are
> seed of the next war.
>
> (*C*, 29; my emphasis)

Another pun later in the volume reinforces the point: ' "The body is mine and the soul is mine" / says the machine . . . / . . . I fill my *tanks* up / and there is war' (*C*, 47; my emphasis). The machine is not a mod con but a deathly con: the tempted Adam is described as 'A slow traveller with all time / to arrive but for the machine's smiling / *undertaking* to get him there sooner' (*MHT*, 17; my emphasis).

'I have looked in / through the windows of their glass / laboratories', Thomas says of the scientists,

> and seen them plotting
> the future, and have put a cross
> there at the bottom
> of the working out of their problems to
> prove to them that they were wrong.
>
> (*ERS*, 89)

'Plotting' has them insidiously conspiring as well as drawing graphs, and Thomas corrects their unholy deductions not only with the examiner's cross (X) but with Christ's. In 'Gradual', Thomas dismisses the 'instruments' of physics as being 'beside the point of / their sharpness' (*LP*, 178), the pun pointedly rejecting the cutting-edge as irrelevant and ineffectual in the search for the metaphysical. Troublingly, however, the mathematicians are shown to be in league with a ludic deity who is also engaged in perverse arithmetical play:

> Take this
> from that, [God] says, and there is everything
> left.
>   . . . the mathematicians
> are best at it.
>   . . . And we are shattered
> by their deductions.
>
> (*F*, 31)

Appropriately, the poem is a game working through a pun: 'deductions' – signifying 'subtractions' as well as 'conclusions' – emphasizes the alliance between the scientists and the god who taunts Creation with paradoxical subtractions. The Lord giveth, and the Lord taketh away.

Face-to-face with the machine in the 'Winter' section of 'The Seasons', humanity sees itself belittled, dismissed:

> We have looked
> it in the *eye*
> and seen how our image
> gradually is *demoted*.
>
> (*MHT*, 69; my emphasis)

'Demoted' is an audacious play on Christ's warning against hypocrisy in Matthew 7: 3–5: 'And why beholdest thou the mote that is in thy brother's eye, but considerest not the beam that is in thine own eye? Or how wilt thou say to thy brother, Let me pull out the mote out of thine eye; and, behold, a beam is in thine own eye?' The pun provocatively asks us to consider whose hypocritical eye needs 'de-moting' – humanity's, or the machine's? – and, of course, whose eye has the beam in it. *Hypocrite Thomas – mon semblable – mon frère?*

The 'Credentials of the Divine'

One of Thomas's most resonant puns is the title of his pivotal 1972 volume, *H'm*, which apostrophizes God (pun intended – this is a deity with gaps and 'unpredictabilities at [his] centre' (*NTF*, 58)), while simultaneously expressing scepticism, wistfulness, contentment and the 'hum of the machine' (*AL*, 26). The multiple suggestiveness of the pun in the metaphysical poetry captures the shifting moods of the believer and of a god described in 'Nuance' as 'the Janus-faced' but also, punningly, as 'two-faced' (*NTF*, 32) – a paradoxical being who, typically, 'con*descends* to be put to death' in '*high* places' ('Jerusalem' (*EA*, 47); my emphasis). In *The Echoes Return Slow*, Thomas writes:

> Faces looked up at the pulpit, knowing the vicar as a player of games . . . Is God funny? . . . What tricks has he beside lightning up his capacious sleeves? And the boys' parents, educating their sons to make *money* as a gentleman should, inclined to concede that religion could be a *capital* concern.
>
> (*ERS*, 54; my emphasis)

As the self-portrait and the quibble at the end emphasize, religion for Thomas the ludic vicar is also a punning concern. The sleeves of Thomas's cassock are as capacious as those of the deity imagined in the above passage. In the 'Incarnation' poems of the second part of *Counterpoint*, he prepares assiduously for a brilliant pun by repeatedly referring to Christ's manger and then ending the section with the lines: 'I have been student of your love / and have not graduated . . . / . . . Time and again I was / caught with a *crib* up my sleeve' (*C*, 34; my emphasis). A poem about trying to cheat God ends, pertinently, with a pun.

Certain words in the priest's lexis cry out to be punned on. There is 'cure', for instance, which recurs throughout the poetry, registering both the search for physical and spiritual health and the responsibility for a parish – and of course the tension between them: 'The cure of souls! Congregations tend to get older. There is no cure for old age' (*ERS*, 62); 'But just when, after such long practice, he was beginning to approach spiritual health, life with that irony that is so dear to it announced that there is a time to retire even from a cure' (*ERS*, 100); 'The priest's cure, not on prescription' (*NTF*, 20; see also *PS*, 41; *BT*, 8; *EA*, 66). A neat paradox in *Experimenting with an Amen* – 'a compulsion to volunteer' (p. 52) – offers a good description of what the following pun from *The Minister* suggests about the pastorship of Reverend Elias Morgan: 'a man *ordained* for ever / To pick his way along the grass-strewn wall / Dividing tact from truth' (*M*, 23; my emphasis). 'Divine' (to foretell, to dowse and, of course, God) is another repeated equivocation: 'They did not divine it but / they bequeathed it to us' (*LS*, 45) – a pun in 'Ffynon [*sic*] Fair (St Mary's Well)' which M. Wynn Thomas sees as a classic instance of maieutic irony leading the reader, retrospectively, to a sudden epiphanic consciousness of the poem as a whole.[72] 'Consumers / of distance at vast cost, / what do they know of the green / twig with which he divines . . .?' (*EA*, 58) – nothing, one might reply, if they don't get the pun. 'Believe' is yet another word exploited, exploded, as in 'it is easy to believe / Yeats was right' (*LS*, 30), where the line-break transmutes a statement of faith into the Yeatsian acknowledgement that the age of faith is merely a phase of the moon that has been displaced by the next cycle of history.[73] The lines hold faith and doubt in balance, as does the ambiguity of statements such as 'To pray true is to say nothing' (*MHT*, 77) and of line-breaks such as 'The supreme vow is no / vow, but a concession / to anger at the exigencies / of language' (*LP*, 188) – lineation which makes us aware of those very 'exigencies of language'. And what is the tonal quality of the final two words of 'Still', one of the late, plangent elegies to Thomas's first wife, Mildred E. Eldridge? 'Last night, as I loitered // where your small bones had their nest'

– an affecting pun on 'rest' – 'the owl blew away from your stone cross / softly as down from a thistle-head. I wondered' (*NTF*, 27). Caught between scepticism and astonishment, it is another *H'm*, as is the following example from 'Anybody's Alphabet': 'Gone, [God] still / gazes upon us. Gracious', where the final word hovers between sardonic irony, exclamation and an acknowledgement of God's grace.

'No time' is a phrase that fascinated Thomas. 'I will simply say that I realised there was really no such thing as time, no beginning and no end but that everything is a fountain welling up endlessly from immortal God', he says of his mystical experience at Maes-yr-Onnen; 'creatures of time and space as we all are', he writes in 'The Making of a Poem', 'we are yet haunted by dreams of eternity' (*Selected Prose*, 37 and 87). Thomas's numerous puns on 'no time' communicate this sense of being 'a seeker / in time for that which is / beyond time' (*F*, 27): 'deep down is as distant / as far out, but it is arrived at / in no time' (on space-travel; *WI*, 28); 'As though there were no time / like the present and that / vanishing' (on God begging to be loved; *LP*, 202); 'What time is it? / . . . It is no time / at all (on violent and momentous events in history; *EA*, 20); 'The blood / ticked from the cross, but it was not / their time it kept. It was no / time at all' (*C*, 40) – all of which (the second and third assisted by the line-breaks) reanimate time-bound, moribund clichés about time with conceptions of space-time and eternity. Thomas also employs the pun in the title – 'No Time' – of another elegy to Elsi in which, after death, she 'comes / to [him] still'; here, the title articulates both a cry of despair at the brevity of life and the miracle of that moment when 'time immolate[s] / itself in love's fire' (*NTF*, 33). Likewise, permanence and transience are beautifully caught in a pun in 'Somewhere': 'Surely these husbands and wives / have dipped their marriages in a *fast* / spring?' (*LS*, 46; my emphasis)

The pun is also a means of contrasting, and to an extent reconciling (since the pun works both ways), the secular and the sacred, 'the quotidian and the sublime' (*NTF*, 61), as in 'Pilgrimages':

> There are those here
> not given to prayer, whose office
> is the blank sea that they say daily.
> (*F*, 51)

The lines describe the farmers and boatmen of Bardsey island, whose observance is very different from the pilgrims' 'office' (in the sense of religious service); the pun broadens the reference to contrast the religious life with the secular city workplace (while perhaps simultaneously hinting that, as 'The Moon in Lleyn' puts it, 'In cities that / have outgrown their promise people / are becoming pilgrims / again' (*LS*, 30)). The pun is also a minor incarnation in which the physical and the spiritual/intellectual cohabit. Christ is described as 'a body the issues / of which were for the conversion / of a soldier' (*EA*, 44), where the spiritual 'issues' of atonement are also the bloody physical discharges of a body suffering crucifixion. The pun returns in a harrowing poem in *The Echoes Return Slow* on the poet's sick mother (in which, as we have come to expect, the son puns nervously and compulsively across line-endings – 'She came to us with her appeal / to die, and we made her live / on'): 'The ambulance came / to rescue us from the issues / of her body' (p. 77). Here, 'issues' suggests both incontinence and the emotional problem the mother has become for the son.[74] (How subtly in the later poem 'Healing' Thomas cleanses the indignity of soiled sheets: 'Sick wards. The *sailed* beds / becalmed'; *MHT*, 45; my emphasis.)

The pun's doubleness is a weapon Thomas deploys against hypocrisy and double standards. In 'Cures', inspired by Emmanuel le Roy Ladurie's classic account, based on Inquisition depositions, of life in a French village at the time of the Cathar heresy, Thomas writes:

> So the deposition
> At Foix. Inquisitor,
> what would you have the soul
> be to escape the rigour
> of your laundering? Your Christ
> died for you; for whom
> would you have these die?
>   (*EA*, 66)

In the context of Thomas's reference to the Crucifixion, the pun enjoins mercy by reminding the Inquisitor of Christ's Deposition from the cross. Quibbles also highlight those aspects of institutionalized Christianity that Thomas finds unpalatable and prompt us to substitute for them worthier values. In *The Echoes Return Slow*, the small is contrasted with the great, Celtic simplicity with militaristic imperialism, the ancient with the modern:

> There were other churches from which the population had withdrawn, Celtic foundations down lanes that one entered with a lifting of the spirit . . . Is God worshipped only in cathedrals, where blood drips from

regimental standards as from the crucified body of love[?] Is there a need for a revised liturgy, for bathetic renderings of the scriptures? The Cross is always *avant-garde*.

(ERS, 82; my emphasis)

The companion poem (and the facing poems and prose pieces in this volume are in a sense puns on each other), celebrates 'the contemporaneity of the Cross', which consolidates the primary meaning of 'avant-garde' in the prose piece. But the literal sense of 'avant-garde' – 'the vanguard of an army' – also haunts the phrase, recapitulating Thomas's earlier reference to the bloody 'regimental standards' displayed in cathedrals. 'I dislike cathedrals on the whole', Thomas said, 'big places, because they are associated in my mind with English imperialism . . . I look upon the Church of England as having betrayed Christianity by its acquiescence in war.'[75] The pun in *The Echoes Return Slow* asks us to reject a Christianity that is in this sense *avant-garde*, martial, crusading, and replace it with one that is eternally contemporary in its pacifism. (Characteristically, Thomas, in a different mood, was later to ask: 'how contemporary/ is the Cross, that long-bow drawn / against love?' (*MHT*, 13)). *Counterpoint* similarly berates institutionalized religion:

> We have over-furnished
> our faith. Our churches
> are as limousines in the procession
> towards heaven. But the verities
> remain: a de-nuclearised
> cross, uncontaminated
> by our coinage . . .
>
> (C, 37)

But the criticism is ambiguously phrased, and therefore ambivalently aimed. 'Coinage' is used in a financial sense, but it also resonates with the sense of linguistic 'coinage' (witness 'de-nuclearised' here, for a start). We therefore glimpse Thomas, whose religious poetry draws much of its distinctiveness and impact from the coinages of sub-atomic physics ('The muse and calculus / In alliance' (*YO*, 21)), questioning the propriety of his own religious vocabulary as well as asking us to consider the extent to which the cross has been 'contaminated' by applied science more generally.

Thomas's god, 'never . . . plain and / out there' (*F*, 52), refuses to be pinned down, and the polysemy of the pun emphasizes that frustrating elusiveness. In *Counterpoint*, Thomas acknowledges our failure 'to *incorporate* / him in the *second person*' (p. 15; my emphasis) – our failure, that is, both to include him meaningfully in our grammar of address (he is, as Thomas was later to put it playfully, 'infinite / in the intensity of [his] / opposition to the incursions / of an implicit Thou'; *NTF*, 89[76]), and to conceive of him as human, incarnate ('in-corporate', 'person') or as the '*Second Person* of the Trinity' ('Belief in the Trinity / for most of humanity / suggests a nonentity', he later jested (*NTF*, 86)). The puns here, in other words, work to stress the impossibility of 'domesticating / an enigma' (*C*, 53). 'I have developed my negatives / of the divine', the speaker of 'Mischief' says, 'and preserved their technicolour / in a make-believe album' (*NTF*, 45). 'Make-believe' suggests a pun, but a better one precedes it: in addition to the fanciful notion of capturing an image of the deity in a photograph, the lines characterize precisely the kind of theological approach to God to which Thomas has subscribed. Conscious of the impossibility of making any affirmative statements about God, Thomas has famously figured him in terms of absences, shadows and traces; 'developed . . . negatives / of the divine', then, puns on the negative theology famously dramatized in such poems as 'Via Negativa': 'Why no! I never thought other than / That God is that great absence / In our lives' (*H'm*, 16).

Punning: everyone's at it, or is the victim of it, including Jesus, Mary and Joseph. In *Frequencies*, a presumably particoloured, harlequin Christ sits down at our Christmas table, complete with party hat and a cracker of a quibble: 'he sits at table / with us with on his head / the *fool's cap* of our *paper* money' (p. 50; my emphasis), where 'paper' animates the pun in 'fool's cap' on 'foolscap'. It was Joseph who taught Christ to pun in the carpenter's workshop: 'I taught him / the true trade: to go / with the grain' (*LS*, 171) – which Christ didn't, of course, thereby 'fashioning / . . . a cross for himself'. Mary can't resist a dark pun on her son, either:

> They looked in under
> my lids and saw
>
> as through a stained glass
> window the hill
> the infant must climb,
>
> the crookedness of
> the kiss he appended
> to his loving epistle.
>
> (*LS*, 171)

'Kiss' and 'epistle' here evoke the once loving *apostle* who gave Christ a crooked kiss in Gethsemane, which resulted in Christ climbing that hill. '[I]t is words' – one might also say puns – 'are the kiss of Judas / that must betray you', Thomas writes in *Mass for Hard Times* (p. 13).

The arch-punster, of course, is Thomas's mischievous, conjuror-deity, whose perversity is expressed through the trickery of puns. In 'The Belfry', Thomas has to negotiate the 'hard *spell* / Of weather that is between God / And himself' (*P*, 28; my emphasis). A pun in *Counterpoint* highlights the contradiction between a loving god and the ruthless scientific deity 'of quasars / and pulsars', 'of the molecule and the atom': 'I have seen the jay, that singer / out of tune, helping itself // to a morsel out of the lark's nest, / and you *beamed* down imperturbably as the sun' (*C*, 51; my emphasis), which catches both a smiling and a destructive, sci-fi god (significantly, it is Satan who 'beams down' in an earlier poem in the volume (*C*, 29)). 'Mischief', a poem on the two-faced god's 'juggling / with the scales' of life, similarly employs a pun to reveal this duality:

> But against
> all this [nothingness] I have seen the lamb
> *gambolling* for a moment, as though
> life were a good thing. This, I have said,
> is God's roguery . . .
>
> (*NTF*, 45; my emphasis)

The existence of such innocence in a world full of 'evil piled / upon evil' proves this juggler-god to be *gambling* with Creation. God as chess-player is the subject of 'Play' –

> His mind shines
> on the black and the white
> squares.
>
> (*F*, 16)

– where the enjambment after 'white' suggests the benevolent Father of all races (with a hint of rain falling alike on the just and the unjust), only to conjure him round the corner as a being for whom Creation is merely a game. In 'Calling', subversive lineation transforms the divine into the satanic:

the temptation

> has come to experiment
> with the code which would put
> me through to *the divine*
> *snarl* at the perimeter of such tameness.
>
> (*EA*, 31; my emphasis)

In the face of this incorrigibly plural deity, puns are charged with heterodox dual perspectives: 'You have answered / us with the image of yourself
/ on a hewn tree, suffering / injustice, pardoning it' (*MHT*, 46): this god
may have suffered injustice on the cross, the pun implies, but does he not
also, perversely, *allow* ('suffer') injustice – and then pardon it? Looking at
a reflection, a 'replica', of himself in a metaphysical window in *Counterpoint* (and appropriately yielding to the double reflection of the pun),
Thomas appears 'hungry for meaning / at life's pane' (*C*, 46) – lines that
remind us that meaning in Thomas's religious poetry is never far from a
pun, or from pain.

Puns on Women and Two Wives

Thomas's highly ambivalent relationship with his mother, and the role
puns play in his representation of her, have already been noted. The concluding section of this essay looks at Thomas's punning representation of
women and the gender politics of the pun. The ekphrastic poems of
Between Here and Now and *Ingrowing Thoughts* in particular have
focused critical attention on what Helen Vendler refers to as Thomas's
'conflicting views of woman – as creatures of fashion, as timid about
"heat", as a natural body, as deceptive in "femininity", and as a potential
sexual partner'[77] and on what Tony Brown identifies as 'the masculine
gaze' of Thomas's speakers.[78] Puns play an important part in articulating
these gendered reflections.

James A. Davies has described the world evoked by the speaker in
Between Here and Now, which responds to a series of Impressionist
paintings, many with female subjects, as a 'fallen' one that 'smoulders
with sexual activity . . . actual . . . suggested . . . [or] latent'.[79] Tony
Brown sees the relations between the sexes dramatized by these poems as
'a matter of elaborate ritual, and subterfuge'; women in this bourgeois
world of surfaces, masks and façades are less disempowered subjects of
patriarchal control than duplicitous, powerfully sexual performers who

evoke anxious, conflicting desires in the male viewer/narrator/poet.[80] Puns register the tension between the speaker's 'innate fleshly instinct' (Davies's phrase) and societal/moral codes governing gender relations; they also suggest some of the dangers of the ekphrastic project for the male poet. A number of these poems warn us against lustful gazing – '[Her] hands, / . . . are, / as ours should be, in / perfect repose, not accessory / to the plucking of her own flower' (*BHN*, 69) – but puns also reveal more anarchic drives. Take Thomas's 'reading' of Degas's *Mademoiselle Dihau at the Piano*, which implicates us in the pun through the use of a disturbingly euphemized 'we':

> Almost
> we could reach out a hand
>   for the mellow-fleshed,
> sun-polished fruit
>   that she is. But her eyes
> are the seeds of a *tart*
>   *apple*, and the score a notice
> against trespassing upon
>   land so privately owned.
>
>   (*BHN*, 25; my emphasis)

On the face of it, the poem emphasizes the resistance of the chaste female subject to the predatoriness of the male gaze, but the bold enjambment confronts us with a very different woman – or with the male's lustful, misogynistic construction of her. Degas's *Musicians in the Orchestra* portrays a group of male musicians beneath a stage on which female ballet dancers perform: 'it is not their ears / but their eyes the conductor // has sealed, lest they behold / on the stage's shore / the skirts' rising and falling / that turns men to swine' (*BHN*, 27). 'Swine' figures the dancers as modern incarnations of Homer's enchantress Circe, and the men, therefore, as victims of female sexuality and guile, but it also represents men as lustful and brutish, as potential violators of women. The nakedness of the women in Renoir's *The Bathers* is there 'for us to gaze / our fill on, but / without lust', but a pun inflames male desire: 'These bodies, / smooth as bells / from art's stroking, toll / an unheard music' (*BHN*, 77); brush-strokes and the stroke of the bell, yes, but the sexual contact the poem warns against, too. Cassatt's *Young Woman Sewing* elicits a pun from the male viewer which emphasizes her status as both debutante and sexual being (and therefore potential sexual partner): 'She is / the chrysalis she / inhabits, but the *blood* // in flower about her / is an indication of the arrival / of her *period* to come / out now and spread her wings' (*BHN*, 55; my emphasis).

Such puns in the painting poems, then, suggest both female duplicity and male lustfulness or violation. This is also to be seen elsewhere in the poetry, as in the lineatory pun at the beginning of 'Passenger', which makes the fault first hers and then his:

> Leaning over her excuse
> me smell of hair smell of
> powder warm smell
> of woman . . .
>
> (*WI*, 27)

'Excuse' is first a noun, then a verb. If the dualities of Wales and the duplicities of a tricksy god prompt puns, so too do Thomas's performing, role-playing women who, with their 'forked laughter' (*H'm*, 27), are both familiar and threateningly other and unknowable. Significantly, language itself at such moments becomes a punning performance, as in 'Duty' (a pun, as will become clear) from the posthumous *Residues*:

> Then there is the lost continent
> of ideas to be re-discovered
> in a woman. For climate
> she gives herself *airs*. Her geology
>
> is *cosmetic*; the fauna
> of her interior that unknown
> to science. Herself being
> her frontier, she is *easy to cross*.
>
> And yet there are *customs*
> to comply with; if her eyes *frisk*
> me, I give them their *due* knowing
> I have imponderables to *declare*.
>
> (*R*, 18; my emphasis)

In such a poem, the pun can be seen as a response to the dualities of the female, who can be represented, it seems, only in language that speaks double. One might (disingenuously) say that for Thomas, women are close to God.

Puns also reveal – movingly, regretfully, ironically – the dynamics of Thomas's marriage (marriages, indeed – two, appropriately, for this punster). The portrait offered in 'Anniversary' is delicately poised between tender celebration and disconcertingly cool documentary: 'And not to be first / To call the meal long / We balance it thoughtfully / On the tip of the tongue, / Careful to maintain / The strict palate' (*T*, 18). The pun, from a poet sharing his 'table', 'air' and 'child' with the artist Mildred E. Eldridge and the accomplished productions of her *palette*, hints at the fact that this wife did far more than merely spend 'Nineteen years . . . / Keeping simple house'. Tony Brown has noted how a pun in 'The Untamed' contrasts the masculine sphere 'Of wild places' – Thomas's – with what the poem constructs as the constraining female space of his wife, symbolized by her enclosed garden: 'Despite my first love, / I take sometimes her hand, / Following *strait* paths / Between flowers' (*BT*, 33; my emphasis).[81] Another pun at the end of the poem emphasizes the disjunction: 'But not for long, windows, / Opening in the trees / Call the mind back / To its true eyrie; I stoop / Here only in play'. 'Stoop' is used in the literal sense (tall Thomas has condescended to bend down to smell the flowers, his nose significantly becoming 'Clogged with their thick scent'); in the context of the earlier reference to the 'wild hawk of the mind' that has been temporarily domesticated by 'the gloved hand' of the garden's 'silence', it also suggests the violent, predatory, unfettered realm of the masculine by evoking the *stoop* – the plunging attack – of a raptor. The pun recurs in *H'm*: 'Sudden flowers / Opened in the sea's / Garden; a white bird / Stooped to them' (p. 13). One might suggest that the husband who makes it plain in 'The Untamed' that his 'stooping' to the feminine is merely temporary and playful is consciously (only in play?) evoking a troubling prototype: that of the murderous husband in Browning's poem about power-games and husband–wife relations, 'My Last Duchess': 'Who'd stoop to blame / This sort of trifling? . . . / E'en then would be some stooping; and I choose / Never to stoop.'

Thomas had a deeply sensuous, even sensual and erotic, side – clear enough to those who knew him, as also to those who read the poetry in any depth. In places, however, puns seem to sublimate the sexual, inscribing it in terms of something else. One might suggest that in the poems on his marriage, puns assist Thomas in the delicate task of representing sexual relations – 'the ultimate intimacies / of the bed' as he puts it in a late elegy to Elsi (*R*, 27) – by effectively broadening the frame of reference, decorously incorporating a measure of intellectual play into highly personal poems.[82] 'Acting', another poem on his relationship with Elsi (and another in which the woman 'performs'), puns thrice in as many lines:

I

Was only the looking-glass she *made up in*.
I *husbanded* the rippling meadow
Of her body. Their eyes *grazed* nightly upon it.

(*H'm*, 11; my emphasis)

'Made up in' catches the female acting and applying cosmetics (and
suggests a link between them); 'husbanded' figures sexuality in terms of
agriculture, leading to the insertion in 'gazed' of a punning consonant.
(An earlier poem, 'Once', describes 'an old farmer whose hands / Played
her thin body's slow / Neglected music' (*T*, 22)). In 'All Right', in which
Elsi preserves a 'serene' and 'cool' indifference to her husband, Thomas
writes: 'My eyes' / *Adjectives*; the way that / I *scan* you; the / *Conjunction*
the flesh / Needs' (*H'm*, 29; my emphasis): sex becomes a grammatical
game; one might say the wife has *declined* him. And in 'Nuptials' from
Mass for Hard Times (the volume was dedicated to Elsi, who had died
the previous year), we read: 'Did she listen / to him, plaiting the basket /
from which he would take / bread? Once the whole loaf: / flesh white,
breasts risen / to his first *kneading*' (p. 29; my emphasis).

Samuel Johnson regarded the tendency of Shakespeare's characters to
quibble in the face of death as transgressive of 'reason, propriety and
truth'.[83] Johnson would also have disapproved of Thomas, who faces
down Elsi's impending death with puns: 'Am I catalyst of her *mettle* that,
/ at my approach, her grimace of pain / turns to a smile?' (*ERS*, 121) –
appropriately, a pun Shakespeare was also fond of. And as we have
already seen, Thomas is also a punning elegist. I want to end with one of
his most moving puns, which occurs in a further elegy to Elsi in *Residues*.
It is in more than one sense the culmination of his punning. Thomas
repeats puns across the oeuvre, and each incarnation accrues new
meanings and resonances. In 'Groping', Thomas invokes Wordsworth,
who turned from 'the great hills / of the north'

to the precipice
of his own mind, and *let himself
down* for the poetry stranded
on the bare ledges.

(*F*, 12; my emphasis)

The enjambments enact the 'perilous ridge' over which the young
Wordsworth suspended himself to gather raven's eggs in the famous
episode in *The Prelude* (1805, I, 339–50). But 'let himself down', from one

who had edited Wordsworth, expresses the view that the institutionalized poet let himself down politically and artistically in later life (Thomas's edition refers to the conservative Wordsworth's 'more orthodox view of things' and to the 'increasing dullness of his later verse'). The pun also reminds us how Wordsworth 'let himself down' *stylistically*, as Thomas also noted: 'He could descend to the bathos of "Spade with which Wilkinson hath tilled his lands".'[84] 'Monday's Child . . .' (typically) uses a punning enjambment to remind us of Thomas's bad birth: 'Let down at birth / into a dark well' (*MHT*, 50). And so to the elegy in *Residues*. It quickly became habitual to say that Thomas's second marriage, a few years after the death of Elsi, seemed to give him a new lease of life. But the sardonic poem 'Repeat' offers a shocking portrait of his second wife as 'the mirror of his dotage' and of marriage the second time round as an 'electric chair'. No doubt there were feelings of guilt. And the elegy to Elsi, 'Comparisons', to which the puns on having *let oneself down* have gathered, confesses an awareness of having in some way failed and betrayed her by remarrying. The 'comparisons' of the poem are not merely those of the first stanza but also those between first and second wives. It is a delicate place to end:

> To all light things
> I compared her; to
> a snowflake, a feather.
>
> . . .
>
>   Snow
> melts, feathers
> are blown away;
>
> *I have let*
> *her ashes down*
> in me like an anchor.
>
>   (*R*, 57; my emphasis)

Notes

1 *Selected Letters of Philip Larkin, 1940–1985*, ed. Anthony Thwaite (London: Faber & Faber, 1992), 260 and 341.

2 Quoted in *On Puns: The Foundation of Letters*, ed. Jonathan Culler (Oxford: Basil Blackwell, 1988), 10.

3 Larkin, of course, puns on his own name in 'The Whitsun Weddings': 'And down the long cool platforms whoops and skirls / I took for porters larking with the mails'.

[4] Walter Redfern, *Puns: More Senses than One* (2nd edn; London: Penguin, 2000), 212.

[5] William V. Davis, 'The Presence of Absence: Mirrors and Mirror Imagery in the Poetry of R. S. Thomas', *Analecta Husserliana*, 73 (2001), 347.

[6] *Essays on Punning and Translation*, ed. Dirk Delabastita (Manchester: St Jerome, 1997), 11.

[7] M. M. Mahood, *Shakespeare's Wordplay* (London: Methuen, 1957), 20–1.

[8] 'R. S. Thomas talks to J. B. Lethbridge', *Anglo-Welsh Review*, 74 (1983), 46.

[9] Ibid.

[10] Calvin Bedient, 'Natural Magic and Moral Profundity', *Three Contemporary Poets: Thom Gunn, Ted Hughes & R. S. Thomas*, ed. A. E. Dyson (Basingstoke: Macmillan, 1990), 204.

[11] Tony Conran, *Frontiers in Anglo-Welsh Poetry* (Cardiff: University of Wales Press, 1997), 198.

[12] M. Wynn Thomas, 'Irony in the Soul: The Religious Poetry of R. S[ocrates] Thomas', *Agenda*, 36:2 (1998). See the same author's *Internal Difference: Twentieth-Century Writing in Wales* (Cardiff: University of Wales Press, 1992), 136–7, 139 and 148.

[13] See Vimala Herman, 'Negativity and Language in the Religious Poetry of R. S. Thomas', *Miraculous Simplicity*, 141 and 157, and Peter Abbs, 'The Revival of the Mythopoeic Imagination: A Study of R. S. Thomas and Ted Hughes', *Critical Writings*, 86–7.

[14] 'Lean Parishes: Patrick Kavanagh's *The Great Hunger* and R. S. Thomas's *The Minister*', *Dangerous Diversity: The Changing Faces of Wales*, ed. Katie Gramich and Andrew Hiscock (Cardiff: University of Wales Press, 1998), 148.

[15] See Elaine Shepherd, *R. S. Thomas: Conceding an Absence – Images of God Explored* (Basingstoke: Macmillan, 1996), 157.

[16] See Thomas, 'Irony in the Soul', 59–68.

[17] Delabastita, *Essays*, 6.

[18] See Ben Astley, ' "Somewhere Between Faith and Doubt": R. S. Thomas and the Poetry of Faith Deconstructed', *WWE*, 4 (1998), 76, 78 and 81.

[19] ' "Welshing on the Language": R. S. Thomas, Oliver Reynolds and Postmodern Wales', *WWE*, 4 (1998), 118–32.

[20] See *Wales: A Problem of Translation* (The 1996 Adam Lecture; Adam Archive Publications/Centre for 20th-Century Cultural Studies, King's College, London, 1996), 12.

[21] See 'The Moor' (*P*, 24): 'Breath held like a cap in the hand', behind which lies the Welsh idiom *gyda'i wynt yn ei ddwrn* – 'with his breath in his fist' (that is, out of breath). This is one of the very idioms Thomas cites in *Wales: A Problem of Translation* as translatable only 'at the cost of much merriment' (p. 12). See also the interlingual pun in 'Nant Gwrtheyrn' (*NTF*, 66): 'The cuckoo returns / to Gwrtheyrn . . . / bluebells tolling over // the blue sea', which plays with the Welsh for bluebells, *clychau'r gog* – 'the cuckoo's bells'. Thomas has, of course, rendered a number of Welsh poems into English: see for example *SF*, 18; *EA*, 15; and *NTF*, 57.

[22] Quoted in Delabastita, *Essays*, 266.

[23] *Cymru or Wales?* (Llandysul: Gomer, 1992), 12, 23, 30.

[24] *Autobiographies*, 22.

[25] See Bobi Jones, 'Anglo-Welsh: More Definition', *Planet*, 16 (February/March 1973), 12.

[26] *Cymru or Wales?*, 10 and 11.

[27] See *Autobiographies*, 77.

[28] Jonathan Culler, *On Deconstruction: Theory and Criticism after Structuralism* (London: Routledge, 1983), 91–2.

[29] Culler, *On Puns*, 143.

[30] *Autobiographies*, 21.

[31] *Autobiographies*, 93.

[32] Delabastita, *Essays*, 49.

[33] *Autobiographies*, 116.

[34] *Page's Drift*, 13.

[35] Thomas, 'Irony in the Soul', 60.

[36] See Christine Meilicke, 'Dualism and Theodicy in R. S. Thomas's Poetry', *Literature and Theology*, 12:4 (1998), 407–18.

[37] *Page's Drift*, 92–3. R. A. Shoaf sees puns working in a similar way in Chaucer's poetry, in which 'the pun is a device for delaying, interrupting or otherwise frustrating closure. Often when a character insists on closure and its unisemy, a restriction of meaning, a pun emerges to suggest polysemy and a ludic re-opening of the text'; see Culler, *On Puns*, 45.

[38] For Thomas's radical lineation, see *Miraculous Simplicity*, 127–30, and *Page's Drift*, 65, 91–2, 127–30, 157.

[39] Christopher Ricks, *The Force of Poetry* (Oxford: Oxford University Press, 1987), 91.

[40] Rowan Williams in *Page's Drift*, 91.

[41] Shepherd, *R. S. Thomas*, 129.

[42] W. Gass quoted in Redfern, *Puns*, 39.

[43] Quoted in Redfern, *Puns*, 66.

[44] See R. A. Shoaf, *Milton: Poet of Duality: A Study of Semiotics in the Poetry and the Prose* (New Haven and London: Yale University Press, 1985), xi and 61.

[45] Quoted in Christopher Ricks, *Milton's Grand Style* (London: Oxford University Press, 1963), 66.

[46] See *Page's Drift*, 14–15.

[47] See *Autobiographies*, 84. See also *ERS*, 88.

[48] See *Autobiographies*, 84. See also *Poetry Wales*, 7:4 (Spring 1972), 53–4.

[49] See Culler, *On Puns*, 15. For God as punster, see Walter Redfern, *All Puns Intended: The Verbal Creation of Jean-Pierre Brisset* (Oxford: Legenda, 2001), 65.

[50] Thomas, 'Irony in the Soul', 52. Discussing the poem 'Country Church', M. Wynn Thomas has referred to 'the metaphysics of its sonic patterns'; see 'R. S. Thomas: War Poet', *WWE*, 2 (1996), 92.

[51] Dennis Brown, *The Poetry of Postmodernity: Anglo/American Encodings* (London: Macmillan, 1994), 122.

[52] *Murphy* (New York: Grove Press, 1938), 65. See also C. J. Ackerley, ' "In the Beginning was the Pun": Samuel Beckett's *Murphy*', *Journal of the Australasian Universities Language and Literature Association*, 55 (1981), 19.

[53] See *Page's Drift*, 93: 'The implication is that there might be a legitimate word or thought, an utterance beyond suspicion, if it held to a point of pure tension, articulated in a way that *showed*, rather than imposing, the co-presence of God and world.' I suggest a pun might be one such word.

[54] Shoaf, *Milton*, 62.

[55] See Kierkegaard's *Concluding Unscientific Postcript* in *The Essential Kierkegaard*, ed. Howard V. Hong and Edna H. Hong (Princeton, NJ: Princeton University Press, 2000), 191–3. See also in this regard William V. Davis, ' "At the Foot of the Precipice of Water . . . Sea Shapes Coming to Celebration": R. S. Thomas and Kierkegaard', *WWE*, 4 (1998), 104–5, and Thomas, 'Irony in the Soul', 60.

[56] See also *Page's Drift*, 19.

[57] 'Popular Fallacies – That the Worst Puns are the Best', *Elia and the Last Essays of Elia*, ed. Jonathan Bate (Oxford: Oxford University Press, 1987), 292.

[58] *Seven Types of Ambiguity* (rev. edn; London: Chatto & Windus, 1956), 108.

[59] *Cymru or Wales?*, 27. See also *Selected Prose*, 131 for a further litany of traductions.

[60] Tony Brown has also noted the pun: see *Page's Drift*, 152, and ' "Eve's Ruse": Identity and Gender in the Poetry of R. S. Thomas', *English*, 49:195 (Autumn 2000), 248.

[61] For this spooneristic pun, see Seamus Heaney's 'Dylan the Durable?' in *The Redress of Poetry* (London: Faber & Faber, 1995), 136.

[62] *Coleridge on Shakespeare*, ed. Terence Hawkes (Harmondsworth: Penguin, 1969), 164.

[63] Mahood, *Shakespeare's Wordplay*, 143.

[64] J. P. Ward, *The Poetry of R. S. Thomas* (2nd edn; Bridgend: Seren, 2001), 200.

[65] *Furious Interiors: Wales, R. S. Thomas and God* (London: HarperCollins, 1996), 397.

[66] 'Living with R. S. Thomas', *Poetry Wales*, 29:1 (July 1993), 13.

[67] Interestingly, Thomas puns on the ouzel's name in his prose writings: 'This is the ring-ouzel's home for a few brief months . . . The air oozes birdsong'; *Selected Prose*, 77 and 78.

[68] See *Miraculous Simplicity*, 76.

[69] 'Brochure'; *University of Wales Review* (Summer 1964), 26.

[70] See *Autobiographies*, 114–15.

[71] Yeats's 'Fragments': 'Locke sank into a swoon; / The Garden died; / God took the spinning-jenny / Out of his side'.

[72] Thomas, 'Irony in the Soul', 65.

[73] Noted by M. Wynn Thomas in 'Irony in the Soul', 67.

[74] See Thomas, *Internal Difference*, 136–7 and Barbara Prys Williams, ' "A Consciousness in Quest of its Own Truth": Some Aspects of R. S. Thomas's *The Echoes Return Slow* as Autobiography', *WWE*, 2 (1996), 109–110.

[75] Lethbridge, 'R. S. Thomas talks to J. B. Lethbridge', 52.

[76] See also *MHT*, 18 and 82.

[77] 'R. S. Thomas and Painting', *Page's Drift*, 68.

[78] Brown, 'Eve's Ruse', 230.

[79] ' "Pessimism and its Counters": *Between Here and Now* and After', *Miraculous Simplicity*, 234.

[80] See Brown, 'Eve's Ruse', 232–7.

[81] Ibid., 242.

[82] P. Bernard Jones and Don Dale-Jones have recently suggested that 'Thomas appears to have a horror of describing the sexual act, often not because of its intrinsic nature . . . but because it can produce children . . . He recognises in his own procreation a reaffirmation of sin'; see *T. H. Jones: Poet of Exile* (Cardiff: University of Wales Press, 2001), 184–5.

[83] See Mahood, *Shakespeare's Wordplay*, 33.

[84] *Selected Prose*, 97 and 95.

8

'Time's Changeling': Autobiography *in* The Echoes Return Slow

M. WYNN THOMAS

Although *The Echoes Return Slow* (1988) is, at least in my estimation, one of R. S. Thomas's most impressive collections, it has received relatively little attention. In overlooking it, readers are, unawares, discounting individual poems of exceptional quality, as well as missing an opportunity to familiarize themselves with aspects of Thomas's background and personal history that shed considerable light on his work as a whole. But the matter is more complex than that. *The Echoes Return Slow* is an innovative work, and is so in ways that even seasoned, let alone casual, readers of Thomas could not have foreseen. It is an exercise in autobiographical writing, but of a highly unusual kind.

Indeed, so unusual a text is it that it seems especially resistant to categorization. Once one has got beyond the stage of excitedly regarding it (in conjunction with *Neb*) as an invaluable quarry of materials relating directly to Thomas's life, and of consequently exploiting it as a rare resource (since he had always been so notoriously reticent about himself),[1] one is likely to begin noting the peculiarity of the terms in which Thomas has chosen to construct his narrative of the self, and to ponder the significance of the methods he has adopted. His text, for instance, consists of a series of pairings of prose and poetry, the former invariably printed on the left-hand page and the latter facing it on the right, with each pair jointly devoted to a consideration of the 'same' period, or occasion, or experience in his life. Frequently, the prose is beautifully crafted and cunningly moulded, so that in some cases it is difficult for a reader to understand in what respect precisely, except for the style of its layout, the prose discourse differs from the poetic discourse. There are many instances, particularly in the prose, when Thomas speaks of himself in the third person (as he does throughout his 'official' autobiography, *Neb*). And although the complete text comprises a chronological narrative tracing the whole course of Thomas's life, from the womb (literally) down to the period of his composing the book, the materials included are selective in ways that are sometimes disconcerting: for instance, very little is revealed about his marriage or his family life, until those enchanting sections very late in the collection that constitute such a wonderfully loving tribute to his first wife.[2]

Any serious attempt, then, to address the autobiographical character of *The Echoes Return Slow* has carefully to consider, and to account for, key features such as these; and it would also be advisable to resist the pressing invitation to offer a purely psychological reading of the text. My suggestion, to be developed in this essay, is that crucial to our under-standing of *The Echoes Return Slow* is the realization that Thomas conceives of the self as essentially a *spiritual* rather than a psychological category. Consequently, the true history of one's self is bound, for him, to take the form of *spiritual autobiography*. But just as his religious poems reflect, in their every aspect, the problem of finding an authentic contemporary means (involving language, style, form) of conveying the complex conditions and the distinctive 'style' of modern belief, so too does his autobiography address the problem of how to develop a contemporary discourse appropriate for exploring the concept (so alien and unsympathetic to modern minds) of the intrinsically spiritual character of the self. It is true that spiritual autobiography is an ancient, sophisticated, and distinguished 'literary' genre, and that as such it would seem to provide modern writers with a great variety of models and templates. But the same is true of the great genre of religious poetry, and yet, as we know, Thomas (although highly appreciative of past achieve-ments) felt compelled, by the very uniqueness of the contemporary situation, to depart from precedent and to embark on a course of radical innovation. And it is the same compulsion, deriving from the same circumstances, that caused him to experiment with unconventional means of narrating the self.

What he is particularly concerned to register – by ensuring it is inscribed in his very discourse – is the way that any valid modern concep-tion of the spiritual self is bound to take very substantially into account those aspects of the development of personal identity that have been so notably identified by such ostensibly 'secular' modern disciplines as psychology and sociology. Thus *The Echoes Return Slow* is careful, for instance, to explore those earliest relations with mother, father and nurturing environment that, it has now become accepted, significantly influence the development of selfhood. Moreover, those relations are, in turn, understood as having been significantly influenced by the specific time and place (the historical culture) within which they operated. This interpenetration of the personal and the extra-personal, an interaction that produces the historical and social components of individual existence, is subtly registered in the prose when Thomas recalls his young parents' first home in Cardiff:

> A scrubbed door-step, clean enough to be defiled by the day's droppings, circulars, newspapers. A threshold of war, unbeknown to the young couple, the child-planners . . .
>
> (*ERS*, 4)

Here the doubling process, by means of which Thomas keeps the radical dualities of existence in sight throughout the volume, takes the form of a sort of extended pun, to which our attention is drawn by a pointed parallelism of phrasing. The scrubbed doorstep is also the threshold of war: the new home, and the marriage it houses, is about to be 'defiled', and redefined, by world conflict. The poem that 'corresponds' to this prose passage contrasts almost violently with it in tone. The foreboding that is controlled by irony in the passage about Cardiff is transposed into a very different key in a poem that recalls the rawness of a primal scream:

> The scales fell from my eyes,
> and I saw faces. I screamed
> at the ineffectuality
> of love to protect me.
>
> (*ERS*, 5)

This change in key corresponds to a change in the very category of the experience being 'recalled'. Whereas the prose is concerned with violence as an aspect of history, the poem is concerned with violence as the naked 'face' of existence per se; a view of life as consisting of what Thomas powerfully calls 'Pain's climate' (*ERS*, 2). And in 'seeing' this, the child (or rather the baby) ironically sees more, and sees further, than do the 'child-planners' themselves.

Prose and poetry are brought together, and used in tandem, here as throughout the volume, in order to explore the multi-dimensional character of a self that relates to time in an extremely complex fashion. 'Time's changeling' (*ERS*, 3) is Thomas's own arresting phrase for this. 'I have no name: / time's changeling . . .'; the phrase thus circumstanced *becomes* the name (that is, identity) he gives himself. It has several ramifications of meaning, which are rendered both as styles of living and as styles of writing in *The Echoes Return Slow*. 'Changeling' can obviously be understood as the noun-form of an adjective such as 'changeable' or 'changeful' – that is, as expressing the mutability to which the self is 'subject', both in the sense of its being helplessly affected (if not effected) by change and in the opposite sense of the self's being itself the author of its own restless changes. Therefore the pejorative meaning of 'changeling' (as the OED reminds us) is a waverer, or turncoat – a name for himself which Thomas contemptuously adopts at several points in *The Echoes Return Slow* ('A will of iron, perforated / by indecision' (p. 59)). And as the dictionary further points out, 'changeling' can also mean 'half-wit', a construction that Thomas seems to be recalling when, in the very poem that follows the one in which he characterizes himself as 'time's changeling', he speaks of his infant self as exhibiting in a photograph:

> A dislocation of mind:
> love photographed
> the imbecility of
> my expression and framed it.
> (*ERS*, 5)

Of the many equivocations of meaning in these lines (as in virtually every passage in *The Echoes Return Slow*) it is the play in the opening phrase that at this point repays attention. 'Dislocation' means, of course, to 'displace', as well as to wrench out of joint, and as such it points up the sense in which the dislocation of mind (like the 'imbecility' with which it has been made cognate) may be understood as the result of the violent removal of the self from its true place and the resiting of it in a bewilderingly, painfully alien situation. And that conveniently brings us to the final meaning of the word 'changeling', namely that of a fairy baby surreptitiously exchanged for a human child. Used in that sense, 'time's changeling' implies that the self may be understood as not really belonging in, or to, the temporal order – that is, as being, instead, the child of eternity foisted onto, and abandoned to the care of, unsuspecting time.

Understood in these several senses, 'time's changeling' is a wonderfully suggestive, compressed definition of the 'existential' self, that concept whose currency in modern theological discussion still owes so much to the profound experimental work undertaken by Kierkegaard, a thinker known to have been important for Thomas.[3] And although *The Echoes*

Return Slow is by no means to be understood as systematically Kierkegaardian in its approach to the life-history of the self, our reading of it is, I would suggest, likely to be enhanced by an awareness of certain of the Danish thinker's modes of apprehending personal existence.

In the opening passage of *The Sickness Unto Death*, Kierkegaard writes as follows: 'Man is spirit. But what is spirit? Spirit is the self. But what is the self? The self is a relation which relates itself to its own self.'[4] This concept of the spiritual self as actually existing only in, and as, a process of self-relating seems relevant to the very way in which *The Echoes Return Slow* emerges out of the interrelating of prose and poetry. Kierkegaard has partly in mind the kind of incessant internal conversations, infinitely recessive in character, that constitute human consciousness even as understood in exclusively secular terms. But even in that connection, his definition of 'relation' differs from the ordinary, as has been noted by H. A. Nielsen:

> the underlying relation to myself that constitutes me a human self is not the presence or potential of inward dialogue *per se*, much less any of the transitory relations we noted before, but rather those parts or threads of the dialogue which deal with matters of what I really think it is worth to have a human life, what I privately judge it is worth to me to have *this* one. The rest of my self-dialogue will doubtless concern some important matters amongst the trivial, but the part of the dialogue Kierkegaard seems to want to isolate and later X-ray concerns in a rather narrow sense how I in my uttermost privacy feel about being the one I am.[5]

Some such concept of the kind of self-relating which truly constitutes the self seems to me to underlie R. S. Thomas's chosen mode of proceeding in *The Echoes Return Slow*, and to account for such features as its manifest selectivity, its compression of style (in the prose almost as much as in the poetry) and the *kind* of privacy to which it so movingly gives us access. Thomas successfully devises strategies for 'committing his silence to paper', as he puts it (*ERS*, 48), and for thus safeguarding the integrity of his inwardness even in the process of making it public. But then his best poetry is not infrequently felt to be a kind of precipitate of silence.

But Kierkegaard specifically denies that the self, in his sense of the term, is susceptible of purely secular definition. For all its subtleties, such a view of the self is bound, for him, to remain a simplistic one – a view he characterizes as so blithely one-dimensional as to amount to no more than the redundant definition of the self as the 'I–am–I'. Such simplification may include immense complexities of psychological (and psychoanalytical) analysis revealing the multi-layered, multi-faceted and virtually unfathomable nature of the self. But simplification it nevertheless remains, since the self viewed in secular terms – even the radically fractured and dispersed self of postmodernist writers – is considered as essentially homogeneous, that is, as wholly belonging to a single category of existence. Kierkegaard, by contrast, sees the self as profoundly paradoxical in its ontological character, precisely because its very existence is a logical impossibility, compounded as it is of those two mutually incompatible states, eternity and time. And the compound self truly discovers itself (that is, it discovers this fundamental aspect of itself) only when it enters into the relationship with God that brings it into being as an 'individual'.

Viewed in this context, *The Echoes Return Slow* might appropriately be subtitled 'an autobiography of an individual', since the book has been constructed in the very image of a self that knows itself as belonging simultaneously to the temporal and the eternal. It is with the self as the continuous, and necessarily paradoxical, product of *this* 'relation' that the volume is primarily concerned. As Wyschogrod has pointed out, this state of 'relating', which is the inescapable existential state of the compound self, generates pathos precisely 'because of the basic incommensurability of [its] ontological ingredients'.[6] In order to reproduce that pathos, Thomas needs faithfully to render the temporal conditions that, paradoxically, provide the spiritual self with the very terms of its existence. In eternity, all will be reconciled, but not in time, which is the realm not of being but of existence:

> When all things are accomplished providence rests in consummation; when all things are accomplished the atonement comes to rest in equilibrium, but they do not *exist*. Faith is therefore the anticipation of the eternal which holds the factors together, the cleavages of existence.[7]

So, in *The Echoes Return Slow*, birth itself is imaged as a reluctant coming to life: 'The marks in the spirit would not heal. The dream would recur, groping his way up to the light, coming to the crack too narrow to squeeze through' (*ERS*, 2). But are we offered historical fact here, or existential myth? After all, one of the inescapable aspects of life in time is that time present denies us full and immediate access to time past. The deliberate acts of recollection that constitute the act of autobiography, of writing the self, are themselves inevitably compromised as to their 'truth' by this fact. Or perhaps we should rather say that in Thomas's view, autobiography's only legitimate *raison d'être* is its search (however ultimately self-defeating) for the kind of 'truth' about the self that is available only on these equivocal existential terms.

Accordingly, he finds ways of dramatizing these very terms, in order to foreground the paradoxical nature of his undertaking. So, for instance, the 'interference' of present with past, the positive aspect of which is maturity of judgement, is part of the point Thomas has 'in mind' when recalling an early occasion of 'Gathering mushrooms by the light of the moon':

> The clouds towered. Their shape was prophetic, but there were no prophets. Through long hours, inhaling the dust that was not injurious, he was prepared with a minimum of effort on the part of himself to 'satisfy the examiners'.
>
> (*ERS*, 10)

Here, the way in which the detonation of the atom bomb irrevocably altered mankind's whole way of seeing the world, including personal memory of a past ostensibly wholly unconnected with that event, is shown also to have involved an alteration of language itself: 'mushroom' and 'dust' are words that can no longer be used in the ways they once could when Thomas was that child. (Such an emphasis is cognate with Geoffrey Hill's observation that etymology is the record of language's fall from innocence, and a synecdoche of humanity's fall from grace.) Thus inscribed in language itself is the fact that recollection is, unavoidably, retrospection. Similarly, when Thomas writes at one point, while remembering the early phase of the Second World War, 'The innocent [that is, himself] could not believe the robin could whistle in deaf ears. Its breast should have been his warning' (*ERS*, 18), he is seeing the robin retrospectively in the light of the bombing of Liverpool, when 'Skies [became] red where no / sun had ever risen / or set' (*ERS*, 19). Again, when he recalls his eventual move to Manafon, and thus to the hill country he had previously viewed only from a nostalgic distance, he writes as follows:

> What had been blue shadows on a longed-for horizon, traced on an inherited background, were shown in time to contain this valley, this village and a church built with stones from the river, where the rectory stood, plangent as a mahogany piano.
>
> (*ERS*, 24)

In this context – that of a prose which is constantly advertising its doubleness of meaning – the phrase 'were shown in time' seems to imply not only 'were shown in due course' but also 'were shown in truth, that is, in that aspect which was theirs in time'. The implication is that the human mind, constantly yearning for escape from the limits and limitations of the temporal (Kierkegaard's 'despair of finitude') is always liable to dream of some place, somewhere, where the operation of such conditions may virtually be suspended. For Thomas, as for Kierkegaard, true existence becomes possible only when such a dream is abandoned ('the despair of infinitude'), and the self is awakened to its paradoxical state as 'shown in time'.

Elsewhere in *The Echoes Return Slow*, the hybrid nature of memory is considered under the more general rubric of the relativity that inescapably characterizes all human acts of comprehension. This is given simple parabolic expression in a poem (deliberately written in the form of a children's story) about the sailors' view of shore from ship and of the children's view of ship from shore (*ERS*, 9). Pondering his own relation to his childhood self as he stands on the Llŷn peninsula, gazing over and back at his native Anglesey, Thomas ruefully notes that 'One headland looks at another headland. What one sees must depend on where one stands, when one stands' (*ERS*, 70). And the accompanying poem brings out the pun in that ostensibly innocent geographical expression, 'headland':

> How shallow the minds
>
> they played by! Not like mine
> now, this dark pool I
> lean over on that same
> headland, knowing it wrinkled
>
> by time's wind, putting my hand
> down, groping with bleeding
> fingers, for truths too
> frightening to be brought up.
> (*ERS*, 71)

If the prose appears, however briefly, to be leaving a door open to belief in the mere relativity, and equal (in)validity of all judgements, then the poem very firmly closes it. Emphasize relativity though Thomas may as a textual strategy for highlighting the self-limiting character of the existential self, he does not mean to imply that all judgements are thereby rendered essentially nugatory. Indeed, from the beginning of *The Echoes Return Slow* he is very particularly concerned to establish the difference between the true and the false, and throughout the volume he remains deeply troubled by the inexhaustible resourcefulness of human beings (including himself) when it comes to practising deception and self-deception. It is an issue beautifully imaged in the picture of himself as a child aboard his father's ship during the First World War, whiling away the time while his parents enjoyed themselves:

> I lay in a bunk while they feasted, turning and turning the glossed pages. The cockroaches should have been a reminder. The shadows from which they crawled were as dark as those where the submarines lurked.
>
> (*ERS*, 6)

Those pages he read were therefore more than 'glossy'; they were 'glossed' in the sense that they were specifically designed to deflect the attention away from the truth by providing the mind with a false textual gloss on events. Thomas's sceptical view of the world – particularly the adult world – recurs throughout the volume, and he frequently focuses on the way language is routinely used to mislead: 'The war to end all wars! After "the hostilities were over", the return to cross-channel' (*ERS*, 8).

What is becoming clear, then, from the above considerations is that for Thomas the act of personal recollection is truly legitimate only when it involves a considered act of understanding, which in turn involves the fullest possible judgement of the self by the self, conducted in the light of its existential experience of its paradoxical state and of its acknowledgement that human apprehension (even the self's apprehension of itself and its history) is, in every instance, fundamentally flawed and narrowly circumscribed. For him, memory is most consequential when it is deliberate, not least in the sense of being the product of those profound acts of deliberation that the paradoxes of existence demand. And it is this measured, considered mode of remembering that Thomas emphasizes through the deliberateness of the composition of his text, regardless of whether it is prose or poetry. Yet, in order for it to retain its existential integrity and authenticity, such deliberation must be constantly qualified, and redeemed, by the humility of uncertainty, an uncertainty with regard both to the finality of judgement, and to the (unreliable) language in which that judgement has to be couched. So, Thomas's writing is constantly destabilizing itself, taking rigidity out of its firmness, and taking the simple firmness out of its affirmations. This is done both through the interplay between the sometimes contrasting discourses of prose and poetry, and through the play of meaning within each of those discourses taken singly. As a simple example, consider parts of the early passage in which Thomas recalls his family's move from

England, and the various ports at which his father had been based, to live
permanently in Holyhead:

> After 'the hostilities were over', the return to cross-channel. So many hours
> at sea, so many more on shore. The salt waters were spat into from Welsh
> mouths.
>
> (*ERS*, 8)

What sort of estimation is being made, in that last sentence, of Holyhead?
It is surely ambiguous. There may be wry affection in it, as Thomas notes
with amusement that *every* aspect of 'home', including the most banal or
unattractive, is liable to have its charms. But the sentence may also be read
as comical, since it is comical to suppose that the sea could care what
nationality was the mouth that was self-importantly spitting into it. Thus
understood, the sentence may be regarded as a comment on the pre-
sumptuousness of human beings, who make so much of distinctions that
are meaningless in a cosmic perspective. But the sentence may also be felt
to be sardonic and satirical in tone: what do the Welsh do to the sea but
spit into it with the ineffectuality that typifies the nation? Even the slightly
unusual readjustment of customary phrasing ('from Welsh mouths' rather
than 'by Welsh mouths') seems to have been determined by a wish to hint
at the distance a Welsh spitter is careful to place between himself and the
sea. Or is it rather intended to emphasize the self-conscious separation of
the human from the realm of the non-human?

Such equivocations of meaning, or multiple suggestiveness, abound in
both prose and poetry in *The Echoes Return Slow*. Indeed, they may
safely be said to be part of the *raison d'être* of the text, and to be what
the text is carefully composed to produce. The results can be disturbingly
powerful, as when Thomas speaks of his first curacy:

> So he was ordained to conduct death, its shabby orchestra of sniffs and
> tears; the Church renowned for its pianissimo in brash scores.
>
> (*ERS*, 16)

The puns here on 'ordained' and 'conduct' are many, and between them
the meanings range with profound resonance over such issues as fate and
free will, authorization and its relations to authority, the human being in
the priest and the priest in the human being, ritual and its potential for
both revelation and deception.

It is, then, in these potent terms that the text in *The Echoes Return
Slow* is always very evidently a composition, not least in being a careful

composite of past and present, of feeling and judicious reflection. As we have seen, in order for it to be genuinely responsive to both the elements that constitute these, and other, dualities, the text needs to take doubleness upon itself, and it is to this end that Thomas avails himself of both prose and poetry. His use of these modes is, however, extremely flexible. They can be interchangeable in function, and sometimes he deliberately minimizes the difference between them, as if to stress that what they have in common – their compositional character – is more important than what separates them. At other times, however, he capitalizes on the different effects of which they are respectively capable, since that allows him to maintain his double vision.

For Thomas, as for Kierkegaard, double vision is all when one is dealing with the human, spiritual, self. And just as doubleness is inscribed everywhere in his text (as pun, parallelism, contrast, dialogue, dialectic, and so on), so too is it explicitly addressed by the text as a psycho-spiritual phenomenon. No wonder Thomas is attracted to the little owl, 'Athene noctua', who may be 'too small for wisdom' (as, in a sense, Thomas feels himself to be), but who, unlike the grander barn owl, is active both night and day: 'at night it was lyrical, its double note sounded under the stars in counterpoint to the fall of the waves' (*ERS*, 78). In such an act of counterpointing, doubleness dizzyingly redoubles itself. But what is playfully, affectionately, touched upon here is considered altogether differently elsewhere. So, for instance, the agony of human consciousness, which derives from its awareness of itself – that consciousness of self that constitutes the very being of the human self – is rendered in a poem depicting man as dancing to the music of time played by 'The piper with the thin lips':

> I only

> look at him as I dance,
> shaming him with the operation
> on the intelligence of
> a creature without anaesthetic.
>   (*ERS*, 99)

Even in an instance as anguished as this, however, Thomas might be understood by some as being essentially concerned only with the secular aspects of human doubleness. For those concerned to identify the specifically spiritual aspects of that condition as registered in *The Echoes Return Slow*, certain comments by Kierkegaard may again prove useful.

In the following passage from his *Journals* Kierkegaard is considering the kind of double-mindedness that for him constitutes the highest mode of self-consciousness:

> Most men are blunted I's. What was given us by nature as a possibility of being sharpened to an I is quickly blunted to a third person (like Baron Münchhausen's dog, a greyhound which wore down its legs and became a dachshund).
> It is quite a different matter to be related objectively to one's own subjectivity.
> Take Socrates: he is not third-personal in the sense that he avoids danger of exposing himself and risking his life, as one would do if one were third-personal and not I. Not at all. But in the midst of danger he is related objectively to his own personality, and at the moment when he is condemned to death he speaks of the condemnation as though he were a third person. He is subjectivity raised to the second power, he is related to objectivity as a true poet wishes to be related to his poetic production: this is the objectivity with which he is related to his own subjectivity. This is a work of art. Otherwise one gets either an objective something, an objective stick of furniture which is supposed to be a man, or a hotch-potch of casual and arbitrary happenings. But to be related objectively to one's own subjectivity is the real task.[8]

It is, I think, useful – and, I believe, proper – to see R. S. Thomas as attempting, by several means, in *The Echoes Return Slow* to relate objectively to his own subjectivity. He can only do so dialectically, that is, by ensuring that both the move towards objectivity and the equal but opposite impulse towards subjectivity are held together in tension, thus preventing the objective from becoming the blandly impersonal and the subjective from becoming mere self-indulgence. The coexistence of both, maintained by an interaction between them, guarantees the authentic spiritual qualities of each. And the alternation between prose and poetry is one (but not the only) essential textual means by which this dialectic is created and preserved.

The way in which prose and poetry interact to this end constantly changes. Any example must, therefore, be a partial one. Allowing for that, however, the following instance may give some indication, at least, of the way in which the process seems to work. Both texts are printed complete, so that the full effect of juxtaposing/combining/contrasting them may be judged:

> Memento mori! But he was young for death. Was the sea calling him on or back? It was a false voice in the trees. Bad days were when three herring-

gulls cried above the valley; or when a shepherd in the high moors said:
You can almost smell the sea to-day. From different motives he assumed a
cure, where that same sound was no longer a trick of the wind, but real
waves on the bar a few miles to the west. He was reminded all too soon
that journeying is not necessarily in the right direction.

> The wrong prayers for the right
> reason? The flesh craves
> what the intelligence
> renounces. Concede
>
> the Amens. With the end
> nowhere, the travelling
> all, how better to get
> there than on one's knees?
>
> (*ERS*, 44–5)

The prose in this instance is deliberately discursive in style, the poem
deliberately elliptical. The prose plays with the idea of sententiousness –
at first rejecting it, through its ironic discounting of 'Memento mori!',
but then quietly assuming the very manner of moralising, of emblem-
atizing the personal and blazoning it as representative, that it had begun
by repudiating. And, of course, the past self is spoken of, rather than for,
in the third person. It is thus re-viewed in the perspectives of both
morality and eternity, its significance thereby being both diminished and
enlarged; diminished by its being reduced to a 'case', and set in a context
that denies it centrality, yet enlarged, or amplified, by its being connected
to universals. The poem, by contrast, is written in the language and
grammar of actual existential experience, and gives us the self agonistes,
through lines that seem to be bent and buckled at their right-hand
margins by the pressure of feeling to which they are almost palpably
subject. The ellipses, like those in Emily Dickinson's poems, belong to an
urgently compressed and curtailed style of mental notation, the poetic
equivalent of the stammered morse code of a mind in the midst of
spiritual emergency.

The main point, however, is that for Thomas autobiography becomes
spiritually authentic only when the history of the self is written
simultaneously in *both* these styles, in a fashion that is consequently both
objective and subjective. And in allowing him to write like this, the
prose–poetry combination also allows him to explore a related concern,
namely the inexhaustibly mysterious question of the origins of poetry,
and of its status as a cognitive instrument. Indeed, it would not be too

much to claim that as well as being specifically a spiritual autobiography, *The Echoes Return Slow* is also necessarily, and not merely incidentally or contingently, a *poet's* autobiography, one of the subjects of which must be the distinctive modus vivendi of a poet's mind. As we read the book, this subject is likely to take the form of a whole nexus of interrelated comments and questions: how on earth did the circumstances and experiences recorded for this period in the prose give rise to *this* poem? Who would have thought that *this* poem would find its point of origin *there*? In what way, if at all, does it make sense to claim that this poem is commensurate with that experience? Is it the prose that, in this instance, is a sort of afterthought, a doubtfully appropriate gloss on the experience of the kind with which Thomas has been particularly taken in the marginal comments to Coleridge's 'The Ancient Mariner'?[9] Or could it be that the poem belies the actual experience, in the interests of intensifying it?

These questions, and many, many more, are likely to come to mind as one reads. And the result is not only that one discovers what a penetrating autobiography of a poet *The Echoes Return Slow* is, but also that one appreciates how, for Thomas, the mystery of poetry is a significant aspect of the mystery of the existential spiritual self. It reveals, once more, the strangely compound character of that self, the ways in which it is, as it were, radically inconsistent with itself, and consists of experiences that coexist yet are incommensurate with each other. One of the sections based on his period at Eglwys-fach brings this out with particular sharpness:

The highway ran through the parish. The main line ran through the parish. Yet there were green turnings, unecclesiastical aisles up which he could walk to the celebration of the marriage of mind and nature. Otters swam in the dykes. Wild geese and wild swans came to winter in the rush-growing meadows. He hummed an air from Tchaikovsky quietly to himself. Yet on still days the air was as clerestories in which the overtones of gossiping voices would not fade.

(ERS, 58)

Several of these sentences seem already to be aspiring to the condition of poetry. There seems to be a poem here struggling to get out, so that it would seem natural for it to be allowed to materialize, to realize itself, on the adjoining page. Instead of which, the prose is followed by one of the most blistering of Thomas's poems of self-accusation, 'A will of iron, perforated / by indecision. A charity / that, beginning at home, / ended in domestication' (*ERS*, 59), and so on in a bitterly witty litany of self-indictment. What has happened is that those 'gossiping voices' that made themselves heard in the concluding sentence of the prose have taken full, malevolent, possession of that part of Thomas's mind, and self, from which poems come. But then, through the response to those voices that is the poem itself, Thomas turns destructive criticism into a devastatingly creative act of self-evaluation. It is a striking example of how poetry does not necessarily originate in the 'poetic', and of how, in Thomas's case, it is most likely to emerge from the most spirit-haunted recesses of himself. That the result may as often be a poetry of radiance as of darkness is beautifully illustrated in the conjunction of texts that relate to his period in Manafon:

> How far can one trust autumn thoughts? Against the deciduousness of man there stand art, music, poetry. The Church was the great patron of such. Why should a country church not hear something of the overtones of a cathedral? As an antidote to Ancient and Modern, why not Byrd and Marcello? But was winter the best time?
>
> (*ERS*, 30)

The poem comes as an answer to that question, and may even be read as Thomas's distinctive response to Wallace Stevens's famous observation that 'one must have a mind of winter':[10]

> It was winter. The church shone.
> The musicians played on
> through the snow, their strings sang
> sharper than robins in the lighted interior.
>
> From outside the white
> face of the land stared in
> with all the hunger of nature
> in it for what it could not digest.
>
> (*ERS*, 31)

In this case, the poem becomes a means of revealing a potential in 'winter' that had previously been hidden, and in the process comes to stand for a state of mind, or condition of self, that can scarcely be made available in, or by, prose. Poetry here powerfully instances the kind of insights that, as the prose concedes, are possible only in art. And art is shown to speak to art, and to inspire it, as the poem here becomes the only form of words that can, in any adequate sense, conform to music.

The poem also, in this instance, becomes an affecting example of that spiritual effect which Kierkegaard characterized as 'repetition'. By this he meant a special kind of sameness-in-difference, the recovery of spiritual understanding from the past, in a way that transfigures the present and transposes it to an entirely different pitch of understanding. Or rather, to use the terms Thomas himself chooses to employ in these passages, 'repetition' is the way in which the mind – for instance, in great art – can miraculously acquire the kind of permanence of insight that the very 'deciduousness' (impermanence, mutability) of man paradoxically makes possible.

'Repetition' is, then, an experience of the self which is both the opposite and necessary complement of what I earlier called 'deliberation'. Whereas 'deliberation' is likely implicitly to value the present above the past, and thus to view the self's progress through time as growth and development, 'repetition' instead views the self as ceaselessly working in effect to stand still, to stand by what was, and is, best. These, along with several other models of the self's existence in time – models that represent a portfolio of possibilities for autobiographical writing, variant readings of the act of writing the self – are consciously entertained and implemented in *The Echoes Return Slow*. (These include instances where the metaphor of space is used for exploring man's situation in time.) And the very title itself, if we refer back to the poem in the volume that gives rise to it, carries several very interesting connotations in this connection. It occurs in a moving poem about visiting the elderly:

> They keep me sober,
> the old ladies
> stiff in their beds,
> mostly with pale eyes
> wintering me.
> Some are like blonde dolls
> their joints twisted;
> life in its brief play
> was a bit rough.
> Some fumble
> with thick tongue for words,
> and are deaf;
> shouting their faint names
> I listen;
> they are far off,
> the echoes return slow.

But without them,
without the subdued light
their smiles kindle,
I would have gone wild,
drinking earth's huge draughts
of joy and woe.

                                                                (*ERS*, 63)

The need for patience when listening for what life – one's own and that of
others – has got to say about its past; the slowness of the self to answer to
any single name, however intimate; the need to use the past as a kind of
tuning fork to keep the present in a sober key; these, and other meanings
important for our understanding of Thomas's way of practising
autobiography, emerge from the poem. But there is also more, which
appears if one takes this poem in conjunction with the prose passage that
accompanies it. There Thomas bleakly notes: 'There is no cure for old
age. And the old tend to be sick. When one should be leading them on to
peer into the future, one is drawn back by them into the past' (*ERS*, 62).
Echo, then, has got its distinctly narcissistic features.[11] Autobiography
may mean no more than an orgy of remembering indulged in so that,
replete with the past, the self may complacently sleep out that future
which leads to eternity. In his pseudonymous work on *Repetition*,
Kierkegaard has Constantine Constantius observe:

> When existence has been circumnavigated, it will be manifest whether one
> has the courage to understand that life is a repetition and has the desire to
> rejoice in it. The person who has not circumnavigated life before beginning
> to live will never live; the person who circumnavigated it but became
> satiated had a poor constitution; the person who chose repetition – he
> lives. He does not run about like a boy chasing butterflies or stand on
> tiptoe to look for the glories of the world, for he knows them. Neither does
> he sit like an old woman turning the spinning wheel of recollection, but
> calmly goes his way, happy in repetition.[12]

It is *against* 'the spinning wheel[s] of recollection', those other, familiar,
versions of autobiography – narrating the progress of the self, or con-
fidently recalling its experiences – that *The Echoes Return Slow* is
written. Attention has already been drawn to some of the means by
which Thomas deliberately avoids falling into this pattern, but there are
many others that, were there space, could be considered. Of these, some
of the most obvious – such as his keeping death constantly in mind, and

his extended exploration, through the image of the sea, of life as the neighbourhood of eternity – are also probably the most important.

The figure of time that particularly fascinated R. S. Thomas was that of the circle, as one might perhaps have expected, given that his poetic career had turned (monotonously, as some would have it) around his own seemingly obsessive return not only to particular subjects (Iago Prytherch, the hidden god) but to the repertoire of phrases and tropes that were, for him, inseparable from those inescapable concerns. *The Echoes Return Slow* is in many ways modelled on that figure, with Thomas even reflecting on the way his career as priest had brought him circling back to near his original point of departure ('For some there is no future but the one that is safeguarded by a return to the past' (*ERS*, 66)). It is appropriate, therefore, that his last published essay should have taken the form of a meditative circling around the epigraph to David Jones's *The Anathémata*: 'It was a dark and stormy night, we sat by the calcined wall; it was said to the tale-teller, tell us a tale, and the tale ran thus: it was a dark and stormy night'.[13] And as epigraph to that essay he printed a poem that itself echoes (or redoubles) many of the concerns of *The Echoes Return Slow*:

> We asked our questions and passed
> on. The answer, discovered
> by others, was to a different question.
> Yet they, too, had the feeling
> of having been here before.
> We are our own ghosts, haunting
> and haunted. We live out a dream,
> unable to equate the face
> with the owner, the voice
> with the speaker, the singer
> with the song. Ah, how we thought
> science would deliver us, when
> all it has done is to set us
> circling a little more swiftly
> about a self that is an echo.
>
> (*DJ*, 153)

The phrases correspond to, and in a sense with, those in *The Echoes Return Slow*, when Thomas speaks of how 'The spirit revolves / on itself and is without / shadow', before proceeding to twin that spiritual movement with the biological movement of 'the twin helix / where the dancing chromosomes / pass one another back / to back to a tune from the abyss' (*ERS*, 109). It is in the echoing coexistence of those two movements – the one seemingly self-determined, the other seemingly determining 'the self' – that Thomas sees the paradox of 'existence', and it is on this paradox that he meditates both in *The Echoes Return Slow* and in the David Jones essay.

In the latter, he notes the fatalism of writers such as Hardy and Yeats, and historians such as Spengler and Toynbee, who believe that 'the same elements, the same characters recur and must go on doing so in accordance with some mysterious but inexorable law' (*DJ*, 155). Although Thomas is in so many ways very deeply drawn, by his own inclination towards pessimism, to such a conclusion himself, he nevertheless resists it, fortified by the observation that exact repetition – of the kind that is significantly called 'mechanical' – is totally impossible for human beings. By way of illustration he invokes examples such as Borges's celebrated story of Pierre Ménard's rewriting of *Don Carlos* and the alteration of meaning by 'repetition' of identical phrases in Beckett's *Krapp's Last Tape*. Of particular significance, though, is the way in which a case of 'repetition' may involve not just an alteration of meaning but a change to a completely different category of experience, a completely different order/conception of 'reality'. Repetition thus becomes radically recreative, and profoundly revealing of the truth that a human being is, in Sir Thomas Browne's celebrated phrase, a great amphibian, existing (simultaneously) in several entirely different elements.

In being recreative, repetition is necessarily a fiction (even when it goes under the name of 'history', or even, perhaps, 'science'), but then fiction, as the Latinist in Thomas knows and points out, comes from 'Fingo, fingere – to fashion, to form' (*DJ*, 158). At root, therefore, it does not mean 'falsehood', but rather a particular 'form' of understanding and truth. And in this 'form', human beings may not only gain access to their own paradoxical nature as existing beings, time's changelings, but may also, as Coleridge famously put it, echo the creative act of the primary imagination. While very willing to admit that, in his time, it is science that has proved the most revelatory of our 'fictions', our creative acts, Thomas ends his essay by doubting whether 'the only truth in life is that which can be repeated by experiment' (*DJ*, 159). He is therefore attracted to the scientific 'truth' 'that as the electrons whirl about their nucleus at dizzying speeds, one will suddenly leap into a new orbit' (*DJ*, 159). This, one might suggest, is also a metaphor for that leap of faith undertaken by Thomas, the move towards a belief that God's grace can shift a human life 'into a new orbit'. And, as recent commentators have stressed, Kierkegaard's conception of 'repetition' was itself a version of that very same belief.[14]

If, then, the Thomas of *The Echoes Return Slow* is 'time's changeling', he is also, to adopt his own phrase for 'D.J'. (David Jones), 'time's disc jockey', commenting through his 'fictions', his compositions of prose and poetry, on the many revolutions of his own life. Repetition – in the ordinary sense of the word – is, as *The Echoes Return Slow* illustrates, the 'form' that autobiography must inevitably take, but Thomas's work obviously emphasizes, and fetishizes, that structural characteristic of recall and recollection, not least by repeating, in poetry, the 'prose' version of a past period or event. He thus underlines the fact that autobiography is always a self-fashioning; always ('Fingo, fingere') a fiction. The existential implications of this rhetorical strategy have already been explored earlier in this essay: it is an attempt to conceive of the self as an 'individual', in Kierkegaard's sense of that term. What now, finally, remains to be suggested is that the strategy can also be understood as signifying the central drama of Thomas's effort at self-understanding, the struggle within him between a fatalistic acknowledgement of the law of recurrence and a belief in the redemptive possibility of 'repetition', in the Kierkegaardian sense.

'Towards the end of one's life, towards the end of the century; worse still towards the end of the millennium, the tempter approaches us as desperation' (*ERS*, 110). The temptation to despair of any possibility, in his own representative case, of the amendment of self was always strong in Thomas, and in the last phase of his life was powerfully expressed through the fateful metaphor of the furies: not only was *No Truce with the Furies* the title of his last published collection; the furies recur as an avenging metaphor in several of the late poems that remain in manuscript. No wonder he had been so drawn to Coleridge's 'The Ancient Mariner' that he had in significant part modelled *The Echoes Return Slow* on that poem about a lost soul condemned to the endless repetition of his terrible autobiographical story. But he concluded his last published essay with an affirmation of the Christian promise 'of an [*sic*] new sphere for the purified soul', recalling Christ's salvific words: 'let him that heareth say "Come". And let him that is athirst come; And whosoever will, let him take the water of life freely' (*DJ*, 159). Perhaps the most rapturous image in *The Echoes Return Slow* of Thomas taking that water is that in which he registers the experience of offering, and receiving, communion:

He lifted

the chalice, that crystal in
which love questioning is love
blinded with excess of light.
          (*ERS*, 69)

But if that is the most intense of those moments when life is transfigured by grace, the most moving and sustained occur in the final pages of *Echoes* when the word 'love' is repeated, not simply within a single line as in the above quotation, but in each of the last two poems, in which Thomas registers that he also is 'in the debt of love' (*ERS*, 119).

One of the books which R. S. Thomas particularly admired was George Steiner's *Real Presences*, in which the following passage occurs:

> Serious painting, music, literature or sculpture make palpable to us, as do no other means of communication, the unassuaged, unhoused instability and estrangement of our condition. We are, at key instants, strangers to ourselves, errant at the gates of our own psyche. We knock blindly at the doors of turbulence, of creativity, of inhibition within the *terra incognita* of our own selves.[15]

The Echoes Return Slow is compelling because it is serious in exactly this way, and so possesses the precious strength that Steiner definitively recognizes:

> Beyond the strength of any other act of witness, literature and the arts tell of the obstinacies of the impenetrable, of the absolutely alien which we come up against in the labyrinth of intimacy . . . It is poetics, in the full sense, which informs us of the visitor's visa in place and in time which defines our status as transients in a house of being whose foundations, whose future history, whose rationale – if any – lie wholly outside our will and comprehension. It is the capacity of the arts . . . to make us, if not at home, at least alertly, answerably peregrine in the unhousedness of our human circumstance.
>
> (*Real Presences*, 139–40)

But it is Kierkegaard who, perhaps, best captures the challenge Thomas set himself in *The Echoes Return Slow* and thus best enables us to appreciate the measure of his achievement in this, one of his most remarkable volumes:

> For . . . existence paradoxically accentuated generates the maximum of passion. To abstract from existence is to remove difficulty. To remain in existence so as to understand one thing in one moment and another thing in another moment, is not to understand oneself. But to understand the greatest oppositions together, and to understand oneself existing in them, is very difficult.[16]

Notes

[1] For an interesting discussion of the volume from this point of view, see Barbara Prys Williams, ' "A Consciousness in Quest of its Own Truth": Some Aspects of R. S. Thomas's *The Echoes Return Slow* as Autobiography', *WWE*, 2 (1996), 98–125.

[2] I discuss Thomas's treatment of his family in his work in ' "Songs of Ignorance and Praise": R. S. Thomas's Poems about the Four People in his Life', *Internal Difference: Twentieth-Century Writing in Wales* (Cardiff: University of Wales Press, 1992), 130–55.

[3] The significance of Kierkegaard for Thomas is discussed in William V. Davis, ' "At the Foot of the Precipice of Water . . . Sea Shapes Coming to Celebration": R. S. Thomas and Kierkegaard', *WWE*, 4 (1998), 92–117; see also M. Wynn Thomas, 'Irony in the Soul: The Religious Poetry of R. S[ocrates] Thomas', *Agenda*, 36:2 (1998), 49–69. In addition to the works cited below, I have found the following particularly useful in considering the significance of Kierkegaard's work for Thomas: Mary Finn, *Writing the Incommensurable: Kierkegaard, Rossetti and Hopkins* (Pennsylvania: Pennsylvania State University Press, 1992); Patrick Gardiner, *Kierkegaard* (Oxford: Oxford University Press, 1988); David Law, *Kierkegaard as Negative Theologian* (Oxford: Clarendon Press, 1993); and Graham Ward, *Barth, Derrida and the Language of Theology* (Cambridge: Cambridge University Press, 1995). It should, however, be noted that throughout this essay I have assumed (on the basis of my own discussions with the poet) that his deeply pondered understanding of Kierkegaard was not in any respect systematic or scholarly, and so I have not respected the distinctions scholars draw between the different periods of Kierkegaard's writing career, nor have I had regard to the complex issue of his use of personae, as examined so profoundly, for instance, in Roger Poole, *Kierkegaard: The Indirect Communication* (Charlottesville and London: University of Virginia Press, 1993).

[4] Quoted in H. A. Nielsen, 'The Anatomy of Self in Kierkegaard', *Essays on Kierkegaard and Wittgenstein*, ed. Richard H. Bell and Ronald E. Hustwit (Ohio: College of Wooster, 1978), 1.

[5] Ibid., 3–4.

[6] Michael Wyschogrod, *Kierkegaard and Heidegger: The Ontology of Existence* (London: Routledge, 1954), 132.

[7] *The Journals of Kierkegaard, 1834–1854*, ed. and trans. Alexander Dru (London: Collins, Fontana Books, 1967), 110.

[8] Kierkegaard, *The Last Years: Journals 1853–1855*, ed. and trans. Ronald Gregor Smith (London: Collins, Fontana Books, 1968), 235.

[9] During his discussions of *The Echoes Return Slow* with me, R. S. Thomas repeatedly noted that 'The Ancient Mariner' had served him as a model.

[10] 'The Snow Man', *The Collected Poems of Wallace Stevens* (New York: Knopf, 1973), 9.

[11] For the Kierkegaardian aspects of Thomas's interest in echo, see Thomas, 'Irony in the Soul'.

[12] *Fear and Trembling/Repetition*, ed. and trans. Howard V. Hong and Edna H. Hong (Princeton, NJ: Princeton University Press, 1983), 132.

[13] Quoted in R. S. Thomas, 'Time's Disc Jockey: Meditations on Some Lines in *The Anathémata*' in *David Jones: Diversity in Unity*, ed. Belinda Humfrey and Anne Price-Owen (Cardiff: University of Wales Press, 2000), 153; hereafter, *DJ*.

[14] There are interesting discussions in *The Cambridge Companion to Kierkegaard*, ed. Alastair Hannay and Gordon D. Marino (Cambridge: Cambridge University Press, 1998), 273 and 282–307.

¹⁵ George Steiner, *Real Presences: Is there Anything in What We Say?* (London: Faber & Faber, 1989), 139.

¹⁶ *Concluding Unscientific Postscript*, trans. David F. Swenson and Walter Lowrie (Princeton, NJ: Princeton University Press, 1941), 316.

9

Suspending the Ethical:
R. S. Thomas and Kierkegaard

ROWAN WILLIAMS

Kierkegaard was a significant presence in R. S. Thomas's imaginative world from a relatively early stage, as commentators have noted.[1] There is a typically brief and tantalising mention in *Neb* of a visit to Denmark in the 1960s, apparently prompted in part by an interest in Kierkegaard (a journey recorded in 'A Grave Unvisited'; *NBF*, 9);[2] and several poems in which Kierkegaard features, including two – 'Kierkegaard' and 'S.K.' – in which he is the chief subject. Allusions, occasionally direct, appear in many other places. My aim here is not to catalogue all of these, but to lay bare a little of the conversation Thomas undertook so many times with that other great articulator of uneasy faith, of the experience of living over dark fathoms. It is a conversation that can, and should, leave hard questions about the nature of honest religious utterance that is still, in spite of all, the utterance of gratitude or praise.

'Kierkegaard' is not in itself one of Thomas's better poems; there is a touch of the formulaic in places (the introductory 'And', the metaphors of possession – 'the deed's terrible lightning', 'life's bars', 'the press sharpened/Its rapier'). But

> Her hair was to be
> The moonlight towards which he leaned
> From darkness.

is a memorable image, and the conclusion offers a couple of simple but potent figures:

> wounded, he crawled
> To the monastery of his chaste thought
> To offer up his crumpled amen.
>
> (*P*, 18)

Overall, however, this is a poem about Kierkegaard's biography – a romantic poem, if one dare use the word here, dealing not with the unfathomable God but with a human separation that issues in some kind of faintly elegiac religious gesture. It contrasts sharply with the late poem 'S.K.', in which some of the central challenges of Thomas's own poetic struggles are 'played off' the figure of Kierkegaard – though Kierkegaard's rejected fiancée, Regine Olsen, appears again 'with her moonlight hair'. Here, though, the 'moonlight' image is made to do rather tougher duty in introducing the theme of Kierkegaard's 'lunacy', supporting at a distance, a little later in the poem, the image of 'the asylum / of his genius'. And the governing motifs are deeper:

> Imagining
> from his emphasis on the self
>
> that God is not other,
> we are arrested by his shadow
> in which the face of the beloved
>
> is as a candle snuffed out
> in the darkness following
> on the mind's dazzling explosion.
>   (NTF, 16)

And in the concluding section, the problem hinted at in these lines (is there a God outside the self?) is addressed head-on:

> The difficulty
> with prayer is the exchange
> of places between I and thou,
> with silence as the answer
> to an imaginary request.
> Is this the price genius
> must pay, that from an emphasis
> on the subjective only
> soliloquy remains? Is prayer
> not a glass that, beginning
> in obscurity as his books
> do, the longer we stare
> into the clearer becomes
> the reflection of a countenance
> in it other than our own?
>   (NTF, 17)

Characteristic but not formulaic this time: the familiar teasing endstops, with their half-meanings, their subterranean problematic ('The difficulty' – where the previous sentence has ended with 'God'; 'the subjective only'; 'pay, that from an emphasis'; and so on), make this an unsettling sequence. The main argument, however, is very plain: Kierkegaard's passion about the subjective, the integrity of the unassimilable, unrepeatable response, 'delivers', the more we look at it, the existence and nature of something that it in turn looks at. The face of the praying and/or thinking philosopher carries the shadow of another face, rather as if, after a blinding flash of light, the after-image were fixed on the retina.

'He cannot say anything, for what he knows he cannot say.'[3] This is how Kierkegaard describes the agony of Abraham's faith in his much-discussed meditation on the abortive sacrifice of Isaac, *Fear and Trembling*. Abraham must act in respect of God as if there were no aspect of his knowledge of God that could be shared or explained. He is not a tragic hero; tragic heroes are such because they can *locate* themselves against an intelligible background, against the background of universal imperatives which collide with the contingencies of the situation here and now. But Abraham cannot articulate 'universal imperatives'; really *cannot*: it isn't that he restrains himself from speech, but that there is nothing he can say to explain, interpret, or defend his obedience, which cuts across all that is said or understood, all ethics and authority. Yet he is not a conscious rebel; earlier in *Fear and Trembling*, Kierkegaard distinguishes between the knight of faith and the 'sectarian' who *decides* to go his own way (in company with a small admiring audience). The sectarian is playing to a satisfying image of heroic isolation or romantic risk; the knight of faith, Abraham, is compelled to an action that no audience will or can applaud. But the point of this is that it is the step beyond language and explicability involved here that establishes, as nothing else can, the relation between the individual and the absolute.[4] Either there is such a relation, or faith is a temptation which Abraham was wrong not to resist; for faith is the unspeakable reality of affirming that relation.[5]

In relation to Thomas's questioning about subjectivity, one can perhaps see how Kierkegaard's account of faith in effect lays the ground for the metaphors of reflection and after-image that Thomas's poems sketch.[6] It is only as one looks, long and hard, at Abraham that one sees the possibility of faith – not (this cannot be said too insistently) an assertion of the will by an individual trying to find self-definition; that would be the sectarian parody of faith. One has to decide whether Abraham's silent and incommunicable obedience is response or not;

whether his behaviour establishes the reality of God. This is where Thomas's reading of Kierkegaard seems so central to the business of his religious poetics: God can never be 'there' for examination, nor is God to be uncovered in an analysis of religious emotion, religious experience, in anything like the usual understanding of such words. God can be established only in the depiction of a face turned towards faith in Kierkegaard's sense:

> He is his own
> spy without the need
> to decode the language
> since he gave it us.
>
> . . .
>
> He is what escapes always
> the vigilance of our lenses,
> the faceless negative
> of himself we dare not expose.
>
> (*ERS*, 113)

and –

> Conversation, soliloquy,
> silence – a descending or an ascending
> scale?
>
> (*ERS*, 115)

and –

> I waited upon
> him as a mirror
> in its anonymity
> waits upon absence.
>
> (*C*, 45)

The mirror recurs several times in *Counterpoint*, notably in a pair of passages early on. The first seems to reduce both fall and redemption to the self's inner processes:

> There is no Trinity
> in a glass. The self looks at the self
> only and tenders its tribute.
>
> (*C*, 11)

But the second picks up the allusion to the Trinity, imagining the selfhood of God as 'two mirrors echoing / one another', with the Holy Spirit as 'the breath clouding them'. A second stanza probes further:

> What is the virginity
> of mirrors? Are they surfaces
> of fathoms which mind
> clouds when examining itself
> too closely? Eden in the dream
> of when it was alone.
>
> (C, 12)

To come too close to the examined self is to cloud the mirror with your breath: 'virginity' is the distance prior to examination, the lonely Eden before the creation of Eve. Yet the implication is that this virginity must be lost if the mind is to approach God's mind, in which there is a 'clouding', the active relationship represented by the Holy Spirit shared between Father and Son. And if so, the self in being itself (its conscious and related self) cannot be alone. The question is already there of whether the self without the wholly other interlocutor can exist at all.

God enters discourse, then, it seems, in a very particular kind of interruption in speech, the place where the speaker's longing to justify (an idea, a policy, a decision) is brought to an end; but not brought to an end simply by frustration or emptiness. The waiting mirror is a suggestive image: it exists *in order to* reflect what it is not, and that is true even when it is not occupied in reflecting my face. There is an orientation towards the absent face, one might say; and the apparently empty waiting on the empty 'face' of the mirror tells us in what relation the mirror stands, where it finds its definition. But when the face is seen, it is also clouded by the awareness of relation; in a very tangled paradox, being aware of relation with the other obscures the actuality of the other. Only the empty mirror tells us who the other is and how the other is real, but the empty mirror is, by definition, not seen by *my* face.

As with Kierkegaard's Abraham, the refusal to fill up the space of explanation and image – to look for an unclouded picture in the mirror – is what constitutes in practice the desire for the unconditioned; the very character of God as absolute is spelled out by this refusal, as is the character of the human subject in its depth. When a person is engaged in desire without determined object, in the absence of an audience or an argument that justifies the decision to stay *still* with the desire, we see what it means to say 'God', and what it means to deny that prayer is talking to oneself.

This, which is a central and defining concern in so much of Thomas's work, has obvious implications with regard to how we think about time. Thomas's often (too often) quoted words, 'The meaning is in the waiting' ('Kneeling'; *NBF*, 32), can be misleading if they suggest that, in the words of D. Z. Phillips's perceptive comment on this line in *R. S. Thomas: Poet of the Hidden God*, 'if God comes to a person faith is lost'.[7] The poem as a whole makes it clear that the waiting is something that is, at one level, chosen: it is what happens when the praying person refuses premature speech, waiting for the unimaginable moment when God is manifest *as* God, not as the end of a human process of justification, not as a performance by a human speaker. God cannot be forced to appear, even when the words we speak are good words, authorized words, words of adoration and worship. Only as time is taken with and in the absence and indeterminacy does the true God become evident; what exact shape that manifestation will take cannot be predetermined, though we do well not to expect anything like an unclouded face. As for Abraham, authentic manifestation of faith, and thus of the true God, appears when there is no audience and no comfortably enfolding context (even, or especially, the context of an image of the self and its needs; it must be said again that one is not dealing here with the subjectivism that assumes the right to decide the truth by consulting the will).

Earlier in his study, D. Z. Phillips discusses Thomas's dramatic poem *The Minister* in relation to Kierkegaard's *Purity of Heart*. Kierkegaard proposes the image of a man who is captivated by the beauty of a map but is unaware of the fact that it is a guide showing us how to move through a real territory – something, that is, that enjoins us to take our time. He is at a loss as to how he should *use* the map when set down in the territory it surveys; he has thought that the territory can be possessed or grasped by the single moment of seeing. Thomas's minister speaks of the night when 'We might have had a revival / If only the organ had kept in time' (*M*, 16). The search for the momentary experience that will change everything is precisely the state of Kierkegaard's map-lover, who does not want to move in the only way that one can move within a landscape – point by point, taking one's time. 'If only the organ had kept in time': somehow the contingency of real time upsets the fantasy of instantaneous change or total possession. Voices and instruments keep an untidy time, and it is, ironically, the eager worshippers who fail to keep 'in', *within*, the real framework.

So the image of the waiting mirror does not imply that absence itself is something we can settle down with. It must still be experienced as absence, because the mirror is there for the face to appear in. But what the appearance involves is frightening ('we dare not expose' the hidden image in ourselves) because it is something that both affirms our absolute singleness and uniqueness as created persons and yet has nothing at all to do with any of the available ways we have of reinforcing our sense of our value or security. So what we know we cannot say; yet this not saying has also to be a showing, not a retreat into privacy. We stare into the glass (to pick up again the concluding image of 'S.K.') until an otherness becomes clear. How long does it take? We cannot tell in advance. The time taken is the time in which so much of Thomas's poetry operates, a time in which the only thing we can honestly do is refuse the pressure of language that will be justifiable.

In this light, one can make some sense of Thomas's repeated use of what could be called 'post-ethical' language. I have in mind here all those images – the raptor, the vivisectionist, the experimenter – which reinforce a sense of divine cruelty (a theme I have explored elsewhere[8]). For Kierkegaard, the religious has to be radically distinguished from the ethical,[9] and can be so distinguished only when the imperative of faith simply cuts across the bonds of ethical imperatives; only in this way do we know that the religious is *not the same*. It is in this spirit that Thomas so insistently – almost obsessionally – returns, especially in the poetry of the 1970s through to the mid-1990s, to the 'amoral' deity whose concern with us is that of the scientist with the material of his experiment. It may be the working of 'a love fiercer / than we can understand', as in the poem on senile dementia, 'Geriatric', which opens *No Truce with the Furies*; but the proscription of understanding is as serious as the use of the word 'love' here. And in 'Hebrews 12^{29}', there is a still harsher evocation: we look this time into the depths of a fire (the scriptural text of the title is 'Our God is a consuming fire'), tempted 'to confer features upon a presence / that is not human; to expect love / from a kiss whose only property is to consume' (*EA*, 11).

For Thomas, as for Kierkegaard, then, the distance between ethical and religious is an intrinsic part of the grammar of the religious itself, something that can be articulated (dangerously, and consciously so) only by 'suspending' the ethical. The categories of ethics are as much a denial of the uniqueness of God as any other categories: to enlist an expression from 'Neither', God might conceivably be 'announced', but not described or explained. And the annunciation is

> a signal
> projected at you and returning quick
> with the unpredictabilities at your centre.
> (*NTF*, 58)

One should notice, yet again, the ambiguity: 'returning quickly' and 'returning *alive*', living with the very force of the unresolvedness of what divinity is.

Some kinds of theologian might object that this cannot be an adequate rendition of Christian faith because of the perfect revelation of God in the Incarnation, in Jesus Christ. But this is where Kierkegaard deploys some of his most original and challenging argumentation. At the end of *The Sickness Unto Death*, Kierkegaard discusses the fundamental offence of Christian teaching on the Incarnation. The Incarnation is both the affirmation of the 'kinship' between God and humanity and that which secures the impossibility of confusing God and humanity or of reducing God to trivially human terms.[10] It is a proximity that guarantees distance – the same basic paradox that Kierkegaard works out with still more detail in the *Philosophical Fragments*, where he writes of the urge of reason towards that absolute paradox which definitively defeats it. It is the very lack of human defence (literally in the human vulnerability of the man Jesus, metaphorically in the lack of explanation for God) that establishes the immeasurable distance of God's being in the depth of the prosaic human life of Jesus. The Incarnation does not say to us that God is, after all, accessible, domesticable, but rather the very opposite – that God is more different than any difference we can imagine. Hence the possibility of 'offence': we cannot fit Jesus Christ into our categories either of humanity or of divinity, and so deny him.

Thomas's doctrine of Christ would be a fruitful subject for further investigation. Here, I shall mention only a few allusions and hints in the later poems which might once more suggest affinities with Kierkegaard. In 'Neither', Thomas once again employs the favoured image of the mirror, but in a drastically new sense. God is

> Impassible
> yet darkening your countenance
> once for a long moment
> as you looked at yourself
> on a hill-top in Judea.
>
> (NTF, 58)

We look into a mirror in prayer, waiting for the face that is not ours to appear, with all the ambiguity we have seen in that connection of the clouding that the breath creates on the glass; God, it seems, looks into the crucified human face to see who he is, to see himself in the centre of the world's suffering (here, we might remember the imagery of one of the early pieces in *Counterpoint* on the Trinity (C, 12)). God does not suffer; but his image is seen only in the suffering man. There is here at least a hint of the same kind of paradox as Kierkegaard defines – a difference that can establish itself within the world only by suffering.

The 'Incarnation' sequence in *No Truce with the Furies* pushes towards a Kierkegaardian conclusion: Incarnation (including Resurrection) is the brick wall which confronts thought, imagination and management:

> the machine
> stalled at an abyss, empty
> as the tomb in Palestine,
> the eternal afterdraught of the bone's dream.
>   (NTF, 37)

The governing metaphor of this rather difficult sequence is that of the child's dream: the infant dreams of the womb; God dreams of the self-emptying of Jesus's life. The child's dreams are 'Bubbles blown for adults / to seek their reflection in'; God's dream, we have to infer, is also for us to seek a reflection in, to find our divine image or divine kinship. This is found only in the breaking of our expectations under 'truth's chisel'. But the divine dreaming is also the guarantee that our human horizons are not final: when the poet asks the future: ' "Show me the dreamless man, // the prose man, the man imprisoned / by his horizons" ', what he sees is the stalling of the machine in the face of God's 'abyss'. The dreamless man cannot be produced by the mechanisms of planning; and in this lies our hope not to be reduced to the slavery of prose. For Kierkegaard, the Incarnation of God is the basis of a certain kind of human freedom or hope – not in any weak moral sense (Jesus as the bearer of an uplifting message or a challenge to liberating action, neither of which would actually change the boundaries within which humanity exists), but in the sense that the Incarnation established an indissoluble relationship between finite life and God, the presence of God's dream as a kind of wound in the fabric of history.

It is never easy to tease out what Thomas might understand by 'salvation'. Most of the conventional Christian thoughts about this are at best unspoken in his work. But if one turns to the gnomically intense 'Revision', one finds a kind of definition, if not exactly of 'salvation', then of that life or awareness that faith creates. It is a dialogue, not between faith and scepticism, but between two levels or idioms of faith (and it uses the address, 'friend', as always in Thomas, to somewhat chilling effect; when apostrophized thus by the poet, the reader should worry). Selfhood is born out of the recognition of hungry absence; instead of a mirror waiting for the face, one has here the wick waiting for the flame. To be oneself is to be kindled by the imagined, longed-for flame, but, as one of Thomas's speakers states in a parody of Jesus's words in John's gospel:

> Whoever believes in this fire,
> although he lives, he shall die.
>
> (*EA*, 22)

The self is nothing without the divine fire; but the divine fire consumes (compare 'Hebrews 12^{29}' in the same collection). Where one part of the relation is present, the other cannot live. The challenging voice of positive faith responds by saying that 'this gulf you have created / can be crossed by prayer' – implying that the incompatibility of God and the self is in some way the self's own work. The negative, 'blasphemous' voice replies that this is not so much a crossing as an endless traversing of 'a rope / over an unfathomable / abyss, which goes on and on / never arriving'. And the conclusion – given, interestingly, to the 'affirmative' interlocutor – is that this is exactly the condition of faith: 'the arrival / is the grace given to maintain / your balance'. The relation is not a consuming by divine fire, but a current constantly running between the poles of God and the self,

> coming
> to song in the nerves, as in the telegraph
> wires, the tighter that they are drawn.
>
> (*EA*, 23)

The quintessential Kierkegaardian metaphor of faith as being poised over an immeasurable abyss is recast here: we are poised on the tightrope over the depths, but the tension of the rope defines a place not only of balance but of utterance, of 'song'. And, thinking back to the questions noted earlier about whether prayer is talking to oneself, the answer intimated here is clear enough: the very idea of *tension*, a tension on which we can balance, presupposes the other pole.

This suggests a very distinctive perspective on how the given reality of God is to be understood: the fact of grasping the present moment as *tension* is what establishes that God is real. To have one's own identity decisively called into question, and yet to find a place to stand or balance, is to see where subjectivity itself 'delivers' the objectivity of God, not as an object among objects, but as ground and condition of the subject's life. Thus Kierkegaard can argue with great complexity in *The Sickness Unto Death* that only in relation to God does the self become a self – that is, a 'conscious synthesis of finitude and infinitude'.[11] A self is the mental and spiritual process of *becoming* self: it is a movement always away from the present, given situation (hence an 'infinitizing' process), yet it thereby situates itself in a concrete and temporal world ('the process of finitizing'). Either element without the other issues in despair – the 'mean-spirited' acceptance of what is given, or the retreat into fantasy. The self is thus also built of the synthesis of possibility and necessity: possibility alone is empty, necessity alone is slavery, and, once again, despair issues from either one in isolation.[12] The non-despairing self is the one which, by willing its becoming in time, accepts its location between finite and infinite; for Kierkegaard, this is thinkable only when relation with the absolute is presupposed.

The significant point here is that, for Kierkegaard, the way in which God is constructed in language is not simply a case of pointing to the silences, the places where reasoning speech fails or is wrecked on the rocks of divine mystery. The embrace of the specific time-bound process of becoming a self is the embrace of God, who is thus (to borrow terms from an older philosophical tradition) both the 'most concrete of beings' and the most inaccessible to category and definition. Finding God in the act of embracing the finite is the essential work of the self, and in it, the reality of both self and God are unanswerably affirmed. In Kierkegaard's work more generally, as has already been suggested above, the Incarnational interruption of thought by the God-made-flesh is the deepest manifestation of the destiny of the self: God has embraced the finite, refusing to speak except in the anonymity of the vulnerable Jesus.

Here again, then, is a strong convergence with Thomas. The subject of the poems is consistently the becoming self, in the sense of a self poised in tension: 'Bird Watching' speaks of the 'the ability of the heart / to migrate, if only momentarily, / between the quotidian and the sublime' (*NTF*, 61), and 'Mischief', having relativized the whole notion of 'accepting the universe' ('I have said "yes" to the universe / so many times its echoes / have returned increasingly as "no" '), proceeds to identify the indissoluble moment of affirmation in which the scales shoot up towards acceptance, under the weight of 'a tear / fallen from the hardest of eyes' (*NTF*, 45). The metaphor is quite the opposite of the variations on the images of balancing I have been noting, yet its effect is the same: the becoming that occurs in what might best be called a vulnerable perception, a perception unplanned and unprotected, of the world involves a taking up of a concrete position within a universe that is received as gift. And it is this unplanned perception that – rather strangely in some ways – assures me that I am not 'an occasion / merely; an event synchronous / with other events' (*ERS*, 33). If the self's identity is only its 'perform-ance', the self is threatened with dissolution; but there is an answer, and it is love:

> But love answers it
> in its turn: I am old now and have died
> many times, but my rebirth is surer
>   than the truth embalming itself
> in the second law of your Thermo-Dynamics.
>   (*ERS*, 33)

Enough has been said by now to make it clear that Thomas's definition of this 'love' is a pretty complex matter. One is not dealing with a simple cosmic benevolence, but with that post-ethical divine regard that can be experienced as the grip of a predator or as the charged emptiness of the mirror just round the corner of our seeing. But if the God of Thomas's poetry is 'real' (if prayer is not soliloquy), that God is also in some way to be spoken of as active; and while God's activity is never just consoling, never what we would have asked for or chosen, for the poet it has ultimately to be related to the very conditions of our being and even our well-being. No less than for Kierkegaard, God, for Thomas, is both the frustration of every expectation and the only exit from despair. And that God is encountered only in the embrace of finitude.

The convergence between Thomas and Kierkegaard is – as will have been apparent – difficult to articulate clearly, yet a dialogue with the Dane is fundamental to much of Thomas's work. Kierkegaard does not merely provide 'sources' for Thomas's 'religious ideas'; one can reason-ably assert that what theology there is in the poetry is deeply marked by Kierkegaard, but the relation goes a good deal deeper. Poetry is the construction of a more deeply and resourcefully intelligible self which is achieved by pushing the inner tensions of language to the point of new discoveries in form and metaphor. Holding with Kierkegaard that the self is unintelligible and un-speakable without the absolute other, yet underlining relentlessly the radical nature of that otherness, Thomas cannot understand his poetic enterprise except as the pursuit of a pre-sence – but a presence that can only be obscure when it is actually present. Poetic 'achievement', then, becomes a paradoxical act of consciousness seeking unselfconsciousness: speaking in such a way as to open up what is not said. And the unsaid is reality as the manifestation of God, God as the ground of what is perceived (including the poet's own self and sensibility).

The action of poetry itself is thus illuminated and anchored by a Kierkegaardian vision of the speaking self. The poetic embrace of the concrete is something more than the repetition or reproduction of what is given; it evokes or realizes the given in a new way, it posits a new world which is the depth of the old, not by denying the particular and immediate but by seeking words for its unspoken setting, its setting within the presence of God. Poetry seeks the impossible goal of showing a world seen from something other than the simply human, readily available perspective, mechanical, functional, impatient. It claims, very boldly, that this poetic apprehension is essential to being a human self (whether or not this or that particular self finds 'poetic' words for it). Even – or especially – when the self tries to see itself truthfully, it is bound to perform the poetic function and see itself in the perspective of the radically other (which is why good poetry is never *simply* autobiographical as one usually understands that word). And all of this best makes sense when read against the backdrop of Kierkegaard's agonized analysis of selfhood and individuality in direct relation to the absolute.

Two passages from *The Echoes Return Slow* may offer a suitable conclusion to these reflections (I use the word advisedly). They turn once more on the mirror as a fundamental image, or nest of images:

> Not from conceit certainly, yet he could not escape from his looking-glass. There it was the concealed likeness, always ahead in its ambush. Imagining the first human, he conceived his astonishment in finding himself face to face with the unknown denizen of the water. With the refinement of the mirror there occurred only the refinement of his dilemma.
>
> (ERS, 108)

And, just as in the poems from *Counterpoint* quoted above (C, 11, 12), the apparent isolation of the self confronted only with itself is immediately given a twist in the poem accompanying this prose movement:

> The poet scans the stars
> and the scientist his equations.
> Life, how often must I
> be brought round to confront

my image in an oblique
glass? The spirit revolves
on itself and is without
shadow, but behind

the mirror is the twin helix
where the dancing chromosomes
pass one another back
to back to a tune from the abyss.

(*ERS*, 109)

The work of the poet is to suggest a trace of that dance, unobservable in itself or as itself, and of the tune beneath the dance, issuing from the abyss – the Kierkegaardian void over which faith balances, more secure and more insecure than anything we can merely explain.

Notes

[1] For Thomas and Kierkegaard, see, for example, William V. Davis, ' "At the Foot of the Precipice of Water . . . Sea Shapes Coming to Celebration": R. S. Thomas and Kierkegaard', *WWE*, 4 (1998), 94–117; M. Wynn Thomas, 'Irony in the Soul: The Religious Poetry of R. S[ocrates] Thomas', *Agenda*, 36:2 (1998), 49–69; and Tony Brown, ' "Over Seventy Thousand Fathoms": The Sea and Self-Definition in the Poetry of R. S. Thomas', *Page's Drift*, 165–7.

[2] *Autobiographies*, 68.

[3] Søren Kierkegaard, *Fear and Trembling*, trans. Walter Lowrie (New York: Anchor Books, 1954), 128.

[4] See Kierkegaard, *Fear and Trembling*, 91 and 129.

[5] See Kierkegaard, *Fear and Trembling*, 80.

[6] See William V. Davis, 'The Presence of Absence: Mirrors and Mirror Imagery in the Poetry of R. S. Thomas', *Analecta Husserliana*, 73 (2001), 355–6.

[7] R. S. Thomas, *Poet of the Hidden God: Meaning and Meditation in the Poetry of R. S. Thomas* (Basingstoke: Macmillan, 1986), 68.

[8] See ' "Adult Geometry": Dangerous Thoughts in R. S. Thomas', *Page's Drift*, 82–98.

[9] See Problem 1 – 'Is there a Teleological Suspension of the Ethical?' – in Kierkegaard, *Fear and Trembling*, 64–77.

[10] See *The Sickness Unto Death*, trans. Walter Lowrie (New York: Anchor Books, 1954), 256.

[11] Kierkegaard, *The Sickness Unto Death*, 162.

[12] See Kierkegaard, *The Sickness Unto Death*, 166, 168–75.

Bibliography

R. S. Thomas: Principal Publications

1. Poetry

The Stones of the Field (Carmarthen: The Druid Press, 1946).
An Acre of Land (Newtown: Montgomeryshire Printing Co., 1952).
The Minister (Newtown: Montgomeryshire Printing Co., 1953).
Song at the Year's Turning: Poems, 1942–1954 (London: Hart-Davis, 1955).
Poetry for Supper (London: Hart-Davis, 1958).
Tares (London: Hart-Davis, 1961).
The Bread of Truth (London: Hart-Davis, 1963).
Pietà (London: Hart-Davis, 1966).
Not That He Brought Flowers (London: Hart-Davis, 1968).
H'm (London: Macmillan, 1972).
Young and Old (London: Chatto & Windus, 1972).
Selected Poems, 1946–1968 (London: Hart-Davis, MacGibbon, 1973).
What is a Welshman? (Llandybïe: Christopher Davies, 1974).
Laboratories of the Spirit (London: Macmillan, 1975).
The Way of It (Sunderland: Coelfrith Press, 1977).
Frequencies (London: Macmillan, 1978).
Between Here and Now (London: Macmillan, 1981).
Later Poems, 1972–1982 (London: Macmillan, 1983).
Destinations (Halford: Celandine Press, 1985).
Ingrowing Thoughts (Bridgend: Poetry Wales Press, 1985).
Experimenting with an Amen (London: Macmillan, 1986).
Welsh Airs (Bridgend: Poetry Wales Press, 1987).
The Echoes Return Slow (London: Macmillan, 1988).
Counterpoint (Newcastle upon Tyne: Bloodaxe Books, 1990).
Frieze (Schondorf am Ammersee: Babel, 1992).
Mass for Hard Times (Newcastle upon Tyne: Bloodaxe Books, 1992).
Collected Poems, 1945–1990 (London: J. M. Dent, 1993).
No Truce with the Furies (Newcastle upon Tyne: Bloodaxe Books, 1995).
Residues (Tarset: Bloodaxe Books, 2002).

2. Prose

ABC Neb, ed. Jason Walford Davies (Caernarfon: Gwasg Gwynedd, 1995).

Abercuawg (Y Ddarlith Lenyddol Flynyddol; Eisteddfod Genedlaethol Cymru, Aberteifi a'r Cylch, 1976).

'Autobiographical Essay', *Contemporary Authors: Autobiographical Series*, 4 (1986), 301–13; reprinted in William V. Davis (ed.), *Miraculous Simplicity: Essays on R. S. Thomas* (see below).

Autobiographies, ed. and trans. Jason Walford Davies (London: J. M. Dent, 1997).

Blwyddyn yn Llŷn (Caernarfon: Gwasg Gwynedd, 1990).

Cymru or Wales? (Llandysul: Gomer, 1992).

'Language, Exile, a Writer and the Future', *The Works*, 1, ed. Christopher Mills (Welsh Union of Writers, 1988), 22–43.

Neb, ed. Gwenno Hywyn (Caernarfon: Gwasg Gwynedd, 1985).

Pe Medrwn yr Iaith ac Ysgrifau Eraill, ed. Tony Brown and Bedwyr Lewis Jones (Abertawe: Christopher Davies, 1988).

Selected Prose, ed. Sandra Anstey (3rd edn; Bridgend: Seren, 1995).

'Time's Disc Jockey: Meditations on Some Lines in *The Anathémata*', *David Jones: Diversity in Unity*, ed. Belinda Humfrey and Anne Price-Owen (Cardiff: University of Wales Press, 2000), 153–9.

Wales: A Problem of Translation (The 1996 Adam Lecture; Adam Archive Publications/Centre for 20th-Century Cultural Studies, King's College, London, 1996).

3. Editions

The Batsford Book of Country Verse (London: Batsford, 1961).

The Penguin Book of Religious Verse (Harmondsworth: Penguin, 1963).

Selected Poems of Edward Thomas (London: Faber & Faber, 1964).

A Choice of George Herbert's Verse (London: Faber & Faber, 1967).

A Choice of Wordsworth's Verse (London: Faber & Faber, 1971).

4. Interviews

'Probings' (interview with Ned Thomas and John Barnie), *Planet*, 80 (April/May 1990), 28–52; reprinted in William V. Davis (ed.), *Miraculous Simplicity: Essays on R. S. Thomas* (see below).

'R. S. Thomas in Conversation with Molly Price Owen', *The David Jones Journal*, 3:1–2 (Summer/Autumn 2001), 93–102.

'R. S. Thomas talks to J. B. Lethbridge', *Anglo-Welsh Review*, 74 (1983), 36–56.

5. Recording

R. S. Thomas Reading the Poems, triple-CD and triple-cassette collection (producer: Damian Walford Davies; Sain Records, SCD 2209 and C2209, 1999).

6. *Select Bibliography of Criticism*
Essays by various hands collected in the volumes edited by Sandra Anstey, A. E. Dyson, William V. Davis and M. Wynn Thomas are not listed separately.

Ackerman, John, 'Man and Nature in the Poetry of R. S. Thomas', *Poetry Wales*, 7:4 (Spring 1972), 15–26.

Allchin, A. M., 'R. S. Thomas: Some Recent Poems', *Agenda*, 36:2 (1998), 70–6.

Anstey, Sandra, (ed.), *Critical Writings on R. S. Thomas* (Bridgend: Poetry Wales Press, 1982; revised and expanded edn, Bridgend: Seren, 1992).

Astley, Ben, 'Iago Prytherch and the Rejection of Western Metaphysics', *Welsh Writing in English: A Yearbook of Critical Essays*, 5 (1999), 101–14.

——, ' "Somewhere Between Faith and Doubt": R. S. Thomas and the Poetry of Theology Deconstructed', *Welsh Writing in English: A Yearbook of Critical Essays*, 4 (1998), 74–93.

Barker, Simon, 'Revisiting the Sources: R. S. Thomas and the Redress of Poetry', *Fire Green as Grass*, ed. Belinda Humfrey (Llandysul: Gomer, 1995), 156–82.

Barnie, John, 'Bread and Beauty', 'Never Forget Your Welsh' and 'Across the Grain', *The King of Ashes* (Llandysul: Gomer, 1989), 3–13, 14–19, and 20–7.

Brown, Dennis, 'R. S. Thomas's "Amen" ', *The Poetry of Postmodernity: Anglo/American Encodings* (London: Macmillan, 1994), 120–33.

——, 'Vernon Watkins and R. S. Thomas', *British Poetry from the 1950s to the 1990s: Politics and Art*, ed. Gary Day and Brian Docherty (Basingstoke: Macmillan, 1997), 221–36.

Brown, Tony, ' "Eve's Ruse": Identity and Gender in the Poetry of R. S. Thomas', *English*, 49:195 (Autumn 2000), 229–50.

——, 'Language, Poetry and Silence: Some Themes in the Poetry of R. S. Thomas', *The Welsh Connection*, ed. William Tydeman (Llandysul: Gomer, 1986), 159–85.

——, 'R. S. Thomas's Elegy for Dylan Thomas', *The Review of English Studies*, 51:203 (2000), 451–5.

——, 'The Romantic Nationalism of R. S. Thomas', *The Literature of Place*, ed. Norman Page and Peter Preston (Basingstoke: Macmillan, 1993), 156–69.

Castay, Marie-Thérèse, 'No Truce with the Furies?', *Agenda*, 36:2 (1998), 77–83.

Conran, Tony, 'Aspects of R. S. Thomas', *The Cost of Strangeness: Essays on the English Poets of Wales* (Llandysul: Gomer, 1982), 220–62.

——, 'The New Frontier: R. S. Thomas', *Frontiers in Anglo-Welsh Poetry* (Cardiff: University of Wales Press, 1997), 188–99.

Crotty, Patrick, 'Lean Parishes: Patrick Kavanagh's *The Great Hunger* and R. S. Thomas's *The Minister*', *Dangerous Diversity: The Changing Faces of Wales*, ed. Katie Gramich and Andrew Hiscock (Cardiff: University of Wales Press, 1998), 131–49.

Davies, James A., 'Participating Readers: Three Poems by R. S. Thomas', *Poetry Wales*, 18:4 (1983), 72–84.

Davies, Grahame, 'Resident Aliens: R. S. Thomas and the Anti-Modern Movement', *Welsh Writing in English: A Yearbook of Critical Essays*, 7 (2001–2), 50–77.

——, *Sefyll yn y Bwlch: R. S. Thomas, Saunders Lewis, T. S. Eliot, a Simone Weil* (Cardiff: University of Wales Press, 1999).

Davies, Walford, 'R. S. Thomas: The Poem's Harsher Conditions', *New Welsh Review*, 11 (Winter 1990–1), 15–26.

——, ' "The Site Inviolate": R. S. Thomas (1913–2000)', *Planet*, 144 (December 2000/January 2001), 16–27.

Davis, William V., ' "An Abstraction Blooded": Wallace Stevens and R. S. Thomas on Blackbirds and Men', *The Wallace Stevens Journal*, 8:2 (1984), 79–82.

——, ' "At the Foot of the Precipice of Water . . . Sea Shapes Coming to Celebration": R. S. Thomas and Kierkegaard', *Welsh Writing in English: A Yearbook of Critical Essays*, 4 (1998), 94–117.

——, 'Going Forward to Meet the Machine: R. S. Thomas's Quarrel with Technology', *Poetry Now: Contemporary British and Irish Poetry in the Making*, ed. Holger Klein et al. (Tübingen: Stauffenberg, 1999), 187–99.

——, (ed.), *Miraculous Simplicity: Essays on R. S. Thomas* (Fayetteville: University of Arkansas Press, 1993).

——, 'The Presence of Absence: Mirrors and Mirror Imagery in the Poetry of R. S. Thomas', *Analecta Husserliana*, 73 (2001), 347–60.

——, ' "This Is What Art Could Do": An Exercise in Exegesis – R. S. Thomas's "Souillac: Le Sacrifice d'Abraham" ', *Religion and the Arts*, 4:3 (2000), 374–97.

Dyson, A. E., (ed.), *Three Contemporary Poets: Thom Gunn, Ted Hughes & R. S. Thomas* (Basingstoke: Macmillan, 1990).

——, *Yeats, Eliot and R. S. Thomas: Riding the Echo* (London: Macmillan, 1981), 285–326.

Garlick, Raymond, 'A Disagreement Between Friends: R. S. Thomas, Language and Poetry', *Planet*, 147 (June/July 2001), 55–8.

Gramich, Johannes, 'R. S. in Munich', *New Welsh Review*, 54 (Winter 2001–2), 20–3.

Hardy, Barbara, 'Region and Nation: R. S. Thomas and Dylan Thomas', *The Literature of Region and Nation*, ed. R. P. Draper (Basingstoke: Macmillan, 1989), 93–107.

Heys, Alistair, 'Kings of Pride and Terror: R. S. Thomas and the Welsh Sublime', *Nations and Relations: Writing Across the British Isles*, ed. Tony Brown and Russell Stephens (Cardiff: New Welsh Review, 2000), 133–55.

Hooker, Jeremy, 'R. S. Thomas: Prytherch and After', *The Presence of the Past: Essays on Modern British and American Poetry* (Bridgend: Poetry Wales Press, 1987), 128–40.

——, ' "The True Wales of my Imagination": Welsh and English in the Poetry of R. S. Thomas, David Jones and Gillian Clarke', *Imagining Wales: A View of Modern Welsh Writing in English* (Cardiff: University of Wales Press, 2001), 28–49.

Lloyd, David, ' "Articulate To The End": R. S. Thomas and the Crisis of Language', *Ariel: A Review of International English Literature*, 30:4 (1999), 99–108.

——, 'Making It New: R. S. Thomas and William Carlos Williams', *Welsh Writing in English: A Yearbook of Critical Essays*, 8 (2003), 121–40.

——, 'Through the Looking Glass: R. S. Thomas's *The Echoes Return Slow* as Poetic Autobiography', *Twentieth Century Literature*, 42:4 (1996), 438–52.

Lord, Peter, 'Parallel Lives?', *Planet*, 128 (June/July 1998), 17–26.

Meilicke, Christine, 'Dualism and Theodicy in R. S. Thomas's Poetry', *Literature and Theology*, 12:4 (1998), 407–18.

Merchant, W. Moelwyn, *R. S. Thomas* (Cardiff: University of Wales Press, 1989).

Minhinnick, Robert, 'Living with R. S. Thomas', *Poetry Wales*, 29:1 (July 1993), 11–14.

Morgan, J. Christopher, '*Destinations*: Roots of Hope in R. S. Thomas', *Welsh Writing in English: A Yearbook of Critical Essays*, 4 (1998), 54–73.

——, *R. S. Thomas: Identity, Environment, and Deity* (Manchester: Manchester University Press, 2003).

Newman, Elizabeth, 'Voices and Perspectives in the Poetry of R. S. Thomas', *Linguistics and the Study of Literature*, ed. Theo D'haen (Amsterdam: Rodopi, 1986), 56–71.

O'Driscoll, Dennis, 'Translating Art: R. S. Thomas and the Poetry of Paintings', *Agenda*, 36:2 (1998), 38–48.

Ormond, John, 'R. S. Thomas: Priest and Poet. A transcript of John Ormond's film for BBC Television, broadcast on April 2nd, 1972; introduced by Sam Adams', *Poetry Wales*, 7:4 (Spring 1972), 47–57.

Perryman, K. A., 'Observation and Observance', *Agenda*, 36:2 (1998), 20–7.

Phillips, Dewi Z., 'Revealing the Hidden', *From Fantasy to Faith: The Philosophy of Religion and Twentieth-Century Literature* (Basingstoke: Macmillan, 1991), 201–11.

——, *R. S. Thomas, Poet of The Hidden God: Meaning and Meditation in the Poetry of R. S. Thomas* (Basingstoke: Macmillan, 1986).

——, 'Seeking the Poem in the Pain: Order and Contingency in the Poetry of

R. S. Thomas', *Through a Darkening Glass: Philosophy, Literature, and Cultural Change* (Oxford: Blackwell, 1982), 165–90.

Pikoulis, John, 'R. S. Thomas's Existential Agony', *Poetry Wales*, 29:1 (July 1993), 26–32.

——, '*The Minister*', *Agenda*, 36:2 (1998), 28–37.

Price-Owen, Molly, 'R. S. Thomas in Conversation with Molly Price-Owen', *The David Jones Journal*, 3:1 and 2 (2001), 93–102.

Reynolds, Rhian, 'Poetry for the Air: *The Minister*, *Sŵn y Gwynt sy'n Chwythu* and *The Dream of Jake Hopkins* as Radio Odes', *Welsh Writing in English: A Yearbook of Critical Essays*, 7 (2001–2), 78–105.

Shepherd, Elaine, *R. S. Thomas: Conceding an Absence – Images of God Explored* (Basingstoke: Macmillan, 1996).

Thomas, Dafydd Elis, 'The Image of Wales in R. S. Thomas's Poetry', *Poetry Wales*, 7:4 (Spring 1972), 59–66.

Thomas, M. Wynn, 'Irony in the Soul: The Religious Poetry of R. S[ocrates] Thomas', *Agenda*, 36:2 (1998), 49–69.

——, 'R. S. Thomas: The Poetry of the Sixties' and ' "Songs of Ignorance and Praise": R. S. Thomas's Poems about the Four People in his Life', *Internal Difference: Twentieth-Century Writing in Wales* (Cardiff: University of Wales Press, 1992), 107–29 and 130–55.

——, 'R. S. Thomas: War Poet', *Welsh Writing in English: A Yearbook of Critical Essays*, 2 (1996), 82–97.

——, (ed.), *R. S. Thomas: Y Cawr Awenydd* (Llandysul: Gomer, 1990).

——, (ed.), *The Page's Drift: R. S. Thomas at Eighty* (Bridgend: Seren, 1993).

Thomas, Ned, 'R. S. Thomas: The Question about Technology', *Planet*, 92 (April/May 1992), 54–60.

Tolkien, Michael, 'A Compulsion to Give Away Assurances: A Note on *The Echoes Return Slow*', *Agenda*, 36:2 (1998), 84–7.

Triggs, Jeffery Alan, 'A Kinship of the Fields: Farming in the Poetry of R. S. Thomas and Wendell Berry', *North Dakota Quarterly*, 57:2 (1989), 92–102.

van Buuren, M. J. J., *Waiting: The Religious Poetry of Ronald Stuart Thomas, Welsh Priest and Poet* (Dordrecht: ICG Printing, 1993).

Volk, Sabine, *Grenzpfähle der Wirklichkeit: Approaches to the Poetry of R. S. Thomas* (Frankfurt am Main: Peter Lang, 1985).

Volk-Birke, Sabine, 'World History from BC to AD: R. S. Thomas's *Counterpoint*', *Literature and Theology*, 9:2 (1995), 199–226.

Walford Davies, Damian, ' "The Frequencies I Commanded": Recording R. S. Thomas', *North American Journal of Welsh Studies*, 2:1 (Winter 2001–2), 12–23.

Walford Davies, Jason, *Gororau'r Iaith: R. S. Thomas a'r Traddodiad Llenyddol Cymraeg* (Cardiff: University of Wales Press, 2003).

——, ' "Thick Ambush of Shadows": Allusions to Welsh Literature in the Work of R. S. Thomas', *Welsh Writing in English: A Yearbook of Critical Essays*, 1 (1995), 75–127.

Ward, John Powell, *The Poetry of R.S. Thomas* (2nd edn; Bridgend: Seren, 2001).

Wigginton, Chris, ' "Welshing on the Language": R. S. Thomas, Oliver Reynolds and Postmodern Wales', *Welsh Writing in English: A Yearbook of Critical Essays*, 4 (1998), 118–32.

Williams, Barbara Prys, ' "A Consciousness in Quest of its Own Truth": Some Aspects of R. S. Thomas's *The Echoes Return Slow* as Autobiography', *Welsh Writing in English: A Yearbook of Critical Essays*, 2 (1996), 98–125.

Wintle, Justin, *Furious Interiors: Wales, R. S. Thomas and God* (London: HarperCollins, 1996).

Index